Living archaeology

Living archaeology

R. A. GOULD
Professor of Anthropology
University of Hawaii at Manoa

CAMBRIDGE UNIVERSITY PRESS

CAMBRIDGE
LONDON · NEW YORK · NEW ROCHELLE
MELBOURNE · SYDNEY

Published by the Press Syndicate of the University of Cambridge
The Pitt Building, Trumpington Street, Cambridge CB2 1RP
32 East 57th Street, New York, NY 10022, USA
296 Beaconsfield Parade, Middle Park, Melbourne 3206,
Australia

First published in 1980

Printed in the United States of America
Typeset by Huron Valley Graphics, Ann Arbor, Michigan
Printed and bound by The Book Press, Brattleboro, Vermont

Library of Congress Cataloging in Publication Data
Gould, Richard A
    Living archaeology.
    (New studies in archaeology)
    Bibliography: p.
    Includes index.
1. Ethnoarchaeology.
2. Australian aborigines – Australia – Western Desert.
3. Australia – Antiquities.
I. Title.   II. Series.
CC79.E85G68   930'.1   79–20788
ISBN 0 521 23093 4

Dedicated to Betsy,
Who was always there . . .

Contents

Preface

This book is an extended essay about an idea whose time has come. There has been a surge of interest during the last few years in the relationship between ethnographic observations of living, human societies and the materials studied by archaeologists. On the one hand, there are books like *Ethnoarchaeology* (1974), edited by Christopher B. Donnan and C. William Clewlow, and *Explorations in Ethnoarchaeology* (1978), edited by the author of this book, in which a number of scholars offer a variety of differing approaches. While it is possible to infer a degree of unanimity in these studies, their very diversity of geographical and topical subjects makes the current status of ethnoarchaeology anything but self-evident.

On the other hand, there are also some admirable new studies that describe and analyze particular contemporary societies from an ethnoarchaeological point of view at a level of detail never before achieved. Foremost among these studies are *Archaeological Approaches to the Present* (1977) by John E. Yellen, and *Nunamiut Ethnoarchaeology* (1978) by Lewis R. Binford, which deal with the !Kung Bushmen of the Kalahari Desert and the Nunamiut Eskimo of Alaska, respectively. Each is a detailed case study stressing particular aspects of hunter–gatherer ethnography in relation to material remains that can be looked at archaeologically. Yellen's study emphasizes !Kung residential patterning in relation to various activities and their physical residues, while Binford's work examines Nunamiut hunting and butchering of game and relates his findings to the larger body of literature on faunal analysis in archaeology.

Both kinds of books give ample evidence of the increasing tempo of efforts in ethnoarchaeological research today. But neither kind represents an attempt to present a unified theory of ethnoarchaeology. For this purpose I realized that it would be better for a single author to draw together materials from a single general region and cultural tradition – in this case, the Australian Aborigines – and use these materials to demonstrate the general principles of this unified theory. So this is also a book about Australian Aborigines and the more recent, innovative aspects of ethnoarchaeological work being done in Australia. The Australian materials are intended to serve as a case study in ethnoarchaeological theory, with the expectation that readers who find these ideas useful will be encouraged to try them out in their own particular areas of expertise.

I chose to title this book, *Living Archaeology* in order to emphasize the active element in ethnoarchaeological research, namely, how one thinks about and actually encounters the linkages between behavior and material residues in the context of living, contemporary human societies. These actions, in turn, imply some effort toward organizing this body of experience into a set of consistent applications to the kinds of problems that archaeologists commonly encounter when excavating and analyzing their data. Living archaeology, in other words, is not being proposed as a new kind of ethnoarchaeology, nor is it presented an alternative to ethnoarchaeology. It is simply ethnoarchaeology in the active voice.

Before setting out to construct a unified theory of ethnoarchaeology, my first priority was to deal with some of the problems that have beset many earlier efforts to discover reliable and consistent relationships between ethnographic and archaeological data. A look at a fairly typical day in the life of an Australian Desert Aborigine group at Tikatika, a habitation base camp in the Western Desert where Aborigines were still living off the land under more or less traditional circumstances in 1966–67, suggests the wealth of social, verbal, and ideational interaction that takes place under such conditions. These would be difficult, if not impossible, to infer by means of direct attempts to recover the "archaeological" by-products of such nonmaterial behavior. Recognition of these difficulties is enhanced by the ambiguities produced in the archaeological record after the abandonment of this campsite, as revealed by a simple mapping study of this site five months later.

One kind of direct approach to the use of ethnographic observations as a way of "explaining" archaeological findings is the use of analogy. Here is an idea whose time has *gone*. An effort is mounted here to mop up the intellectual wreckage this concept has produced in ethnoarchaeology. For some scholars, this may seem unnecessary, since the argument by analogy has already fallen into disrepute among many if not most ethnoarchaeologists. But a critical review of this concept and its applications is needed here if we are to reconstitute our approach on a more satisfying and convincing basis.

The first element of any convincing approach to ethnoarchaeology involves establishing a basis for uniformitarianist kinds of generalizations about human behavior that are not subject to alteration or amendment through symbolic or ideational manipulations by the human beings we propose to study. Here the discussion turns to ecology as one area of study that has produced general principles of a uniformitarianist nature that can be used to understand and explain important aspects of human behavior. By looking first at the general relations between ecological variables and particular adaptive responses by human beings in specific societies, we can establish a baseline against which to measure the effects of symbolic and ideational variables in such situations. So at this point the discussion centers on the geography and ecology of Australia as a theater for human adaptation, turning first to arid Australia, where extreme conditions prevail that have always made human settlement difficult and risky, and turning then to other, more benign habitats in Australia, where we have new evidence for a variety of remarkable human adaptations.

Using this generalizing approach, we can take a closer look at certain material aspects of Australian Aborigine behavior and ask how or to what extent these can serve as the basis for archaeological signatures of adaptive behavior. Here I chose to emphasize stone technology because this is one aspect of traditional Western Desert Aborigine material culture that was still functioning and was pretty much intact when these field studies were made. But I could just as easily and usefully have studied other aspects of Aborigine behavior in relation to materials such as faunal remains, domestic architecture, settlement characteristics, and even the recycling and discard of cars, tin cans, cloth, and other European-introduced items.

From this detailed treatment of the relationship between Aborigine lithic technology and adaptive behavior in the Western Desert of Australia, there emerges a clear and convincing alternative to the argument by analogy – namely, the *argument by anomaly*. The remainder of the book develops this approach and applies it to archaeological and ethnographic findings in other parts of Australia. Only by looking for and recognizing anomalies to general patterns of conformity to utilitarian expectations in human behavior can we reliably infer when and under what conditions symbolic and ideational factors make a difference in the ways people actually behave. It is this contrast between actual as opposed to anticipated human behavior that characterizes ethnoarchaeology at its best, and Western Desert and other Australian examples are used to demonstrate how the argument by anomaly effectively confronts and explains complexities of human behavior in relation to the procurement, manufacture or processing, use, and discard of materials. The principal argument here is that ethnoarchaeologists are concerned with observing and explaining the totality of human behavior relating to material residues, which means they must embrace a philosophy of science that includes both a search for and a use of general principles with a recognition of idiosyncrasies and deviations from those principles. In short, human beings are not particles or inanimate entities whose behavior can be explained solely in relation to general laws like those used in the physical and natural sciences. If ethnoarchaeology is to be a viable part of social science, the search for general laws must be combined with a willingness to recognize the importance of anomalies and to use such anomalies as a primary tool for discovering behavioral relationships that may have no counterpart in any contemporary or known historic human societies.

If all this seems pretty abstract, let me reassure the reader that these general principles are demonstrated in relation to specific cases that show how such an approach can do much to enliven our view of archaeology. In particular, there have been studies in Australia during the last few years that range from the enigmatic abandonment of fishing by prehistoric Tasmanians to the archaeological and ethnohistoric reconstruction of a remarkable adaptation by Aborigines in the eastern highlands of Australia to moth hunting as part of their primary subsistence behavior; these studies all serve to illustrate aspects of this approach as well as to pose special problems in ethnoarchaeological explanation. The final part of this book extends the argument by anomaly into areas outside Australia in a brief, trial effort to show the wider applicability of this approach. It also ventures into areas of Aborigine behavior which *remain* anomalous and will require further study, such as the apparently inexplicable absence of skin waterbags in the Western Desert of Australia. The purpose of this last part of the book is to say, essentially, that while we do not yet know all the answers, we do at least have an approach that will direct our attention to the right questions.

R. A. G.

Acknowledgments

The ideas presented in this book represent products of research carried out over the last twelve years, and I wish to thank those funding organizations and other institutions that supported this research at various stages along the way. Initial ethnographic fieldwork in the Western Desert of Australia in 1966–7 was funded by the Social Science Research Council (New York) and in 1969–70 by the Frederick G. Voss Anthropology and Archaeology Fund (Department of Anthropology, American Museum of Natural History, New York), with supplemental assistance in the form of a Landrover furnished on both occasions by the Australian Institute of Aboriginal Studies (Canberra). Fieldwork in the Central Desert of Australia in 1973–4 was supported by the National Science Foundation (Research Grant No. BNS 73-09088-A02). Finally, archival studies of unpublished manuscripts and dissertations on Australian prehistory and ethnoarchaeology were facilitated by a Visiting Fellowship at the Department of Prehistory, Research School of Pacific Studies (The Australian National University, Canberra) in 1977.

Other institutional affiliations have also done much to assist in the preparation of this book. The Department of Anthropology, University of Western Australia (Nedlands), the Western Australian Museum (Perth), and the South Australian Museum (Adelaide) all helped in various ways and did much to ensure the success of these studies. The actual writing was done while I was a Visiting Fellow at Corpus Christi College, Cambridge University, in 1977–8, and valuable assistance in typing the manuscript and preparation of tables was furnished by the Social Science Research Institute (University of Hawaii, Honolulu). I am grateful to all of these funding agencies and scholarly institutions for their many services and valuable support.

In undertaking this book, I sought the advice of scholars in different parts of the world, many of whom are acknowledged by name in the text together with the particular ideas they proposed. Others, however, made general suggestions which were not specifically mentioned in the text but were important, nevertheless. Worthy of special mention in this regard are the late Prof. N. W. G. Macintosh (Department of Anatomy, University of Sydney) and the late Dr. Charles P. Mountford (The South Australian Museum, Adelaide) as well as Dr. Norman B. Tindale (The South Australian Museum, Adelaide), Prof. Ronald M. Berndt and Dr. Catherine H. Berndt (University of Western Australia, Nedlands), Dr. Robert Tonkinson (University of Oregon, Eugene), Dr. Nicolas Peterson (Australian National University, Canberra), M. E. Lofgren (The Western Australian Museum, Perth), and Cecil J. Hackett, M.D. (Royal Society of Medicine, London) for their expertise and advice about traditional behavior among Australian Aborigines. Special thanks go to Dr. Hackett for allowing me to read his unpublished notes and diaries of field trips into the Western Desert during the 1930s. With regard to advice on various aspects of Australian prehistory, I wish to thank Prof. D. J. Mulvaney, J. M. Bowler, F. W. Shawcross, and Michael McIntyre (Australian National University, Canberra), R. V. S. Wright (University of Sydney, N.S.W.), Graeme Pretty (The South Australian Museum, Adelaide), Charles Dortch (The Western Australian Museum, Perth), Dr. P. J. Coutts (Victoria Archaeological Survey, Melbourne), Dr. D. R. Horton (Australian Institute of Aboriginal Studies, Canberra), F. P. Dickson (Macquarie University, North Ryde, N.S.W.), R. J. Lampert (The Australian Museum, Sydney), Prof. V. R. Kabo (Institute of Ethnography, Academy of Science, Moscow, U.S.S.R.), Sandra Bowdler (University of New England, N.S.W.), and Dr. Goeffry Bailey (Department of Archaeology, Cambridge University, England).

Useful suggestions about ethnoarchaeology in general were provided by numerous individuals, including Dr. Paul Mellars and Robin Torrance (University of Sheffield, England), Prof. G. Connah (University of New England, N.S.W.), Prof. C. B. M. McBurney (Department of Archaeology, Cambridge University, England), Dr. P. Bion Griffin (University of Hawaii, Honolulu), Dr. Michael Schiffer (University of Arizona, Tucson), Dr. Karl L. Hutterer, (University of Michigan, Ann Arbor), Dr. Mark P. Leone (University of Maryland, College Park), Dr. Michael Stanislawski (Museum of New Mexico, Santa Fe), Dr. Douglas Schwartz (School of American Research, Santa Fe), Dr. Ari Siirianen (National Board of Antiquities and Historical Monuments, Helsinki, Finland), Dr. D. T. Bayard (University of Otago, Dunedin, New Zealand), and Dr. Peter Gathercole (Museum of Archaeology and Ethnology, Cambridge University, England). I am grateful for the many excellent suggestions offered by these individuals and those mentioned in the text, although I remain entirely responsible for the views presented in this book.

Others have played an important part in assisting with various expertise and help in preparing this book. Special thanks go to Peter

Latz (Arid Zone Research Institute, Alice Springs, N.T.) for his advice on fire ecology and botany in the Central Desert, to Dr. Douglas Haynes (Western Mining Corporation Pty. Ltd., Canberra) for expertise on the geology of the Warburton Ranges area, to Mr. Arthur Court (Director), Dr. Ian Telford, and Dr. Michael Crisp (Herbarium, Canberra Botanic Gardens, A.C.T.) for their advice on the botany of various Australian plants, to Ms. Clare Davies-Jones (Cambridge University Press, Trumpington St., Cambridge) for her sound criticism of the manuscript as it was being written, and to Mr. Nicholas Amorosi (American Museum of Anthropology, New York) for drawing the illustrations in Figs. 2, 3, and 5. It is no easy matter to produce a book of this scope, and I am grateful for the competent advice and help these individuals and institutions provided.

Finally, I wish to thank the Australian Institute of Aboriginal Studies (Canberra) for permitting me to cite some of the data and conclusions in Chapter 5 (including Tables 8–10) that I published earlier in a paper titled "Ethno-archaeology; or, where do models come from?" appearing in *Stone tools as cultural markers*, edited by R. V. S. Wright, 1977. Thanks, too, to the American Museum of Natural History for allowing me to recycle data and ideas about Puntutjarpa Rockshelter that first appeared in "Puntutjarpa Rockshelter and the Australian desert culture," *Anthropological Papers of the American Museum of Natural History*, **54**(1977), and to Robert S. O. Harding and Geza Teleki, editors of *Omnivorous primates: Gathering and hunting in human evolution* (Columbia University Press, New York, in press), for letting me develop ideas about home bases and fire (or the lack of it) that first appeared in my paper in this volume, titled "To have and have not: The ecology of food-sharing behavior among contemporary hunter–gatherers and early hominids." Similar thanks go to *The American Anthropologist*, for permitting me to reuse some of the data and ideas that appeared in my paper, "The anthropology of human residues," **80** (1978).

Introduction: archaeology and the totality of human behavior

For several years it has been fashionable among prehistorians to refer to archaeology as "fossilized human behavior," following a call to arms issued by Binford in 1964 (p. 425). Enough has happened in the field since then to cause archaeologists working on both sides of the Atlantic and in the Pacific as well to start asking whether such a goal – namely, the application of deductive arguments to archaeological evidence in order to discover how human beings in different prehistoric societies behaved in the past – is realistic. Certainly, to someone outside the field of archaeology, this goal might seem to be the height of presumption. One does not have to be a trained archaeologist to understand how the ravages of weathering and decomposition affect perishable remains of past communities; and when one adds to this the recognition that material remains account for only a small part of the total range of human behavior, most of which consists of symbols (i.e., language, social organization, ideas) that are manipulated in various ways, most of which are nonmaterial in nature, the problem must seem insurmountable.

The trained archaeologist knows, too, that the obvious limitations posed by decay and the material nature of the evidence are further compounded by other sources of error that can affect his behavioral interpretations. Sampling error, faulty or imprecise chronologies, disturbed sediments and site deposits, and a multitude of other factors rise up like armed men to obstruct the archaeologist in his quest for satisfying knowledge about past human behavior. The question is: Are archaeologists engaged in such a quest really informing us about past human behavior? Or are they merely sowing more dragon's teeth; that is, creating more ambiguities and difficulties for themselves by attempting to study behavior? Perhaps, as some might argue, archaeologists would be better off to confine their efforts to constructing chronologies and recording the spatial distributions of various artifacts and other remains. Why do we persist in this difficult quest when it would be so much easier to limit our interests to the traditional time – space frameworks that have been a basic part of archaeology from the beginning? No one is seriously suggesting that the need for such time–space frameworks in archaeology is over, so why not leave it at that?

More and more archaeologists today would answer this question by stating that archaeology simply for the sake of chronicling past human events is the dullest form of intellectual stamp-collecting imaginable. While time–space relationships are a necessary first step in understanding the prehistory of any region, they would argue that these are only a means to a larger end, namely, the behavioral explanation of those relationships. Can one discover why the material remains of prehistoric peoples vary in time and space? Inevitably even the dullest chronicler of events must wonder how these events came to be the way they were, and such wonderings lead one, willy-nilly, to consider processes of human behavior that might account for such events.

So the problem is not one of deciding whether or not archaeologists should attempt to understand past human behavior. Rather, the problem is basically the same as it has always been since the beginnings of archaeology as a discipline–finding and improving ways to overcome the limitations posed by the nature of archaeological evidence. The application of principles of stratigraphy to archaeology, the use of various kinds of sequence dating, radiocarbon and other radioactive decay dating techniques, fossil pollen studies, faunal analysis, and many other methods stand as landmarks in this process. Each of these methods calls for particular skills and training, and as a result there has developed within archaeology a natural tendency to specialize. In other words, as archaeologists develop different ways to overcome the limitations posed by their evidence, they move in different directions according to the special demands imposed by their choice of approach. It becomes more and more difficult for archaeologists to obtain useful results in their own particular specialties and still keep a wider view of archaeology as a social science. Other social scientists, too, find it increasingly difficult to understand what is happening in archaeology as the literature becomes more diverse and specialized. What possible relevance, they ask, does archaeology have for their kind of social science?

Anthropologists in particular have been ambivalent toward archaeology. In part this ambivalence arises from basic differences in the histories of archaeology and anthropology, especially in Great Britain and America. Until recently, as Leone (1972:16) and Smith (1976:275–6) point out, social and cultural anthropology usually were the "donor disciplines" when it came to the development of a new theoretical framework, with archaeology acting as a kind of passive "recipient" of these ideas. Archaeologists persistently mined the anthropological literature in search of useful ideas about human behavior that could be used to interpret the prehistoric evidence. Social and cultural anthropologists, for their part, could not help but wonder if archaeology could ever be as rewarding as their approach, since archaeologists were limited to studying the material remains of human behavior. Only in living human societies, they might argue, could one expect to understand the operation of the really important and interesting aspects of human behavior, namely those having to do with the human use of symbols. Since these are mainly nonmaterial in nature, it seemed reasonable to conclude that archaeologists, with their reliance on material remains, could never hope to do more than deal with a limited and rather unimportant part of the story of the human species. Indeed, the historic precedent for such a view within archaeology was strong, since the pioneering work of Radcliffe-Brown and Malinowski was as much concerned with supplanting earlier preoccupations with conjectural history by evolutionary and diffusionist anthropologists as it was with developing new analytical approaches to the study of living human societies. The problem more recently has been that, as archaeologists have shown an increased interest in understanding processes of past human behavior, they have also increasingly run the risk of adopting a kind of client relationship toward social and cultural anthropology in order to obtain ideas that would enliven their discipline. Such a dependency relationship is always uncomfortable for both the donor and the recipient discipline. For a time, then, archaeology has seemed directed toward an inescapable dilemma. The more archaeologists tried to enliven their interpretations of the past by applying ideas about the past derived from social and cultural anthropology, the more they exposed themselves to the criticism of social and cultural anthropologists whose studies encompassed a wider and presumably more satisfying range of human behavior. Was archaeology destined ever to become anything more than either a collective attempt at chronicling human prehistory or a kind of conjectural history based at second hand upon social and cultural anthropology?

With this question in mind we can perhaps begin to understand a phenomenon that has grown into an important new development within archaeology during the last decade – the detailed ethnographic study of contemporary, living human societies by trained archaeologists. Termed ethnoarchaeology in most quarters, this approach represents an attempt by archaeologists to overcome the limitations of their data in interpreting past human behavior without a correspondingly increased dependence upon the theoretical approaches favored by social and cultural anthropologists. Or, to put it even more simply for the sake of argument, *we are now seeing the development of a new kind of anthropology that is based upon the observational and interpretive skills that are peculiar to archaeology*. The rise of this approach signals an effort by archaeologists to apply a theoretically self-conscious set of methods to the discovery and testing of general principles about human behavior in relation to materials and material residues. Archaeologists, for so long dependent upon social and cultural anthropologists for ideas about human behavior upon which to base their interpretations, are now in the process of developing an approach which will enable archaeology to make its own unique contribution to social science. This is not to suggest, of course, that archaeologists must limit their explanations to purely material aspects of human behavior; as we shall see later on, the archaeologist is always concerned with explaining the totality of human behavior, including social and symbolic relations and "unique" events in prehistory.

What probably distinguishes this approach more than anything else from earlier efforts by archaeologists to use anthropological data and theory is the importance placed upon the archaeologist or archaeologically trained ethnographer doing his or her own first-hand field studies of living, contemporary societies. This activity I shall call *living archaeology*, as opposed to the wider definition of ethnoarchaeology as a theoretical and methodological subdiscipline. That is, I shall primarily explore how archaeologists do[1] ethnoarchaeology, rather than worrying at length about what ethnoarchaeology is. The ethnoarchaeologist is concerned primarily with examining human behavior in relation to materials and material residues as a means of discovering relationships within contemporary societies that allow him to specify when and under what circumstances certain kinds of behavior may have been important in relation to overall processes of human adaptation. Hence the title of this book and also the emphasis on fieldwork, both of my own and that of colleagues, done in Australia. Using Australian Aborigines as a source of case studies and primary observations, I shall demonstrate what seem to be key principles in carrying out and applying this approach to our wider understanding of the behavior of the human species in general. I have published some of the ideas and data presented in this book in other places, but there does seem to be value in trying to unify this work by bringing it together as a coherent whole.

At this point I should note that much valuable research in ethnoarchaeology is currently going on among living people in many different parts of the world and at every level of sociolcultural complexity. There is no necessary reason for ethnoarchaeologists to limit their interests to traditional or semitraditional hunter–gatherer societies or to one particular geographical area like Australia. Right now, valuable work of this kind is continuing among several hunter–gatherer societies (for example, by Wilmsen and by Yellen among the !Kung of the Kalahari Desert in Africa; by L. Binford among the Eskimo of the Anaktuvuk Pass region of Alaska; by Griffin among the Agta of northeast Luzon in the Philippines; by Meehan and Jones among the Anbara Aborigines of Arnhem Land, Australia; and by O'Connell among the Alyawara Aborigines of the Central Desert of Australia) as well as among farming and herding societies (for example, by Longacre among the Kalinga of Luzon, Philippines; by Stanislawski among the Hopi Indians of Arizona; by Hole among the Baharvand nomads of Iran; by Kirch among Western Polynesian farmers and fishermen; by David among the Fulani of Africa; by Hodder among the Pokot and other societies of West Kenya; and by J. P. White, Lauer, and others in New Guinea) and even among modern, complex societies (like "Le Projét du Garbage" by Rathje in Tucson, Arizona). While these and other studies will be referred to, the primary emphasis here is on Australia for the rather arbitary-sounding reasons that this, too, has been a productive area for this approach and happens to be this author's main area of regional competence. The general principles derived from an examination of living archaeology in Australia should, however, be applicable anywhere in the world and to a wider field of social science than just archaeology.

These general principles and demonstrations of them by means of material derived from recent work in Australia constitute a first step toward an unified theory of ethnoarchaeology. So much discussion has occurred recently about the nature and direction of ethnoarchaeology that it seemed timely to attempt this exercise. This will not be an attempt to reconcile all of the differing views that currently exist about ethnoarchaeology, since many of these views are contradictory and cannot be reconciled. Instead, I shall try to select and develop those views that appear to point in the direction that will be most productive. I realize that an overly doctrinaire presentation could have a chilling effect on the use of this approach, so I should make it clear now that my aim is to open doors to productive research rather than to close them. While my theoretical and methodological eclecticism will be tempered by personal preferences and choices, I hope this personal effort on my part will give a unity to this approach that could not be attained by any group of scholars attempting to do this jointly. Ethnoarchaeology, and its offspring, living archaeology, are not beasts that can be bred successfully by a committee.

With these general comments in mind, let us now examine how living archaeology is done and what its importance might be for our understanding of human behavior in general.

1

TIKATIKA

Nothing should begin to reveal the essential problems of archaeological interpretation in relation to behavior better than a close look at contemporary behavior in the context of a reasonably well-bounded physical locus comparable to what archaeologists habitually refer to as a site. The locus I have chosen for this exercise is the habitation camp at the waterhole called Tikatika in the Western Desert of Australia, as it was occupied by a group of 13 Ngatatjara-speaking Aborigines on one day during the summer of 1966. This fine-focus description of the activities occurring at that site will then be compared with the physical remains left at the site following its abandonment.

In this description I am taking several literary liberties that should in no way affect the validity of the observations. Not all of the social activities described here actually took place on this single day, but they did occur in the context described, mainly at or close to the time that I have chosen, and they involved the actual people included in this account. In a limited sense, this "day in the life of. . ." is a composite account of behavior observed over the course of several days, since it was clearly impossible for my wife and me to have all thirteen people directly in view continuously during this period. As Wobst (1978:303–5) correctly notes, even the most empirical attempts at observation must necessarily have certain gaps and discontinuities. These can be filled in as one observes a community over a period of time and gets to know the people better. Also, I shall not be using the personal names of individuals in this camp but will refer to them instead by their subsection names. While nothing of a compromising nature is being reported here, this kind of anonymity for one's informants is now accepted practice among anthropologists in matters of publication. The use of subsection instead of proper names should adequately preserve confidentiality without affecting the verissimilitude of the situations I shall be describing.

A Western Desert Aborigine habitation base-camp near the
Clutterbuck Hills, about 65 kilometers west of Tikatika, Febru-
ary 1967. Despite the cast-off European clothing they wore,
these people were entirely dependent upon wild food products
for their subsistence.

As it was . . . Tikatika: December 26, 1966

Among the Western Desert people, activity began at first light. As
the first band of yellow light appeared on the horizon, the morning
bird chorus commenced along with the appearance of the first of
what became hordes of flies later in the day. In each family's camp
one could hear stirrings and conversation as someone in each camp
built up the fires and threw out the dogs. The air was dead still, so
voices carried easily between camps. The smoke rose straight up,
creating a filmy layer of blue haze over the camp that seemed to be
part of the landscape itself. Yet this fine smoke haze was as transient
here today as the hunting-and-gathering way of life that my wife
and I were observing among these desert Aborigines. It was still
quite dark, but a shout from Tjupurula's camp brought everyone
over. Tjupurula and the younger of his two wives, Nyapanyangka
(2), had a baby daughter, Nyakamara, who was approaching the age
when she should be able to take her first steps and start to walk.

Tjupurula and Nyapanyangka (2) were seated about 2½ meters (8 ft.) apart on opposite sides of their camp. In the firelight, Tjupurula held little Nyakamara out at arms' length while Nyapanyangka (2) extended her arms toward Nyakamara, urging her to walk across the gap of about a meter on her own.

This had been going on for some time each morning, but the reason for all the excitement this morning was that, for the first time, Nyakamara had succeeded in walking across the gap. Tjupurula called everyone over to have a look at Nyakamara's footprints in the sand. With some excitement, he and Nyapanyangka (2) pointed to the tiny tracks, and everyone looked and commented. The interest was more in the tracks than in the act of walking for the first time. This did not surprise us, considering the importance of tracks and tracking in the lives of these people. European observers have remarked on the almost uncanny ability of Aborigines to follow and identify the tracks of individuals whom they know by the sight of their tracks. These accounts do not exaggerate, but, of course, there is nothing uncanny about this skill either. From the very first steps a child takes, the entire community takes an interest and notes the tracks so well that, in a short time, they become as much a part of a person's social personality as his or her physiognomy and kinship.

After this initial excitement, people retired to their own family camps and ate some leftover food from the previous day's foraging. There are no formal meals or mealtimes among these desert people, but some plant foods that are processed after collection are always kept around and eaten the following morning. In this case, the only hot item on the menu was tea boiled in a billycan. (Tea, along with the billycan, tobacco, and various colored yarns, is among the few nonnutritive gifts that we could give these people as a partial reward for their patience in allowing us to camp with them and make these observations. Tea is not a traditional part of the Aboriginal diet.) This morning, large balls of kampurarpa (*Solanum centrale*), fashioned by grinding the raisinlike, sun-dried fruit into a paste and compressing the paste into a ball about the size of a large grapefruit, were passed around within each family camp while each family member broke off a piece and ate it. The other item on this morning's menu consisted of the sun-dried husks of ngaru (*Solanum chippendalei*), which were pulled off long sticks on which they had been strung and eaten. Like kampurarpa, the ngaru husks were shared with everyone in each family camp, and only a small amount of both of these wild plant foods was left by the time everyone was finished. Meanwhile, a child from each of the two family camps was sent over to the waterhole, about 180 meters (600 ft.) away, to get water for more tea.

Once it became light enough to see around, we could assess the

A Western Desert Aborigine woman grinding kampuṛarpa
(*Solanum centrale*) at a habitation base-camp near the Clutterbuck Hills, Western Australia. This is one of several edible
plant species that provide the bulk of the diet for these people
most of the time.

physical surroundings with greater clarity. Tikatika is, in fact, a "native well," that is, several holes in the ground where there is a localized subsurface water table (in this case about 2½ meters below the
ground surface) in a relatively impermeable layer of conglomerate
with a hardness intermediate between soil and true rock. Water
sources like this are enlarged by people and no doubt by animals,

too, as it becomes necessary to dig deeper for water, and also whenever the camp is revisited and one needs to clean out slumped soil
and other debris that has accumulated since the last visit.

The habitation campsite at Tikatika on this occasion contained five
windbreaks: three large ones (for Tjupurula's, Tjungurayi's, and
Tjampitjin's families, respectively) and two small ones (one for Tjapaltjari, an as yet unattached young man, and the other for Nyungurayi, Tjungurayi's widowed sister). Each windbreak consisted of a
row of mulga boughs arranged in a linear fashion alongside an
oval-shaped area of cleared ground and a series of hearths. Each of
the three larger windbreaks had a large stone seed-grinding slab and
one or two hand-held seed-grinding stones, either next to the windbreak or cached not far away in some grass. The center of the
cluster of windbreaks was situated 186 meters (610 ft.) southeast of
the waterhole, in an area that was burned clear of spinifex and other
grasses in order to drive away snakes. As the weather got hotter, the
men said they would construct slightly more substantial shade-
shelters made of mulga boughs. But for now the shade of the mulga
trees around the camp was sufficient for comfort during the heat of
the day. The remains of two shade shelters from a previous summer
occupation were visible about 30 meters (100 ft.) southwest of the
waterhole, along with the scattered remains of a hunting blind of
boughs that was formerly constructed close to the waterhole.

When these people first arrived here on this visit, the women
immediately went to the old camps and dragged their large seed-
grinding slabs out of the grass, where they were cached, to their new
camps. In a couple of instances, they also tore down old bough
shelters and dragged the boughs over to their new camps for firewood. They also lit small fires around the bases of about a dozen
large, dead mulga trees at various distances from camp up to about
240 meters (800 ft.), and during the first few nights here the stillness
of the night air was punctuated wtih the sound of falling trees as one
after another of these mulga trees was burned through at the base
and toppled over – providing an ample source of firewood, which
was dragged into camp when needed.

The three families, totaling thirteen people, had been camped
here for the last eleven days, having walked to this location via a
series of smaller, surface waterholes to the east. To reach Tikatika
they crossed open terrain that is flat except for low undulations of
clay conglomerate knolls alternating with rows of parallel sandhills.
Close to Tikatika there is a low outcrop of conglomerate that serves
as a landmark for people crossing this otherwise relatively featureless area, and about 64 kilometers (40 miles) further to the west,
there is a series of low rocky ridges (indicated on the map as the
Clutterbuck Hills) separated from Tikatika by a further series of

alternating conglomerate knolls and sandhills. This region, situated about 160 kilometers northwest of the Warburton Ranges Mission, Western Australia, is typical of the sort of country described as the "Great Undulating Desert of Gravel" by the explorer David Carnegie (1898:207) when he crossed it in 1896. The sandhills and flat interdunal corridors are dominated by spinifex (*Triodia sp.*), a unique Australian desert plant that has the combined qualities of grass and cactus. It grows in pale green tufts up to three or four feet high with grass stems emerging from the upper part of the plant from a cushionlike base of thorny spines. This "grass" is often highly resinous, but, at least in this region, it is not edible. Along with spinifex, one finds other plants growing in the sandhills, such as *Crotolaria cunninghamii*, a small, straight-stemmed shrub with a silvery-green, velvety covering on its stem and leaves, and a pale yellow-green flower. This plant characteristically occurs in the otherwise bare, sandy tops of the sandhills and is much sought-after by the Aborigines during the summer for its supple bark, which is used in making sandals. Except for occasional *Hakea* and *Acacia* shrubs, these sandhills are relatively sterile of edible plants, at least in their pristine, unaltered state. Although there were rains this particular summer in other parts of the Western Desert, it remained dry here at Tikatika. Large storm clouds, offshoots of monsoons from the tropical North of Australia many hundreds of miles away, had been seen at times. But no rain had fallen here, and the spinifex was brittle and yellow in color.

The vegetation of the clay conglomerate knolls is much the same, although one finds fairly dense stands of mulga (*Acacia aneura*), a short tree with extremely hard wood, along with other acacias and shrubs in flat or undulating areas where there is a high clay content in the soil. These areas of mulga scrub provide the best available cover for kangaroos, which on the whole are scarce in this region. One conspicuous feature of the mulga scrub immediately around Tikatika and everywhere else in this area is the large amount of dead wood lying about. The trunks and branches of dead trees, with their shaggy gray bark, are visible everywhere, even though white ants (termites) usually consume them rapidly. What one sees, in fact, is vegetation that is very limited in terms of the number of species, and shows evidence of catastrophes (in this case, severe droughts) that occur frequently enough to kill trees faster than they can be consumed by the formidable number of white ants in the area.

Although less visibly apparent on one's first look around, the array of fauna in the Tikatika region is also quite limited, both in terms of the number of species and also in relation to the number and sizes of individual animals. There is a relative profusion of bird life, but one seldom sees large animals of any kind. Kangaroos and

Aerial view of sandhill country in the Simpson Desert, Central Australia. Large areas of both the Central and Western Deserts consist of this kind of terrain. The sandhills shown in the photograph average about 10–15 meters high.

emus occur here sometimes, and one sees their tracks enough around the waterhole at Tikatika to warrant setting up brush blinds near the water for hunting them. But none were known to be in the vicinity at this time, although the prospect of catching a fast-digging and elusive small marsupial, the rabbit-eared bandicoot (*Macrotis lagotis*), was discussed by both the men and women in camp this morning. Not only is this rare marsupial good to eat, but its white-tipped, furry tail is a favorite hair ornament. And digging for one presents a hunting challenge that few Aborigines can resist.

More important, however, is the fact that the sandhills and sand-plains around Tikatika abound with small goanna lizards (*Varanus gouldii*) – called kurkati by these desert people – which can be caught with relative ease. While Nyapanyangka (1), Tjupurula's older wife, and Nyangala, the wife of Tjungurayi, considered the possibility of hunting a bandicoot, they said in the end that they were more likely to catch lizards and other small game like feral cats along the way than they were to catch a bandicoot. The decision was finally made to forage for kampuṛarpa in a locality about 9½ kilometers (6 miles) to the north of Tikatika, and then search afterwards for a bandicoot.

Tjupurula, Tjampitjin, and Tjungurayi, the three older men, and Tjapaltjari, a young man, meanwhile discussed the prospects of making a longer trip to the south, where they hoped to pick up tracks of kangaroos moving through this area and also perhaps catch a bush turkey (i.e., the bustard, *Eupodotis australis*) out in the spinifex. This discussion, with all the adult men and women participating, lasted over 45 minutes and included several contingency plans. For example, if the women saw any fresh kangaroo tracks, they would put up a smoke signal to call the men over. Furthermore, they said they would light the fires in a sequence to indicate the direction in which the kangaroos were traveling. Once these plans were agreed upon, there was a simultaneous move by everyone to gather up the implements needed for the day's activities. The men took their spears and spearthrowers, and each man had a belt of human hairstring and a firestick (nothing more than a smoldering piece of mulga wood taken from the fire). The women took wooden bowls – small flattened ones for digging, and large, deep ones which they fill with water for the outward trip and fill with harvested fruit for the trip back – and wooden digging-sticks. Nyapanyangka (1) had a metal digging stick which was made originally from the push-rod on a mechanical windmill and was traded to her by a relative living over 320 kilometers (200 miles) away. The children and dogs accompanied the women, while the men went off unaccompanied. (At this point I should mention that my wife Betsy and I would usually go our separate ways, I with the men and she with the women, or else I would sometimes go with the women myself. Some sort of composite account here is inevitable.)

The departure was quite early (6:45 a.m.), and there was a slight chill in the air which the men overcame periodically by stopping to ignite a spinifex plant with their firesticks. These resinous plants burst into flame, while the men stood around the fire to get warm. Tjupurula, the oldest man present, always complained about the cold, even when, to me at least, it did not seem cold at all. The men stopped constantly to allow him time to "light up," and, since no one attempted to extinguish these fires, we soon had a large area of spinifex burning behind us. The men continued their hunt in the manner of a leisurely stroll, following a meandering route and stopping frequently to examine an old animal track or any other detail of potential use in the landscape. At one point, Tjapaltjari spotted the fresh tracks of a goanna and followed it at a lope for about 5 minutes until he reached the entrance to its burrow. Sandplain goannas live in shallow, short burrows, so Tjapaltjari's technique was first to stamp heavily with his heel in an arc around the burrow on the side away from the entrance, in order to immobilize the creature inside, and then to take a short stick lying nearby and use this as an impromptu digging-stick to dig into the burrow entrance. In this case, he hardly had to dig at all, since the goanna's tail stuck out of the sand just inside the entrance. A quick grab into the burrow sealed the lizard's fate, and it was hauled out and immediately hit on the head to kill it. Then it was gutted and secured under his hair-string belt, leaving his hands free for further activity. Altogether, this hunting episode took 7½ minutes from the first sight of the tracks until the lizard was secured for carrying, and the animal weighed 1.24 kilograms (2¾ lb.) – a slightly bigger-than-average go-anna obtained in slightly less than the average amount of time for hunting episodes connected with this species. Tjapaltjari was understandably pleased, but in fact this kind of "kill" is a foregone conclusion once the tracks are seen. At the end of this study in 1966–70, my notes showed that on only four out of 220 episodes when I observed Aborigine men, women, or children begin their pursuit of fresh goanna tracks did they fail to obtain at least one animal for their efforts. While small, these lizards are a fairly common resource that is easy and reliable to obtain. Before this day was over, two more of these goannas were caught by the men, while the women brought back a goanna, a small blue-tongue lizard (*Tiliqua scincoides*), and a small "mountain-devil" lizard (*Moloch horridus*), totaling just over 4 kilograms (9 lb.) in body weight (nearly all of which was also meat-weight, for reasons that will be explained later).

After three hours, or around mid-morning, we reached a small and nearly dry waterhole called Tjalputjalpu. A fresh set of kanga-roo tracks had been seen heading in this general direction, so the three men set about constructing a brush blind about 12 meters (40 ft.) from the waterhole. They agreed that there was enough water to attract game, but they had considerable discussion about where to position the blind. The problem at Tjalputjalpu is that the waterhole is situated in the open, along the top of a knoll of conglomerate. There are no natural defiles or gullies to restrict movement of game, and, consequently, it is hard to know from what direction kangaroos or emus might come. As I was beginning to learn, open waterholes like this are poor places for hunting. Nevertheless we spent most of the remainder of the day there, sitting quietly within the semicircu-lar blind of mulga boughs. From time to time each man in the hunting party used the chipped stone flake attached to the end of his spearthrower to resharpen the wooden tips of his spears. In Tjampitjin's case the stone flake had been reused and resharpened so often that it was worn down to a narrow slug, and it popped out of its haft and was left on the ground within the blind. Tjampitjin borrowed Tjungurayi's spearthrower to finish the sharpening task he had begun with his own hafted adze flake. Tjampitjin and Tjun-gurayi shared the use of a steel axehead back in camp. The axe was acquired in trade from distant relatives, but it is too heavy to bring along for woodworking tasks on one-day trips away from camp like this one.

Fortunately this was a fairly comfortable place to wait for game, mainly thanks to a big mulga tree next to the blind that gave adequate shade most of the time. Altogether we waited for about six hours without ever seeing any game at all. Finally the men decided they were hungry, and we lit a small fire and boiled a billycan of tea (the billycan, tea, sugar, and some damper coming out of my pack, of course) and sat around making small-talk for a while before setting off for camp. We headed back in the same leisurely and circuitous manner as we took in the morning, stopping frequently to pursue lizards and take little "snacks" of edible fruits from bushes along the way. In particular, there was a shrub called yarnguli (the botanical identification is unknown) that produces a fairly tasty berry in small quantities, and these were picked and eaten whenever seen. None, however, were carried back to camp. We also stopped at one point to dig out a grub from the rotting base of a desert poplar tree (botanical identification unknown), but only one of these was found, and it, too, was eaten on the run. Under circumstances such as these grubs are eaten raw, but if a sufficient number are collected they may be carried back to camp and roasted lightly before being consumed.

On the way back, Tjungurayi and Tjapaltjari walked together, and Tjungurayi teased Tjapaltjari about his intentions regarding Nyakamara, Tjupurula's oldest daughter. On this occasion, the matter was something for mild joking, but it was no secret that Tjapaltjari's interest in camping on his own with these families had to do with his interest in marrying Nyakamara. According to the rules of kinship and subsection relationships, there is no obstacle to such a marriage, and Tjapaltjari and Nyakamara appeared to be genuinely fond of each other. Tjupurula was not opposed either, although to my knowledge there had been no earlier betrothal of the girl by him to Tjapaltjari. Tjapaltjari's behavior toward Tjupurula was circumspect, as required by rules of avoidance behavior that encompass even potential in-laws and are strongly maintained in the Western Desert generally. Even mild joking would be unthinkable between Tjapaltjari and Tjupurula, and in camp Tjapaltjari averts his head and makes a conscious effort to avoid direct discourse with Nyapanyanaka (1), Tjupurula's older wife and mother of Nyakamara. Even in the light banter with Tjungurayi there was a slight note of tension, since the issue remained unresolved.

We arrived back in camp around 5:30 p.m. For the men it had been a low-key kind of day addressed mainly to the business of hunting. Although the effort in hunting made by the men on this day was not great, the time expended was considerable (i.e., 36 full man hours) for rather small returns. In this case, the day's catch for the men consisted of three small goannas, totaling slightly more than 3 kilograms (7 lb.) in body weight, along with assorted bits of edible plant food and one grub of undetermined total weight, eaten along the way.

The men arrived back shortly before the women, and Tjungurayi decided on the return trip to start manufacturing a replacement for his spearthrower, which had a bad crack in it that his repairs had not been able to mend with any success. He saw a fairly straight mulga tree about a kilometer from camp on the way in, and, having got his steel axehead, he headed back to the tree to cut a spearthrower blank before it got dark. Using the steel axehead, Tjungurayi first made a V-shaped cut in the tree trunk and then carved two wedges of mulga wood to insert in the wood just above these cuts. Taking a large rock lying nearby, he pounded the outer surface of the tree trunk above the V-shaped cut to loosen the wood surface and then pounded the wedges into the wood until a flitch of wood began to lift away from the tree trunk. As the slab separated from the tree trunk, he shifted the position of each wedge farther up the trunk, with the result that a 660 millimeter (26 in.) slab of wood was speedily detached. Later in camp, Tjungurayi said he would shape this piece into the characteristic broad and somewhat flattened shape of a Western Desert type of spearthrower (although, in fact, he did not work again on this artifact for over a week). Before he and Tjampitjin acquired this metal axe, Tjungurayi had used a simple stone chopper to make the initial V-shaped cut. The chopper might be a rock with a naturally sharp edge or a stone that he retouched by direct percussion with a hammerstone to give it a single sharp edge. In either case, as I have observed on other occasions, a large rock found somewhere near the place where the removal of the wooden slab took place would be used, and this rock invariably was abandoned neare the base of the tree when the work was completed. In this case, the rock pounder and wooden wedges were left next to the base of the tree when we returned to camp. I doubt that Tjungurayi would have used his steel axehead for this job if the tree had not been situated fairly close to camp, where he could conveniently bring this rather heavy implement (1.8 kg. or almost 4 lb.) to it. By the time the two of us arrived back in camp it was almost dark, and the women and children had returned.

The women's day had been just as low-key as the men's, but it was more productive. Unlike the men, the women walked briskly and directly to their main objective – an area situated in sandhills about six miles from camp. When they arrived, the children set up a small "play camp" complete with a campfire lit by a firestick brought by

Nyapanyangka (1), while, about 30 meters (100 ft.) away Nyapany-angka (1), Nyapangati, Nyungurayi, Nyapanyangka (2), and Nyan-gala immediately started collecting kampuṛarpa fruit. The vegeta-tion in this area of the sandhills is noticeably more varied than is true for the country the men had passed through on the way out (and indeed for most of the spinifex country around Tikatika). Al-though no one commented on this at the time, I learned later that this area had been burned over several years ago following fires that were lit to chase a feral cat during a hunt. The hunt for the cat was vividly recalled back in camp, but the use of fire during the hunt was only an incidental part of the story. However, here, as in all other instances when my wife and I were present to observe, these fires were allowed to burn themselves out and consumed a large area of spinifex encompassing several square miles before stopping. The plants that grew back into the burned-over area included these edi-ble *Solanaceae* that the women were harvesting today.

Today, as on other similar occasions before, it was apparent that Nyangala and Nyapangati were close friends and inseparable com-panions. The strong affective ties between these two individuals ap-peared to be the real social "glue" that best explains why at least these two families were camped together here at Tikatika (as they had been before, even at Warburton). Their respective husbands and children got along well together, too, so no friction had arisen that might have caused them to camp apart. The kin ties that existed between these two families were not close enough to explain the fact that they consistently camped together, although the kin relations between Tjungurayi and Tjupurula were closer and might go far-ther toward explaining why Tjupurula's family was camped here with the other two families. Watching their behavior from day to day, I formed the inescapable, albeit rather subjective, conclusion that sentiment may at times outweight kinship in determining co-residence. Times like these, when laughter resounded between Ny-apangati and Nyangala from one sandhill to the next, were a power-ful corrective to any mechanistic attitude one might be tempted to adopt toward kinship as a determinant of behavior among the desert Aborigines.

The kampuṛarpa plants themselves are low, brown-colored bushes with dry leaves and numerous fine bristles or spikes. The fruits, which had fallen off the plants some time previously, were shrunken and wrinkled by the dry heat of the sun and looked like large raisins. Having found what they were looking for, the women and children all drank the water contained in the wooden bowls, and the women and most of the children set about picking up the sun-dried fruits and placing them in the bowls. Except for the two smallest children, who stayed close by in the "play camp," everyone worked steadily to harvest kampurarpa, and within an hour a full load had been collected. Indeed, the collection of fruit was so prodigious that before long the women were building up the sides of the bowls with grass and sticks in order to enlarge their carrying capacity. Much more fruit remained behind on the ground, and this spot was revisited for several more weeks. Finally, each woman took a twist of grass from nearby and fashioned an impromptu circlet to use in cushioning the fruit-laden bowls when they carried them back to camp on their heads. Women and children then started back to camp together, moving in a direct line and with few stops or detours. Although the children amused themselves by chasing small lizards that appeared along the way, they were told by their mothers to keep up, with the result that no lizards were actually caught. By shortly after noon they were back at camp with 10.1 kilograms (22½ lb.) of dry fruit.

After boiling a billy for some tea, the women poured water into the bowls of fruit and began to grind the kampurarpa into a seedy paste using large, flat stone-grinding slabs and hand-held stone grinders. As when the actual collecting was being done, the atmosphere was relaxed and sociable, with much small talk and joking, despite the obvious efficiency of the operations being performed. By far the most tedious and time-consuming activity in the collection and preparation of kampurarpa this day was the walk to and from camp, which took a total of about 4½ hours.

When the kampurarpa paste was packed into balls, the women sat or lay around for a while, and Nyapanyangka (1) aired her views concerning Tjapaltjari's interest in her oldest daughter. Unlike Tjupurula, she was opposed to the marriage, at least for now. First, she said, Nyakamara was too young. (Actually, she was no younger than many Aborigine girls when they marry, and I estimated that she was around 14 years old.) Second, and perhaps more important from her point of view, she felt that Tjapaltjari would be a poor match for her daughter. Nyapanyangka (1), as I had learned from having observed her in the past, was an intelligent and thoughtful woman who habitually analyzed situations and tried to plan ahead. Usually she was reserved and did not express her views, in contrast to the outgoing Nyapangati; but on this occasion, when it affected her own family directly, she was willing to speak out. And she had a compelling argument. Tjapaltjari was generally well liked and would, under completely traditional circumstances, make a good husband. He was an effective hunter and had advanced to the point in the sacred life where he was eligible to marry (i.e., he had been subincised). And he belonged to the appropriate subsection and category of kinship for such a marriage. Were it not for the fact that these three families and Tjapaltjari had previously come in from the desert and lived for over a year at Laverton and the Warburton Ranges

Mission, the marriage might be all right. But Nyapanyangka (1) knew that their return to the desert could not last indefinitely, and she was planning ahead for the time when, inevitably, they would have to return and reside in close proximity to Europeans and Aborigines from other parts of the desert.

While they were living at Warburton and Laverton, these "desert people" found themselves largely cut off from any access to the European-introduced goods that were circulating widely in the camps. Rifles, blankets, footwear, and other manufactured items were in great demand, but the desert people, lacking the education and contacts – not to mention the ability to speak English – of the Aborigines who had been resident at these places for much longer, were unable to get more than the bare essentials for their existence there. Tea, flour, sugar, and some tinned food found their way to the desert people at Warburton and Laverton along with a few odd steel axes and knives and some cast-off European clothing, but compared with the "mission people" and the Europeans, they were impoverished. (Gould, 1969:165–89 gives a fuller account of the state of affairs that existed at Warburton and Laverton at this time.)

As far as the desert people were concerned, the main strategy they considered effective for remedying this situation was to establish kin-ties with mission-based families through intermarriage. This would have the effect of involving the desert and mission Aborigines in kin-sharing networks that would overcome the social gap and material disparity between these two factions. At this time, however, no such marriages between these factions had occurred, and conditions at Warburton had grown worse as more and more exploitation of the desert people (particularly of the young, marriageable girls) had taken place. This exploitation took the form of sexual abuses, but for the desert people as a whole, perhaps the most important problem was the disadvantages they faced in obtaining any kind of employment or financial aid when forced to compete with long-time residents at Warburton. This was the paramount reason these three families voiced for their having returned to the desert several months ago, and it was something that was still uppermost in Nyapanyangka (1)'s mind. She would rather see Nyakamara married to an Aborigine man from the Warburton Mission settlement if possible. In broaching this idea, Nyapanyangka (1) was adapting a traditional notion of marriage as an alliance between kin groups to a new set of economic circumstances engendered by European contact and settlement in the Western Desert. I could not help but be impressed by how quickly and accurately Nyapanyangka sized up this new situation which, for these three families at least, had not existed before 1965.

So Nyapanyangka (1) opposed the marriage, at least for now,

and she thought it would be better for everyone, including her daughter, to discourage Tjapaltjari and hold out for a more propitious marriage partner from among the eligible men residing at the Warburton Mission. Nyapanyangka (1)'s arguments were compelling, and the other women quickly voiced their assent. Nyapangati, the most outspoken woman in the group camped at Tikatika, said she would support Nyapanyangka (1) in this matter, which meant that Nyapanyangka (1) had won for herself a powerful and persuasive ally.

(Over a year later this coalition was put to the test when Nyapangati and Nyapanyangka (1) managed, by means of public persuasion through singing aloud their grievances, to rally their male kin to drive Tjapaltjari out of the camp where they were living – about 40 kilometers (25 miles) from Warburton. Tjapaltjari at that time was paying special attention to Nyakamara by sporting cowboy boots, belt, hat, and so forth, in an unconvincing effort to prove that he, too, had "made it" at the Mission. On that occasion, the adult men, including Tjupurula, Tjungurayi, and Tjampitjin, as well as several others, publicly threatened to spear Tjapaltjari if he did not leave; and Tjapaltjari, faced with this overwhelming show of unity, left with as much dignity as he could muster. Interestingly, throughout the period here at Tikatika and later, it was apparent that Tjapaltjari was well liked by all concerned. The arguments and fights were without passion or real animosity, revealing a marked contrast between individually voiced feelings about Tjapaltjari as a person and the unity of their expected public behavior toward Tjapaltjari.)

The discussion was carried out in the shade of the mulga trees around the camp at Tikatika, and, after the heat of the day had passed, Nyapangati suggested that they should all go out and hunt for the bandicoot they had discussed earlier. This idea was taken up eagerly, and around 3:00 p.m. the women gathered up all the balls of processed kampurarpa fruit and placed them in wooden bowls that were stored in the boughs of the trees near camp. Camp dogs (fourteen in all for this group) are not fed by the Aborigines and must forage for food from the scraps and offal lying about the camp. As their emaciated appearance showed, they were underfed, and the desert people always stored food in trees or on top of their shelters to keep it away from the dogs. The women then set off again, carrying wooden bowls and digging-sticks as before, only now in a westerly direction, accompanied by the children and dogs. However, unlike their earlier trip, the route was more meandering and the pace was more erratic as women and children paused often to inspect an old lizard burrow or a set of tracks.

No bandicoots were seen, but everyone, including the children, was able to get a few handfuls of yarnguli berries. At one point, two

The confrontation between Tjapaltjari (extreme left) and Nyakamara's male kin at Mulyangiri, a desert camp about 23 kilometers from the Warburton Ranges Mission. This dispute,
which Tjapaltjari lost, arose from his attempts to marry Nyakamara in 1966–7. What, if any, evidence of such social behavior could be expected to survive in the archaeological record?

of the older children spotted the fresh tracks of a sandplains goanna
and captured it within a few minutes using the time-honored and
effective approach of stamping in the burrow and digging the animal out tail-first. On their own, the children pursued and caught
two more small lizards. The women, however, seemed more interested in continuing their earlier discussion about Tjapaltjari's marital
ambitions than in serious foraging, and I noticed that they stayed together as a group and talked constantly. Ordinarily the women fan
out in ones and twos and are much quieter as they move through the
bush. Every so often, though, the conversation was interrupted by
someone pointing out an unusually straight tree (straight trees are
uncommon in the desert, and the men would want to know about
this one for future reference when a new spear-thrower or throw-
ing-stick was needed) or an especially fine patch of taliwanti (*Crotolaria cunninghamii*) – for use in making sandals when the weather got
hotter. Despite the casual quality of this afternoon's walk through
the bush, there was a constant acquisition of information about useful plants and other resources by the women.

A small prize awaited in a tongue of sandhills that extends into the
conglomerate terrain not more than a mile from Tikatika. Here the
women discovered a few plants of wild tobacco. Despite the fact that
Betsy and I are generous with tobacco, these Aborigines said they
preferred the wild variety, which is a true native tobacco (*Nicotiana*

excelsior), and they collected it whenever they could. In a few minutes the plants were picked, later to be dried and chewed, mixed with ash to give extra potency. It was evident that the women were surprised by this find, which is not something that happens too often. Indeed, most basic food resources, that is, edible plants and smaller animals, are mentally inventoried so completely by the women that their location and probable condition are well known at any given time. Foraging for these items, we have found, has about the same degree of certainty as when a housewife in a modern, European society goes to the supermarket to shop. Each knows exactly where to look, with a reasonable certainty that the goods will be "on the shelf." Sometimes, of course, the goods are not, but for the Aborigine women this is no more a problem than it is for a modern housewife. Alternative sources are always kept in mind, and, except in times of fierce drought, the women never return to camp empty-handed. The foraging I observed this morning was akin to the "grocery shopping" we already know well from our own culture, whereas this afternoon's light foraging was more in the manner of a reconnaissance or perhaps a form of "exploratory shopping." If these women seemed inordinately pleased by their find of a few handfuls of tobacco this afternoon, perhaps their pleasure is best understood as something derived from the unexpected nature of the find – an extra treat.

The women returned to camp from their brief afternoon excursion just as it was getting dark, and the day's catch was discussed immediately as the fires were built up in front of each windbreak. When the fires burned down to coals, the lizards were placed in them and the coals heaped over. These were allowed to roast until the coals cooled – about 35–40 minutes – then they were pulled out and placed on the flat rock-grinding slabs and pounded vigorously with impromptu stone pounders (one of which, I noticed, was an old chopper that had been formerly used for some woodworking task). This pounding soon reduced each lizard to a pulpy mass of flesh, skin, and cartilege that was eaten in its entirety with the result that total body weight virtually equaled edible meat weight. Portions were broken off from this mass and passed to each member of the family, so that everyone got a share, even if the share was little more than a mouthful. Tonight Nyungurayi and Tjapaltjari both sat next to Tjungurayi's windbreak and shared in his family's catch together, of course, with their own contribution. Portions of prepared kampurarpa fruit were also eaten at this time, and the atmosphere in camp was relaxed and sociable. No one commented on the failure of the men to catch any kangaroos or other large game, and already there was talk of perhaps going off in another direction tomorrow to hunt for kangaroos. Although some conversation between the camps continued until about 8:30

Sandplains goannas (*Varanus gouldii*) about to be roasted in the coals of a small fire by one of Tjupurula's wives at Tikatika.

p.m., things were quiet and people asleep soon after. The only disturbance came around 9:00 p.m., when, for no apparent reason, several of the dogs began to bark. Conversation ensued between the camps to the effect that the dogs must have seen or heard a *mamu* (i.e., a ghost, or, to be more accurate, a part of the soul-substance of a dead relative that hovers around camp at night and allegedly has cannibalistic properties). Dogs are credited with the ability to recognize *mamu* at night and are thought to drive them away with their barking.

As it was . . . Tikatika: May 22, 1967
The foregoing account of a more or less typical day among a small group of Western Desert Aborigines during the Australian summer cannot do full justice to the complexity of these people's lives, even for so short a period. Yet even this rather meager account poses certain basic questions for the ethnoarchaeologist. In the simplest terms, these questions involve the problem of what Deetz (1968:281–5) has referred to as "archaeological visibility." It should be apparent that most of the behavior observed on this day, as on other days, cannot be reliably inferred from any material remains that are likely

to be abandoned at or around Tikatika. How are we ever to know, for example, about the approaching crisis of Tjapaltjari's marital expectations? Indeed, we cannot even see any obvious way to determine whether or not such a society, if represented only by its material remains, was polygynous (as these people are). It is true, in other words, that much of the richness of the ideational realm of human behavior will either be expunged from the archaeological record altogether or else be rendered ambiguous. Such criticisms have been made so often in the literature as to constitute a veritable library of "cautionary tales" (Lee, 1966; Heider, 1967; Bonnichsen, 1973; Gould, 1974; White, Modjeska and Hipuya, 1977). The criticisms presented in these and other cautionary papers are valid, but they can easily create the impression of ethnoarchaeology as a negatively directed discipline. Such an impression was recently echoed by Yellen (1977:8) when he referred to one of the legitimate approaches in ethnoarchaeology as the "spoiler technique," in which the aim is to encourage archaeologists to avoid major methodological difficulties. While this is true, it is also important to say that if ethnoarchaeology were concerned primarily with such criticism, it would amount to little more than a minor footnote in the development of archaeology in general.

Rather than moan about how little of the behavioral record observed at Tikatika remains for the archaeologist to infer, I would prefer to ask: How much of this behavior can be discovered through the use of ethnoarchaeological approaches? As we observe the living archaeology of the people of Tikatika, we must look for ways to establish reliable linkages between human behavior and materials, especially materials that are left behind in their final context of discard. Such linkages, once firmly posited on the basis of empirical observations of living human societies, can be used for making positive statements about past behavior as well as for understanding aspects of contemporary human behavior that are generally not well understood by social scientists.

To get a fuller picture of the magnitude of this problem, let us turn now to Tikatika as it appeared in May 1967, about five months after its abandonment by these people.

Birds and the wind are the only sounds one can hear today at Tikatika. The Aborigines have moved to the Mission, and the desert is empty of the sound of shouting by the women on their way to harvest kampuṛarpa or some other important plant or of excited conversations between camps in the still air of early morning. It has been five months since the desert people left this camp, when they moved on to Partjaṛ, a large drowned creekbed, or "billabong," in the Clutterbuck Hills farther to the west. A couple of months later they were brought back to the Warburton Ranges Mission by a min-

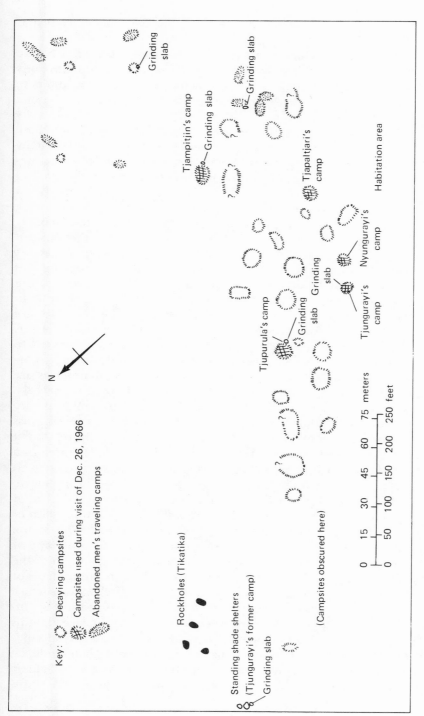

Fig. 1. Tikatika site.

ing survey party. What remains here of that day in December and the other days like it?

I have made this latest visit to Tikatika with a friend, a Native Welfare Officer from the Warburton Mission, who did not have any anthropological training. He is assisting me in my mapping and note taking, but I am especially grateful for his questions about the site, which are "naive" questions in the sense that they are unaffected by any prior knowledge of the detailed conditions under which these particular people had lived. His presence is a useful corrective to my own peculiar kind of ethnocentrism, namely, the unconscious tendency to assume that the patterns we are recording on the ground were necessarily all due to the activities that my wife and I had earlier observed among these desert Aborigines. My friend can look at these remains afresh, without preconceptions about what "should" be on the ground, and his questions sometimes reveal the ambiguities that these remains can represent.

Figure 1 shows the map of Tikatika we produced during this visit. It shows individual camps during December that were being lived in and used at that time. Now, five months later, these individual and family camps are still visible, although their features are becoming indistinct and clearly will not be visible much longer. Strong winds have eroded portions of the cleared areas next to each windbreak. The same wind has scattered and obscured portions of the hearths in each camp. The windbreaks themselves are dry and brittle now and can be expected to decompose rapidly. Indeed, these camps, now abandoned for only four months, are almost indistinguishable from the surrounding terrain. New grass has grown up within the habitation area of the campsite, and it covers the former cleared areas as well as the rest of the area as a whole. Sand and balls of rolling thorn grass (resembling nothing so much as American tumbleweeds) have partially filled in the native well at Tikatika. The only human remains that have any degree of permanence in this setting are the large, flat seed-grinding slabs of stone and scatters of small stone flakes and discarded tools in the vicinity of each camp. Even these stone flakes and tools are of dubious archaeological value, since there is no physical depth to the soil deposits here. This means that we are looking at the remains of an open-air campsite that has become nothing more than a surface scatter of stone artifacts, with items from every past period of human habitation now mixed together on the same surface – in this case, the same 25–50 millimeters (1–2 inches) of wind-stirred sand. Many more stone flakes and tools are visible today than could be seen on the surface of these same camps five months ago. As Table 1 shows, the overall difference within each camp between the num-

Table 1. *Stone artifacts visible on surface of Tikatika Campsites*[a]

December 26, 1966			May 22, 1967		
Tjupu-rula's camp	Tjungurayi's camp (including Nyungurayi)	Tjam-pitjin's camp	Tjupu-rula's camp	Tjungurayi's camp (including Nyungurayi)	Tjam-pitjin's camp
8	14	4	67	131	20

[a] Including flakes, cores, and seed-grinding implements. No stone artifacts were seen at Tjapaltjari's camp.

ber of artifacts visible on the surface in December and the number visible today is roughly 8:1. That is, about eight times as many stone artifacts are visible today, thanks to the scouring action of the wind in eroding the fine sandy surfaces of these camps. The irony here is that, from an archaeological point of view, the apparently greater richness of the site in stone artifacts is in fact a sign of stratigraphic disturbance and mixing that renders the site almost useless for any later attempt to sort out its chronology or to dis-cover the former loci or most of the activities that produced this debris. Wind and weather cannot move the stone seed grinders, however, and they alone have stayed exactly as they were left be-hind. Everything else has changed to some degree.

The physical appearance of Tikatika in May 1967 seems to sup-port Deetz's argument (1968:285) that the sites of most pedestrian hunter–gatherers would tend to fall below the threshold of archaeo-logical visibility. While stone artifacts in general remain visible, only certain kinds, namely large seed-grinding slabs, have remained within the same context as when they were abandoned. One can even say that, because the soil matrix where they rest has shifted, their context has shifted, too. The point is that while this class of objects has not moved, their context of association has been eroded away. In fact, nothing at Tikatika is reliably associated with anything else except for the general facts that: (1) There is an aggregation of stone artifacts of indeterminate age scattered in weak clusters on the surface of a large area; and (2) This area of artifact scatter lies several hundred feet from a waterhole.

The case of Tikatika is a powerful example of the futility of trying to draw direct archaeological conclusions from ethnographic obser-vations. Studies of this kind, in which one attempts to compare behav-ior with its "archaeological" manifestations, tend in most cases to be cautionary tales. While we cannot dispute the conclusions reached by

Lee (1966) in a parallel comparison of behavior and physical remains among the !Kung at the Kalahari-1 site, we may legitimately ask if this approach of direct comparison is ever likely to produce anything more than cautionary conclusions of this sort. Tikatika shows that direct comparisons and the cautionary conclusions they tend to produce have only a limited use for archaeology. This use hardly justifies the scholarly and logistical efforts one usually has to put into the study of living archaeology, and it cannot serve as a basis for making such studies if they are to be productive. Before we can ask what living archaeology *is*, we must ask ourselves what it *is not*, and the first thing it is not is the simple, direct comparison of living people with the physical remains they leave behind. As science lurches on, it sometimes takes paths that lead to dead ends. The case of Tikatika is an example of one such methodological cul de sac, and we are still left with the haunting problem of how to do justice to the richness and complexity of behavior observed in the Western Desert on that day in December 1966, and on many other days while these remarkable people, the desert Aborigines, were still living directly off the land.

2

Beyond analogy

While direct comparison of ethnographically observed behavior with "archaeological" patterning may be unrewarding, the use of ethnoarchaeology to discover analogies to the prehistoric past is downright misleading. Among the problems that have sprung up to plague archaeologists, like the armed soldiers from the proverbial dragon's teeth, the problem of analogy has been the most vexing and has generated a literature out of all proportion to its importance (for example, Ascher, 1961; Binford, 1967; Freeman, 1968; Gould, 1974; Yellen, 1977:1–4). Perhaps we would do better here to remember Winston Churchill's famous remark about an argument by a political colleague that ". . . there is less here than meets the eye."

Analogy's last hurrah
According to the *Shorter Oxford English Dictionary*, an analogy is an "Equivalency or likeness of relations," or, again, "A simile or similitude." More to the point, the *Fontana Dictionary of Modern Thought* defines analogy as:

> Likeness or similarity, usually with the implication that the likeness in question is systematic or structural. To argue by analogy is to infer from the fact that one thing is in some respects similar to another that the two things will also correspond in other, as yet unexamined, respects. . . [In logic] It is a form of reasoning that is peculiarly liable to yield false conclusions from true premises.

The obvious problem with all ethnographic analogies in archaeology is that they are self-limiting by their very nature. That is, they encourage us to assume the very things we should be trying to find out about human behavior. As Stanislawski (1973: 11) and others have noted, the use of analogy in archaeology constitutes an example of the "fallacy of affirming the consequent," which is really just a heightened form of wishful thinking.

There have undoubtedly been many prehistoric adaptations that have no existing counterpart in the ethnographic or historic record. Yet our whole stock of analogies must, of necessity, be derived entirely from historically and ethnographically known societies. It is already apparent that many important archaeologically known human adaptations cannot be understood through the direct application of analogy, if for no other reason than the fact that no historic counterparts for these societies were ever studied or described. For example, the pedestrian big-game hunters of the late Pleistocene in North America and Europe cannot effectively be understood by direct analagous comparisons with ethnographic Eskimos (most of whom hunt sea mammals or have other, specialized adaptations) or the bison-hunting Indians of the Great Plains of North America (who, except for Casteñada's brief account in 1541 [Winship, 1896], are known to us only after they had acquired the horse and became mounted hunters). No historic counterpart exists for this Pleistocene mode of adaptation.

This problem is even more acute when one attempts to understand the social behavior of early man, that is, pre-*sapiens*. It is in this area that the use of direct analogies drawn from ethnographic and ethnological studies has been especially insidious. It is difficult nowadays to break free of unexamined assumptions about the nature of early man and the hominization process that have been accreting like so much marine growth on a ship's bottom. The idea that hunting was essential to the hominization process has become inescapable (Ardrey, 1975; Washburn, 1976). Flowing from this central assumption are others that render the issue more confused than ever – for example, the widespread idea that all hunters share meat and the further notion that meat-sharing is really the only important form of sharing of food and access to resources that occurs among living hunter–gatherers and, by implication, with early man. Yet the conditions under which life was lived by pre-*sapiens* were fundamentally different from what they are today, and these differences have to be considered in any attempt to understand the social behavior of early man.

For example, Schaller has pointed out that no living social carnivores (i.e., lions, wolves, hyenas, hunting dogs, etc.) actually transport kills back to their lairs. The meat from the kill is always eaten at or near the site of the kill except in the unusual case of male African hunting dogs, which carry chunks of meat back to the lair in their stomachs and regurgitate them for the females, who have remained back at the lair with the pups. Even in this case, the regurgitated meat is consumed immediately and completely, with the result that no offal is left in the vicinity of the lair. Schaller's argument is that bringing a carcass to the lair would endanger the young by attracting other carnivores and scavengers. From an ecological and evolutionary point of view, such behavior would be maladaptive, because it would threaten the survival of the offspring and thus the reproductive survival of the species (Schaller, 1973: 275). These same ecological constraints would have applied to early hominids, meaning of course that prior to the use of fire by early man, there would have been no way that they could have effectively defended their lair or home base from predation, especially at night when considerable predation occurs. Thus the use of fire changed the "ground rules" for survival, enabling early man for the first time to bring his kill to camp and consume and share it there without undue risk to the young from predation. Contemporary hunter–gatherers all use fire and thus are freer of this particular constraint than other full- or part-time carnivores. So any attempt to draw analogies directly from modern or historic hunter–gatherers in order to understand early hominid behavior is immediately at risk, since we have reason to think that early man's treatment of kills before the use of fire was substantially different from what it became later on.

Clear evidence for the use of fire by man in Africa is quite late and does not appear in the archaeological record during the period between 3 million and 1 million years ago, when the existence of home bases has been widely assumed (Pfeiffer, 1972: 97). A collection of 3,510 faunal specimens was made from the "Zinjanthropus" occupation floor at Olduvai Gorge, 1,090 of which belonged to the larger mammals and reptiles (Leakey, 1971: 251–3). Since this living surface approximates what archaeologists expect a home base to look like (see especially Isaac, 1978), the presence of this fauna, most of which was broken into small pieces found in the central area of the living floor, is of special interest. While there is no evidence of an established pattern of big-game hunting in this material, there is the possibility of sufficient accumulation of offal around the living area to have attracted unwelcome predators. It has even been suggested that the arc-shaped area of almost bare ground between two portions of this living floor ws the base of a brush windbreak that served as a barrier against predators (Pfeiffer, 1972: 97).

But when we consider the role of fire – or, in this case, the implications of its absence – the evidence presents us with more questions than answers. For example, what was the relative importance of plant foods vis-à-vis meat in the total diet of the hominids living at this site? I can see no reason to assume that butchering, sharing, and consumption of meat was the primary economic activity here, even though there has been a tendency in some quarters to equate "home base" with "hunting base." Plant foods, which would not produce the offal to attract predators, might have been of equal or greater economic importance at this site. And how effective would a windbreak have been in keeping away predators in the absence of fire? Perhaps the home base in this case was a locus for foragers who mainly shared and consumed plant foods there and occasionally brought small and large animals to the site for consumption as well. They may have been ill-equipped to ward off competing predators, so any large concentration of offal in the camp would have been maladaptive. The faunal evidence at Olduvai is ambiguous about the actual numbers of animals involved and the rate at which they were consumed, so our comprehension of what a "home base" might have been like during the period of 3 million to 1 million years ago in Africa in the absence of fire – demonstrably the most effective means of securing such a base against predation – remains incomplete and open to speculation.

One of the more seductive notions built into the use of ethnographic analogy is the idea that the principle of uniformitarianism, a cornerstone of the natural and physical sciences, is applicable without qualification to the study of past human behavior. In arguing for what he called the "new analogy," Ascher enjoined archaeologists to ". . . seek analogies in cultures which manipulate similar environments in similar ways" (1961: 319). Mindful of the many abuses brought about by the uncontrolled use of analogy by archaeologists, Ascher was trying to introduce controls that would render the use of analogy more reliable. Yet, any attempt by archaeologists to understand past human adaptations from analogies of present-day adaptations, however similar in appearance, still presupposes that they are similar. Given such a framework, one cannot know more about the past than one already knows about the present. Even the suggestion by Ascher that examination of multiple analogies might be possible for a single archaeological phenomenon, while valid, cannot by itself provide a way for us to know more about the past than we already do about the present, since we are still bound by the present as the source of these alternatives. However, I see this latter argument as an important step forward in evolving an approach to ethnoarchaeology that will allow us to dispense with analogies altogether.

Binford's much discussed paper on smudge pits and hide smoking (1967), while claiming to refute the use of analogy in archaeology, is in fact an elaborate example of exactly the kind of "new analogy" that Ascher was arguing for. Instead of basing his analogy on simple cases of "look alikes" in ethnology and archaeology, Binford has compared complex "look alikes," in which the inherent probabilities of such similarities – between historic Upper Midwestern Indian smudge pits and those found archaeologically in the same general region – being due to coincidence is low. This may be a better and more controlled use of analogy than has been common in archaeology, but it is still analogy and is just as limited by uniformitarianist assumptions. What other possible interpretations for these archaeo-

logical pits might there be beyond the ones suggested by ethnographic and historic sources for that region? Could these pits have
served any other purpose than the one proposed for historic Midwestern Indians? Again, we are assuming that the prehistoric Indians of this region behaved toward materials in a manner uniformly
identical with the historic indigenes of the area, when in fact there is
no necessary reason for us to think that they did.

A similarly uniformitarianist sentiment was echoed by Wilmsen
when he asserted, "Archaeologists must assume that, other things
being equal, those processes which structure the ethnographic record
have also structured the archaeological record" (1970: 1). The problem with this assertion is that while some processes may be subject to
the principle of uniformitarianism, others may not. Golson (pers.
comm.) has recently shown how the requirements for raising pigs in
pioneer farming settlements in Australia during the nineteenth century reveal that there are certain essential characteristics in the relationship between man and pigs that may also have been true when
pigs became established in New Guinea over 9,000 years ago. Golson
sees this as an argument in favor of the early introduction of pigs as a
domesticant into New Guinea by man, basing his argument on the
idea that the essential features of this relationship are intrinsic to the
ecology of pigs as a species, which cannot become feral until after this
relationship has been severed. In other words, Golson is arguing that
pigs could not have entered New Guinea and established themselves
there as a wild species by themselves. Rather, they required the presence of man for this and became feral only in those areas where the
symbiotic relationship was broken and pigs, no longer being fed by
man, became feral. In New Guinea, as in Australia, feral pigs ordinarily occur only in areas adjacent to those already colonized by human
farmers. What makes this a convincing argument is that the process of
feralization described by Golson is based upon the intrinsic properties
of the pig in a region of the world (New Guinea and Australia) where
we already know that the pig (along with other placental mammals)
did not live prior to the arrival of man.

Yet, if we examine the role of pigs in different societies, we can
see that other processes of cultural adaptation to pig-raising may not
be as uniform or predictable as the one proposed by Golson. Compare how, for example, cultural attitudes toward pigs vary from one
society to another. At one extreme we find societies in the Middle
East where the pig is abhorred and religious prohibitions exist that
forbid people to eat pork, while at the opposite pole we find societies
like those of Highland New Guinea today where pigs are highly
regarded and are eaten with gusto. Here is where the principle of
uniformitarianism lets us down badly, since, given such variability,
we cannot safely assume that processes of human behavior, espe-

cially in relation to the manipulation of symbols, are always uniformly structured in time and space. Instead of assuming that uniformities always exist, why not develop ways of finding out when and under what conditions different kinds of human behavior can be expected to occur? Wilmsen's statement applies more to ecological conditions pertaining to the feralization process for pigs in Australia and New Guinea than it does to the processes by which people in different societies have historically developed different symbolic attitudes toward the same animal.

In the light of considerations such as these, I have had to reevaluate my own views toward the problem of uniformitarianism in the use of analogy. In an earlier paper (1974) I suggested that there were two kinds of analogy that ethnoarchaeologists could usefully employ. One kind, referred to as "discontinuous," was comparable to Ascher's new analogy in the way it furnished models of cultural adaptation that arise in areas that are widely separated in time and/ or space yet possess essentially similar ecological and environmental characteristics. A good example of a discontinuous analogy can be seen in the interpretation offered by White and Peterson (1969) of the post-Pleistocene archaeological assemblages from a series of sites excavated in the Oenpelli area of Arnhem Land, in the tropical north of Australia. These sites occur in two contrasting habitats, coastal plain and interior plateau, each of which offers differing resources at different seasons of the year. These economic activities were reflected in the archaeological remains at these various sites, and a model was needed to explain this variation between sites. Did these intersite differences reflect different prehistoric subcultures? Or did they reflect different seasonal aspects of the same culture? The seasonal–economic model was chosen as the most economical explanation of the existing evidence, based on an analogue derived from a classic ethnographic study of the Wik Munkan Aborigines of the Cape York Peninsula of northeastern Australia by Thomson (1939). Thomson has shown that these Aborigines followed an annual seasonal economic cycle of seasonal transhumance. That is, they moved from one habitat to another on a regular seasonal basis, exploiting completely different resources and using different technologies in each situation. Thomson had argued that, were an archaeologist to uncover these artifacts in their different seasonal sites without the benefit of ethnographic observations, he might well conclude that these were two different societies or subcultures. Differences of the same magnitude arising in the context of the annual alternation of wet and dry seasons in the Australian tropics occur both in Cape York and Arnhem Land. Despite the fact that the Wik Munkan area is over 960 kilometers (600 miles) from Oenpelli on a direct line, the environmental similarities between these two areas were sufficiently close to permit the use of a discontinuous analogue based on Wik Munkan ethnography.

The other kind of analogy, referred to as "continuous," was akin to the direct historical approach that was favored by American anthropologists and archaeologists of an earlier generation (Steward, 1942). In this case, the prehistoric adaptation being studied by the archaeologist could be linked stratigraphically and historically in an unbroken sequence to the historic cultural adaptations in the same area. Even if changes had occurred during the cultural sequence in question, the idea was that these could be explained in relation to the environmental changes observed within that same sequence.

Excavations at Puntutjarpa Rockshelter in the Western Desert of Australia (Gould, 1977) provide an example of a continuous analogue. Here, ethnographic Ngatatjara Aborigines were observed in the same general area where the excavations later took place. Unlike the example from Oenpelli, the ethnographic adaptation in this region was opportunistic and nonseasonal, since there are no regular, predictable wet and dry seasons in the Western Desert. Throughout nearly all of its 10,000 year history of human occupation, the Puntutjarpa site shows signs of having been a hunting base-camp, along lines exactly similar to those observed ethnographically in the same region. The "fit" between the ethnographically observed behavior under these conditions and the array of artifacts, site features, and faunal and floristic remains occurring archaeologically, is close; in other words, the predictions furnished by the ethnographic model were generally borne out by what was found in the excavations. At Puntutjarpa we can see evidence for a conservative adaptation to an essentially unchanging but extremely stressful habitat continuously throughout the post-Pleistocene period culminating in the present-day Ngatatjara people of that region.

Continuous models were seen as having an inherently greater probability of being accurate approximations of behavioral realities than discontinuous models, but the fact is that both kinds are still analogues of contemporary ethnographic behavior with all of the built-in limitations of analogy generally. To get beyond these limitations, I proposed that one could use these analogues as a basis for comparison with prehistoric patterning, rather in the manner of "predicting the past" proposed by Thomas (1974). That is, each kind of model could furnish predictions that could be tested against the actual accurrences discovered archaeologically. In this discussion I stressed that the differences or contrasts arising from such comparisons could prove more rewarding than the similarities. Similarities, after all, could only confirm what one already knew from present-day observations, but contrasts could force us to recognize how the prehistoric past may have differed from present-day analogues.

But we are still left with the job of finding some kind of satisfying explanations for those archaeological patterns that lie outside the range of what we might predict on the basis of ethnographic analogues. If, as was suggested earlier, there were prehistoric societies whose behavior has no ethnographic or historic counterparts, then how are we to develop models that will provide us with satisfactory interpretations of such cases? The "contrastive approach" may overcome some of the uniformitarianist assumptions that have plagued attempts at ethnoarchaeological interpretation in the past, but it does not in itself provide the basis for convincing explanations of prehistoric behavior that do not conform to expectations provided by present-day analogues. Thus I suspect that the contrastive approach to the use of analogues in ethnoarchaeology may be "Analogy's Last Hurrah." Like some kind of ancient, steam-driven locomotive, we have pushed the idea of analogy about as far as it will go, with due regard for the condition of the tracks – namely, the empirical accuracy of each ethnographic and archaeological case and its respective ecological context – and we are still not much farther along than we were when we started. Even the strongest analogies based on well controlled continuous or discontinuous models cannot inform us adequately about prehistoric adaptations that have no modern counterparts. So Freeman was correct when he said:

> The use of analogy has demanded that prehistorians adopt the frames of reference of anthropologists who study modern populations and attempt to force their data into those frames, a process which will eventually cause serious errors in prehistoric analysis, if it has not done so already. [1968: 262]

Perhaps in the end it can be said that analogues are better at informing archaeologists about what they do not know about the past than about what they do know or can expect to know. In this sense, analogies, even if controlled with respect to appropriateness and accuracy of detail, are still nothing more than a way of providing rather elaborate cautionary tales for the archaeologist. Like the exercise in the preceding chapter, they represent an effort to make direct comparisons between archaeological and ethnographic data. We are only now becoming aware of the inadequacies of direct comparison between ethnographic and archaeological evidence, both at the level of inter- and intrasite variability and at the higher level of comparing models of whole cultural systems.

Law and disorder

One way archaeologists have tried to go beyond the limitations posed by simple, direct comparisons of ethnographic and archaeological evidence is to argue for the importance of discovering universal laws of human behavior by means of archaeology. So much has been written on this subject in the last few years that the archaeological literature has begun to resemble the musings of medieval scholastics, with a possibly excessive concern for classifying and subdividing all conceivable kinds of logic that one can apply to archaeological issues. (Good summary reviews of this interest in archaeology appear in Plog, 1973; Stickel and Chartkoff, 1973; and Schiffer, 1975). Although this began as a refreshing trend by archaeologists to consider the philosophical underpinnings of their kind of science, at times it has become obsessive. Archaeologists nowadays do not speak entirely in jest when referring to "law-and-order archaeologists," thereby conjuring up a kind of Wild-West image of young, maverick generalists challenging the particularlist gunfighters of an earlier generation in archaeology. In the tone of these arguments, one can almost smell the smoke of the shootout and see the saloon doors swinging.

Although Nagel (1961) and others have noted that there are different kinds of scientific laws, all of which, as Stickel and Chartkoff (1973) point out, are used by archaeologists, it seems fair to say that all scientific laws have the irreducible properties of stating relationships (be they causal, quantitative, or historical) that are invariable in time and space. Moreover, these laws are derived from observing regularities in time and space. How these regularities are observed and translated into archaeologically usable laws has been the subject of a series of recent papers and a book by Schiffer (1972, 1975, 1976).

Thanks to Schiffer and others like Tuggle, Townshend, and Riley (1972), the discussion about laws in archaeology has begun to shift away from philosophy and closer to a concern for the realities of human behavior. Tuggle, Townshend, and Riley attack the use of covering laws in archaeology for their dependence upon uniformitarianist assumptions. They ask: Are processes of human behavior really as uniform in time and space as these laws suppose? This is really an unsafe assumption, since, as shown earlier, some aspects of human behavior may be more in accord with uniformitarian principles than others. Perhaps we are on safer ground when we apply uniformitarianist notions to those aspects of human behavior most closely tied to or dependent upon the natural world, where such assumptions are warranted, than in those areas of human behavior that are susceptible to manipulation, especially areas of symbolic and ideational behavior.

The implication of this line of argument is, of course, that scientific archaeology should concern itself exclusively with those aspects of human behavior that can reliably be covered by laws. That is, only those aspects of human behavior that can be measured and reduced to manageable properties should be included in the study of scientific archaeology. The rest, being essentially untestable, would be relegated to the outer darkness of humanism or science fiction. This implication has evidently been accepted by many archaeologists and even some ethnoarchaeologists. Thus it is that we can understand one recent statement about the goals of the archaeologist:

> Although I think its aims are noble, I myself do not espouse an explicitly *scientific approach* to archaeology. I believe that the various proponents of the scientific approach share three underlying assumptions: first, that the proper goals of archaeology may be explicitly defined and limited; second, that statements not verified or ultimately capable of verification are not worth making; and, finally, that almost all questions are susceptible to explication if only the archaeologist is clever and patient enough. In conjunction with these beliefs, I often find an unfounded optimism and undeniable arrogance. My own outlook is quite different; it accepts as probable that many aspects of past hominid behavior will never be fully understood, that some may be guessed at but never proven, and that the actual materials with which the archaeologist works are scanty and highly biased at best. [Yellen, 1977: 12]

To this might be added the further recognition that it may be precisely those aspects of human behavior that have proven least susceptible to measurement and scientific analysis that could prove, in the end, to be the most decisive. Could it be that the more restrictively quantitative archaeology tries to become, the more trivial it becomes, too? What assurance do we have that those aspects of behavior we can measure and validate are really important in terms of explaining how human beings got to be the way they are? It seems to me that the arrogance Yellen refers to rests largely upon this point of faith, namely that science and scientifically validatable hypotheses and laws are better at explaining human prehistory than other aspects of human behavior that are less easy to verify. We have thus come around full circle to the argument posed by social and cultural anthropologists who belabor archaeologists for their inability to deal with ideational and symbolic behavior because of the limitations of their evidence. Of course, if we seek to regard archaeology as a form of social science, we must be willing to limit our objectives to those that can be examined according to the rules of science. This means, among other things, artificially restricting the possibilities of what is to be studied to those matters that can be validated. The rules of the "game of science" depend on this, and in order to play the game, archaeologists must be willing to abide by these rules. Pfeiffer (pers.

comm.) recently posed the following problem to me: "Infanticide may have declined or vanished in certain places because prehistoric women rebelled against having to kill their infants." The point Pfeiffer makes is that this possibility is automatically excluded from the domain of science unless it can be validated in some way. As Pfeiffer suggests, we have absolutely no assurance that those aspects of human behavior that we can validate scientifically are really important or worth knowing. No doubt some archaeologists will wind up demonstrating trivia, but, as Pfeiffer notes, we have managed to get quite far even with these self-imposed limitations.

The view I shall propose is less modest than Yellen's. It would, indeed, be arrogant to suggest that archaeologists, by the clever and patient application of scientific methods, can expect to know all, or even what is most important, about human behavior. But certainly it is not arrogant to argue that we can know more than we presently do about human behavior, and, moreover, that systematic, scientific study can provide us with more satisfying explanations than unsystematic (though sometimes inspired) brain-storming. Perhaps the view of the scientific approach described by Yellen and by other archaeologists is too narrow and fails to do justice to the potential that a wider view has to offer for the study of human behavior. If we can put aside analogies and laws, with their uniformitarianist assumptions about how human beings *ought to* behave, and instead explore methods that will help us find out how they *really do* behave, perhaps we will develop wider and more satisfying explanations. Heretical as it may sound to some, the abandonment of analogies and laws does not signal an abandonment of the search for general principles of human behavior.

Suffering from irregularity?

In late 1967, after a long field trip to Australia, my wife and I returned to New York City. Before long we found ourselves back in our old routine, riding subways and buses to get to and from work. We experienced more real culture shock in returning to New York from the Australian desert than we ever felt when we went to Australia, but we were comforted to find that some things had not changed. One of the things that never changes in New York is an advertisement that is as much a part of the subway scene as the drunks and the graffiti. The ad reads: "Suffering from irregularity? Then try Brand X laxative." Gross as it sounds, it's little things like this that make one feel right at home in a place like New York. Just think, during the entire eighteen months that we had been away on this field trip, good old Brand X had been keeping people regular!

When I got back to my office I realized that I had a lot of catching up to do in my reading. During the time we had been away, I had not received any of the current journals or books in archaeology and anthropology, and I needed to reacquaint myself with the literature in my field. So, as soon as I could, I set about doing just that. In due course, as I read more and more papers and attended lectures by colleagues, I realized that a peculiar thing was happening in my field – something that I had missed out on completely while I was away. It began to look as if many archaeologists had taken the ad in the subway very much to heart. They felt themselves to be suffering from a form of intellectual irregularity called particularism.

As I continued to analyze my data from Australia in the quiet confines of the American Museum of Natural History, I became aware that more and increasingly shrill proclamations were being issued by archaeologists to show how they would combat this insidious intellectual ailment. In various ways I, along with other archaeologists, was being cajoled to search for patterned regularities in our evidence that would, as these arguments developed, lead us to discover laws of human behavior. The search for patterns and regularities in archaeological evidence was nothing new, but the attempt to rationalize these as the basis for general laws of human behavior was a trend in a new direction that has continued right up to the present. In some quarters this trend was viewed as an attempt by archaeologists to become more scientific in their reasoning and in interpreting their data. A laudable effort, I thought to myself, although as more and more terms like "nomothethic," "paradigm," "hypothetico-deductive," and others began to appear in the literature, I began to feel as if I were being set up for a dose of Brand X. I wondered if I was one of those perverse particularists who seem more interested in studying the culture sequences and adaptations of a particular region or group, or if perhaps, if I saw the light, I could find a way to employ my particular findings to some general ideas about human behavior. As one who had always been interested in general principles of behavior, the problem for me was to find the best way to do this. Should I try Brand X? I wondered.

Underlying the overall attack on archaeological particularism was the notion that it is the regularities in the archaeological data that will provide the basis for laws or lawlike propositions about human behavior. This view was succinctly expressed by a cultural anthropologist who likened the scientific study of archaeology to Boyle's Law of Gases (Carneiro, 1970: 494), according to which a gas introduced into a vacuum chamber will, given time, expand to fill the interior of that chamber evenly. This result is brought about through the action of gas molecules rebounding against each other in the course of their random movement. This activity, called Brownian Movement in physics, creates the pressure necessary to spread the introduced gas evenly throughout the chamber. This is what Stickel and Chartkoff (1973), following Nagel (1961), classify as a "Functional dependence law without time element," which is a law that can ". . . prescribe the nature of the functional interdependence of phenomena" (Stickel and Chartkoff, 1973: 665). The most important part of Carneiro's argument, however, does not concern itself with what kind of a law this is, but makes a point that is true for all scientific laws in archaeology. Boyle's Law predicts the general trend of movement by gas molecules in the aggregate. It does not attempt to predict the movement of individual molecules. Carneiro's idea here is that archaeologists (and social scientists generally) ought to be concerned with predicting the general trend of human behavior in the aggregate instead of worrying about the particular histories of individuals or even perhaps of individual communities. Given such a framework, it appears that archaeologists should seek to explain the dominant regularities presented by their evidence and leave the idiosyncrasies in their data aside.

Tuggle, Townshend, and Riley (1972) criticized this view, pointing out that archaeologists need to be at least as concerned with the idiosyncrasies in their evidence as with the regularities. I would add that the search for all-inclusive laws could lead archaeologists to ignore a vital component of their data that may be at least as interesting and important as the regularities. In other words, archaeologists should be concerned with the totality of behavior represented by the remains they study. In adopting such a view, I am implicitly suggesting that many of the so-called laws in archaeology today, while proposing regularities of a lawlike nature and susceptible to disproof, have not been tested to anything like the extent required for one to be confident that they are anything more than interesting propositions. I am not suggesting that such propositions should not be formulated or tested; only that these are far from being what scientists generally accept as laws or even lawlike statements. In the search for general principles of human behavior, such "laws" or "lawlike statements" as Naroll's (1962) often-cited relationship between floor space in covered dwellings and population size, fall short of the status of laws in the physical and natural sciences because they have not been tested widely or intensively enough to lead social scientists to feel confident that they are likely to be true under all foreseeable conditions where they might apply. In short, there is something presumptuous about the use of the word law for something that is much less than a law as these are commonly understood in the physical and natural sciences. Logically argued, these propositions may look like laws, but they have not been experienced as laws by social scientists generally. So I am compelled to raise the same basic questions as Tuggle, Townshend, and Riley: Should archaeology be concerned with laws at all, since these presuppose an overemphasis on regularities of behavior? Wouldn't we be better off to state general *propositions* about human behavior that posit relationships that are invariable in time and space and are susceptible to testing without assigning them the exalted status of law? By looking at the problem in this way, we avoid the necessity of omitting idiosyncratic behavior or patterns that are less pervasive than the dominant regularities preserved in our data. Thus we can clear the way for understanding the totality of human behavior represented by archaeological evidence. If, as archaeologists, we want to avoid taking an overly restrictive view of human behavior as we attempt to explain our evidence, then we would be better off to avoid Brand X, namely, laws that necessitate exclusive recognition of the regularities in past human activity.

Culture with a capital "K"

There is an idealized notion of culture, as something that exists above the level of interaction between different components of human behavior in relation to each other and to the physical and biotic environment, that has been widely used by anthropologists and is what I shall refer to as "culture with a capital 'K.' " Having doubted the value of analogy and laws in archaeology, all that remains now is for me to commit the ultimate heresy by suggesting that the time-honored, traditional concepts of culture employed by anthropologists since the days of E. B. Tylor are also inappropriate and even counterproductive for ethnoarchaeology. It sounds wicked to propose that this notion, which is one of the first we so often present to our unsuspecting undergraduates in introductory courses, is inadequate. After all, linguists study language, sociologists study society, and economists study economy. We would agree that these are all valid fields of study that encompass important areas of human activity. So what's wrong with anthropologists and archaeologists studying culture?

Of course there are many ways of doing anthropology, and for scholars interested in human use of symbols, the widely accepted normative ideas about culture are perfectly acceptable. I am not denying that people share values and beliefs which enable them to interact in consistent and even predictable ways. But for the new kind of anthropology being proposed here, namely, the study of human residue behavior, such normative attitudes cannot be assumed but must be discovered anew, if possible, in each case. As anthropologists we may be willing to accept the culture concept as valid, but in our own work as ethnoarchaeologists we cannot. The irony of this position is that, in order to discover how symbolic and ideational factors may actually affect human behavior, we must abandon the idea of culture with a capital "K"–that is, the assumption that there is such a thing as a "culture," in the ideal sense, that we should expect to discover, either in the present or in the prehistoric past.

The culture concept, whether defined in terms of older notions of a kind of "superorganic" (Kroeber, 1952: 22–51; Kroeber and Kluckhohn, 1963: 175–6) or looked at as norms within societies, in the manner widely favored in anthropology today, is of little use to the ethnoarchaeologist who is trying to observe relationships between the essential requirements for sustaining human life in given kinds of situations and the ways in which people behave in response to these requirements. Examination of human residue behavior provides an empirical means of discovering adaptive relationships within ecosystems. We are primarily concerned with understanding the essential nature of these relationships, not with discovering a "thing" called culture or even particular cultures. Searching for this latter entity, whatever it may be, can only distract us from our main task of discovering and explaining these relationships. One could, of course, redefine culture along the lines taken by White (1959: 8) and by Binford (1962: 218) to refer to "man's extrasomatic means of adaptation," but then why bother with the term "culture" at all? Why not just study man's extrasomatic means of adaptation and leave it at that?

The foregoing argument suggests that the culture concept is unnecessary intellectual baggage for the ethnoarchaeologist. However, in another and more basic sense, it may actually be misdirecting our efforts. In the history of ideas in Western thought about man and his relations to the environment, there has been a continuous and influential tradition that has viewed man as separate from the natural world, encouraging the view of man as a subduer and controller of nature (Glacken, 1956). This tradition extends back at least as far as the early Christian era when it was expressed in various ways by St. Augustine in relation to Biblical injunctions to man to "Be fruitful and multiply, and fill the earth and subdue it; and have dominion over the fish of the sea and over the birds of the air and over every living thing that moves upon the earth" (Genesis 1:28). At the same time, though, it should be remembered that other early Christian philosophers like St. Francis were involved with discovering (or, more correctly, rediscovering) the unity of nature and man, particularly as they thought it had existed before the Fall of Adam. St. Francis was one among several early Christian thinkers who regarded nature as a sort of book that man should learn to read (through observation and close association) in order to understand man's place within it; hence his famous encounter with the birds, which had a profound meaning that is usually glossed over in the rather saccharine version that has come down to us today. Like the Augustinian view, this one drew upon orthodox Christian traditions and has continued, in an unbroken history, to the present day. Of course, each of these traditions has undergone transformations and reinterpretation, sometimes of a quite unexpected nature. The persistence of both of these views of man and nature to the present has meant that scholars who are involved with this problem must make certain choices in line with their own philosophies. The fact that man is a controller and subduer of nature is plainly visible almost anywhere in the modern world, especially in industrialized areas. Yet the consequences of this activity make it equally apparent that man is not in a position to ignore the natural world, of which his societies and industries are an integral part.

The culture concept, most strongly in its "superorganic" aspect but also to a lesser degree in relation to normative ideas about culture, presupposes a degree of separation of man from nature – that is, a kind of "culture versus nature" dichotomy. Such a dichotomy makes it difficult for archaeologists and anthropologists to discover systemic interrelationships that exist between certain kinds of human behavior on the one hand and ecological variables on the other. From the early 1900s until the late 1940s, a preoccupation with superorganic concepts of culture led many scholars like Wissler, Kroeber, and others into the intellectual morass of the culture-area approach, in which they attempted increasingly elaborate correlations of natural and cultural phenomena that their definition of culture had already led them to dichotomize. The rise of ecological anthropology since then, with its emphasis on discovering relationships of human behavior to the total ecosystems in which they occur, was possible only when the superorganic view of culture as somehow separate from nature was gradually abandoned. Today we hear more about cultural adaptations that describe interactions between behavior and ecological variables (including variables that are part of the social environment) than about culture as such, or what I have called "culture with a capital 'K.' "

For ethnoarchaeologists, who are deeply involved with understanding how human beings living under different conditions and in different societies adapt, any idea that posits an artificial separation between man and the natural world is bound to be misleading. Culture concepts in use today are not generally useful in ethnoarchaeology, because they all imply some degree of this kind of separation. This is not to deny that there are such things as traditions and traditional behavior in human society or to suggest that these traditions are unimportant. Traditions are an essential part of the human ecosystem, and an accurate recognition of their importance can be decisive in explaining behavior. Ethnoarchaeologists examine human behavior in relation to materials and material residues in order to discover relationships that explain how and under what conditions certain kinds of traditional behavior may have been important in relation to overall processes of human adaptation. They can do a better job of discovering the real, as opposed to the assumed, importance of traditions to the ways human beings adapt by abandoning concepts of culture with a capital "K" and concentrating instead on these relationships.

The error of guilt by association
In America in the 1950s, the expression "guilt by association" was widely used and acquired sinister connotations. Individuals whose only "crime" had been some fleeting, past association with the Communist party – perhaps nothing more than attendance at a rally in support of the Republican cause during the 1936–39 civil war in Spain – were brought before public hearings by federal and state officials and accused of being covert Communists. In the fearful atmosphere generated by these hearings, many of these people had their careers ruined and friendships broken by the assumption generated in many peoples' minds that any association with the Communist party automatically meant that one was a Communist. Later examination showed how baseless these charges had been, for mere association cannot establish guilt. A person who attended a Communist rally in 1936 did not necessarily become a Communist as a result (in fact, some became strongly anti-Communist). The public hysteria of the 1950s was based upon the widespread acceptance of a false assumption that mere association connotes some kind of necessary relationship. This bizarre aberration in American political history demonstrates the danger of making false assumptions of this kind.

In general, the field of archaeology is not excessively concerned with politics, and any false assumptions archaeologists make are unlikely to have public repercussions. The consequences of a false assumption in archaeology, while less public, may be all the more persistent and pervasive because these assumptions may go unexamined for a very long time. One assumption that archaeologists, in particular, must guard against is the idea that a physical association of human residues and/or geological and biotic remains involves any kind of necessary relationship beyond mere contemporaneity. As archaeological interest in explaining past human behavior increases, so does the inclination to impute necessity to associations that seem to imply some kind of behavioral relationship. How tempting it is to exercise one's imagination and "see" a past behavioral relationship in the context of physically associated remains in an archaeological site.

We are probably all guilty of doing this at one time or another. As a graduate student in 1963, I was asked to supervise a small-scale student excavation of a portion of the old Emeryville Shellmound on the east shore of San Francisco Bay. It was hoped that the small portion of this once immense site that we were about to excavate was still undisturbed. We placed our initial trench in a small, weed-covered lot between a paint factory and one of those marvellous auto wrecking yards where dead cars are dropped into a mechanical device that crushes them into small cubes of metal. Although it seemed an unlikely place to find the remains of one of the largest aboriginal Indian settlements in California, we began right away to encounter dark, midden soil containing shells, fire-cracked stones, obsidian flakes, and finely made artifacts of obsidian. As we continued deeper in our excavations, we encountered a compact cluster of large clam-shells, a large rounded cobble, and a well-fashioned wedge made of antler, all occurring at the same level and in apparently undisturbed midden deposits. It looked as if we had found an activity area in which someone had taken an antler wedge and pounded on it in order to open these big clams. How reasonable and inevitable it all seemed at the time. Later, however, we dug through this level and continued deeper. About two feet directly below our presumed activity area we found a complete and unmistakably modern Coca Cola bottle, again with no obvious sign of disturbance in the soil around it. A few more finds like this showed us that the entire midden deposit had been thoroughly homogenized by various kinds of disturbances and that our clamshell-wedge-pounder association was entirely fortuitous. Yet, even if the association had proved stratigraphically valid, how far would we have been justified in regarding this as an activity area along the lines that we had been speculating? This was a humbling experience, because it showed how wrong one's wishful thinking, based upon the assumption that items which occur in association together had some necessary behavioral relationship, could be. This experience also showed me how easy it is for an archaeologist to fall into this kind of error of interpretation.

Associations in archaeology represent nothing more than physical correlations of various kinds of data, and, like all correlations in science, they do not, in themselves, imply any kind of necessary relationships. Relationships, in such cases, are not intrinsic to the data but are products of interpretation. R. G. Collingwood (1946: 282) was right when he argued that the past is really over, and that it can be perceived only in terms of our present-day ideas about it. The interpretation that most economically accounts for all of the observed correlations, according to the principle of parsimony (Occam's Razor), is the one to be regarded as most valid. When new data is discovered, new or modified interpretations may be required. But, as always in science, the simplest interpretation of the available evidence must be regarded as the best. This point of view, which is widely accepted among archaeologists, has a corollary that is not generally considered by archaeologists. Given this hypothesis-testing approach, it follows that there is no such thing as the final or ultimate interpretation – only better and better approximations of past reality. So, while one cannot expect to know everything about past human behavior, one can know more than is already known. There is no Truth in archaeology; but there are better and better truths as new evidence is acquired and new and economical interpretations are applied to it. Hence Yellen's pessimism, referred to earlier, and my optimism about the potential of ethnoarchaeology. Our views are two sides of the same scientific coin, and the question now, after all of this negative probing, is whether or not that coin is sound and has good value. Having put aside expectations and assumptions that will prove misleading or counterproductive, it will be possible now to determine how well the approach called living archaeology works in providing economical and convincing explanations for present and past human behavior.

3

Behavior and adaptation

In looking at general relationships between human behavior and material residues, the first thing to consider is the total ecosystem in which this behavior takes place. The ecosystemic view, a product of evolutionary biology, is one variant of a general systems approach that is currently seeing wide use among archaeologists, and it is an essential part of living archaeology. At an early state in any ethnoarchaeological treatment of human behavior, there has to be an effort to model the basic relationships of environmental resources and constraints in relation to human behavior and population. Just as an ecologist in the biological sciences must construct his model of a natural ecosystem out of systematic and reasonably long-term monitoring of inputs and outputs within and between different components of the total system he is studying, so, too, the ethnoarchaeologist must observe human behavior in particular ecosystems, noting the flow of materials through the system and seeing what effects the human components of the system are having on the final disposal of these materials. Since most of the literature in anthropology does not look at human behavior from this point of view or monitor the flow and discard of materials with anything like the empirical detail required for archaeological interpretation, this ethnographic task is usually performed in the field by trained archaeologists. In general, it is easier for a trained archaeologist to acquire the necessary skills in ethnology to do living archaeology than it is for an ethnographer, trained as most social and cultural anthropologists are, to make archaeologically useful observations of living human societies.

The "ecological connection"
As with the biological scientist, the ethnoarchaeologist is concerned with discovering relationships between components of the total ecosystem that might otherwise appear to be unrelated. The growing worldwide interest in nature conservation and the environmental impact of human industry and other activities in the modern world is predicated upon the recognition of relationships between appar-

ently unrelated components of the total ecosystem. Alter the status of one component, and one may also change the condition of another – sometimes drastically and out of all proportion to the initial change. For example, Rachel Carson's influential book, *Silent Spring* (1962), showed how the introduction of pesticides like DDT, even in relatively small amounts, into an area could lead to massive destruction of the local fauna – including man. She traced the movement of these toxic pesticides through the entire food chain, revealing how they increased at each higher level as residual poisons were retained and concentrated within the liver and other organs. The accumulated concentrations of these toxins were passed on to the next higher trophic level until a lethal dose was present. The most immediate victims of this process were birds, hence the title of her book to describe a damaged environment devoid of bird songs, but cases of human illness and death as a result of this same process were documented, too.

Carson also noted how the insects that were supposed to be eliminated by these chemical pesticides evolved rapidly in a way that passed on inherited tolerances to these chemicals, with the long-term result that it was the birds and mammals (including man) rather than the insects who suffered most from these pesticides. Based as it was on sound biological principles, Carson's book made these relationships common knowledge outside the field of biology and gave impetus to the outlawing of DDT and to other conservationist measures. The essence of her contribution to these measures lay in her ability to point out the chain of interrelationships that exists between variable *A over here* and variable *B over there*, in another part of the total system. Instead of applying simple linear causality to the problem, she explained the results as products of the interaction and feedback of these variables within the total ecosystem. Thus introduction of DDT led ultimately to the poisoning of birds, mammals, and man, while at the same time leading to increased resistance by insects to these poisons. These insects eventually multiplied, leading to the human response of introducing still greater amounts of DDT or other chemicals to combat them, with the net effect of hardier and more numerous insect pests on the one hand (as their genetic resistance to these chemicals increased through the process of natural selection and also as their predators died off from the poisons) and greater illness and mortality among birds, mammals, and man. It was the firm establishment of linkages between disparate variables within the total system that made Carson's arguments convincing, and it is upon this same kind of argument that the effectiveness of living archaeology depends.

Living archaeology depends upon a similarly ecosystemic view of the interrelationships of things, but it is linked to ecology in another, more direct way. In Chapter 1, I argued that one must recognize the potential pitfalls of applying the principles of uniformitarianism to human behavior. But those remarks were not intended to eliminate uniformitarianist principles from consideration in explaining human behavior. Indeed, many principles developed in evolutionary biology and ecology can safely be assumed to have operated uniformly in the past as they do in the present, and they can usefully be applied to the study of the human species provided one accepts the notion that human traditions may expand the total ecosystem to include social and symbolic components. So those aspects of human behavior that are most closely related to physical and biological processes are also those that most reliably lend themselves to the uniformitarianist assumption. In other words, the more clearly one can show the interrelatedness of human behavior to the biological and physical requirements for human life in any given area, the more securely one can make uniformitarian assumptions about how that behavior, given similar circumstances, may have operated in the past. This is what is meant here by the "ecological connection." If one accepts these arguments, then it follows that one of the first tasks of living archaeology is to determine to what extent ecological principles derived from the biological sciences can adequately account for the observed behavior of a living human society or a particular mode of adaptation.

At this point, someone in the back of the room is bound to call out, "Whoa! That sounds suspiciously like environmental determinism to me!" This rather tiresome objection is one of the oldest straw men in the social sciences, but it is raised so often that some discussion is required in order to lay it to rest, at least for the moment. Environmental determinism has meant many things to many different people, but there are certain general ideas that seem to characterize it. One of these is linear causality. Whenever someone asserts that *A* causes *B*, he is using linear causality, or, to be more precise, unilinear causality, since the causality being employed in such explanations is unidirectional. Such thinking about the environment and its effects upon man go back in Western thought at least as far as Classical Greece – for example, Herodotus' well-known idea that people living in cold, northern climates are sluggish and phlegmatic in temperament, while people in the southern Mediterranean regions of warmer climate are lively and volatile in temper. Yet even someone who was as allegedly determined an environmental determinist as Friedrich Ratzel was, by 1904, arguing for the importance of social traditions in explaining human behavior. How, he asked, can we hope to explain the behavior of the seventeenth-century Puritan colonists of Massachusetts Bay without understanding their previous history in England? He pointed out that one cannot understand the society simply from knowing about the climatic conditions and resources of New England, although these were, of course, important factors. The problem is that, both before and after Ratzel, there have been people who have assigned prime-mover status to some aspect of the environment and proceeded to apply this in a unilinear manner to explain human behavior in particular cases. This combination of arbitrary and unilineal causality is generally what is meant by environmental determinism. It is a straw man because, with the exception of certain popularizers, very few ecologists or social scientists today argue from such a point of view.

· If, on the other hand, we approach man–nature relationships from the systemic point of view advocated earlier, this problem of arbitrary and unilineal causality dissolves into a big blob of papaya mush. Instead, what we have are ecological variables and different kinds of human behavior that are interrelated in a consistent and predictable manner. Such consistencies do imply causality, but it is a multi-dimensional causality within a web of systemic relations. Our tiresome fellow at the back of the room might then say, "But isn't what you are describing simply circular reasoning, that is, a tautology?" The best reply I have heard to such a query came from Marvin Harris, who once noted that, "Some tautologies are better than others" (pers. comm.). In fact, all of our explanations for behavior in social science are tautologies, since what we are attempting to explain are correlated stases or shifts between variables. The best of these so-called tautologies are those that have taken the widest possible range of observable variables into account, controlled their observations of occurrence most carefully, and employed appropriate tests of significance to these correlations. Explanations structured along these lines are regarded as most convincing in the biological sciences, and there is no reason why such an ecosystemic view cannot be applied to the study of human behavior as well. In doing this, however, we must keep Ratzel's original dictum in mind; namely, that social and symbolic traditions are as much a part of the total ecosystem as climate, resources, and other more strictly physical and biotic factors.

In considering how human societies adapt, it is not necessary to demonstrate that all kinds of human behavior are adaptive. Indeed, this would be a serious error, since we cannot safely assume that all aspects of behavior in a given society are or must be adaptive. To do this would be to repeat errors that arose in connection with functionalist anthropology, where it was sometimes assumed that all components of a society must be consistently and functionally related to all other components. Such total social integration, if it exists at all, must be discovered rather than assumed. All it is necessary to do is demonstrate that various kinds of behavior, if they are not obviously adaptive, are at least not maladaptive to the extent that they undermine the adaptive system. This idea might be called "neutral determinism." In using an ecosystemic approach to explain human behavior, one is under no obligation to explain the particular details or embellishments of all aspects of human behavior as long as they do not grossly contradict the basic adaptive model. Thus such aspects of behavior as artistic styles and elaborations of belief will not necessarily require an obvious ecological explanation. Such explanations, in fact, often prove to be unconvincing and simplistic. It is perfectly possible for many aspects of human behavior, especially those allied to symbolic aspects of behavior, to vary according to rules that are largely independent of ecological constraints except for the minimal requirement that they not be appreciably maladaptive.

Once we have laid the straw man of environmental determinism to rest, can we perceive any ecological principles that might facilitate the modeling of adaptive relations within living and past human societies? In fact, there are quite a few, but for the purposes of argument I shall focus my attention on one that has proved especially useful: the principle of the limiting factor. This idea is derived from Liebig's Law of the Minimum, a concept of long standing that has had sufficient testing and use to have attained the status of a law in the biological sciences. That is, it appears so far to be true for all living species, everywhere, and at all times. A limiting factor is something in the total environment that sets an upper limit on the number of individuals of a given species that can survive periods of maximum stress. Sometimes the limiting factor is obvious and overriding, as, for example, the availability of water in desert habitats; at other times the factor may be subtle although decisive when scarcity or stress occur. An example of this would be various trace elements, which, although a miniscule part of the diet, can be essential to the growth and well-being of livestock and of human beings. As Odum (1975:107–8) and other ecologists have pointed out, looking for limiting factors can enable one to begin to understand the key relationships within a complex ecosystem without becoming bogged down in trying to calculate the overall carrying capacity vis-a-vis the population of a particular species in a given habitat. Ecologists have long been aware that it is not the optimal availability of resources that determines the population size of a species in the long run, but the periods of maximum stress or instances of scarcity as they restrict population to certain limits. In applying this principle to the explanation of human behavior, we must keep in mind the fact that traditional skills, knowledge, and technology can all serve to overcome such limiting factors, and we must recognize the further possibility that particular traditions may, themselves, act as limiting factors under certain conditions (for example, warfare). With these provisos in mind, we can take the principle of the limiting factor and apply it to the problem of modeling adaptive relations among different Australian Aborigine societies.

The Australian "bull's eye"

The last fifteen years have witnessed a significant increase in our knowledge of the geography and ecology of Australia, especially in the more remote interior regions. Although the basic patterns of Australian ecology have been apparent for a long time, improved levels of detail, especially from quantitative studies in biology, have led to a finer perception of these patterns (see especially the recent treatments by Gibbs, 1969; Gentilli, 1972; and Fitzpatrick and Nix, 1973), which can serve as a basic framework for considering human adaptive behavior on the Australian continent. As Birdsell (1975:34) has pointed out, Australia provides an ideal natural laboratory for examining human adaptation.

The overwhelming factor in Aboriginal and European settlement in Australia is the availability of water. If one looks at rainfall maps of Australia (Figs. 2 and 3), the basic bull's-eye pattern of the continent's rainfall and biota starts to emerge. There are some notable exceptions, but in general one finds the areas of highest rainfall (along with coordinated drainage patterns that include permanent, freshwater rivers and springs) occurring closest to the coastlines, both in the temperate southeast and southwest and in the tropical north. Farther inland, one encounters areas of progressively lower rainfalls correlated with characteristic vegetation patterns involving dry sclerophyll forest ("mallee," as it is known to most Australians), areas of acacia (termed "mulga" and dominated by *Acacia aneura*) comparable to areas of thornscrub noted in other semiarid regions of the world (Riley and Young, 1966:65–8), and finally wide areas of desert dominated by spinifex or other, comparable grasses. In some areas, clumpings of mulga and mallee may occur within savannah grasslands, and one often finds areas of mulga scrub, sometimes quite thick, occurring in and around sandhills and spinifex. In the northwest area of Australia, between the Pilbara and Kimberley Districts, there is a broad corridor of sandhill and spinifex habitat that extends to the coast. And across the south-central coastlines of the continent extends the Nullarbor Plain, which, as its name suggests, is a vast and flat treeless plain whose desertlike appearance is more a product of underlying formations of limestone – which drain away moisture – than of poor rainfall. So the simple bull's-eye pattern is really not as simple as it seems, but it is a useful way to start thinking about the overall distribution of Australian flora in relation to rainfall.

Australian rainfall and climate are dominated by a northerly weather system of monsoonal regularity (hot summers with torren-

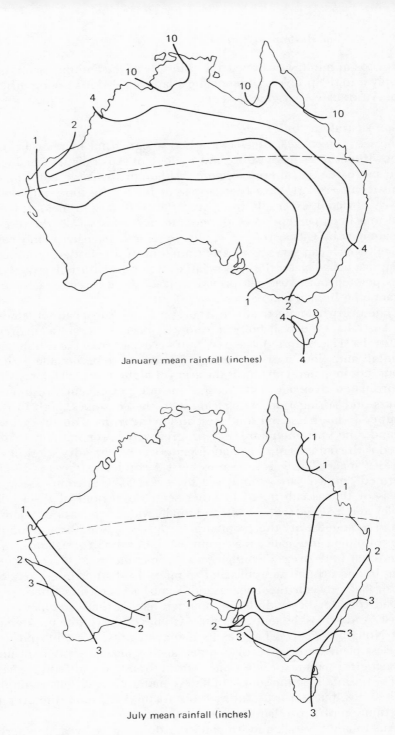

January mean rainfall (inches)

July mean rainfall (inches)

Fig. 2. Mean rainfall in Australia.

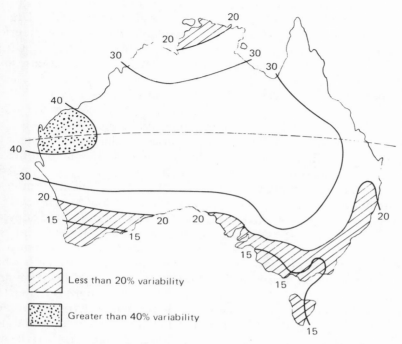

Fig. 3. Percentage mean variability from annual mean rainfall in Australia.

tial rains and dry, though not much cooler, winters) and southerly weather systems emanating from the Antarctic (bringing more or less steady winter rains, with warm, dry summers). The interior of Australia can thus be viewed as a marginal zone into which these two large weather systems alternately penetrate (Gardner, 1944). The problem for the Australian interior districts is that they usually receive the tail ends of the rainfall from each respective weather system. In summer, the monsoons break up as they move south, with the result that rainfall is often torrential but scattered and unpredictable. Similarly, the southerly system discharges most of its moisture before reaching the arid interior, with the result that winter rains in the desert usually consist of nothing more than a cold drizzle. With the possible exception of the highlands of Tasmania and southeastern Australia, there are no large mountain ranges or other landforms that might be expected to modify the overall effects of these competing weather systems to any significant degree. Set against this relatively meager and unpredictable rainfall regime is the fact that the interior of Australia is subject everywhere to high rates of evaporation.

Along the coastal periphery of most of Australia there are many rivers and streams that flow all year and drain areas of extensive forest, but most of these are small by world standards. The largest river system, the Murray-Darling, actually drains a large interior district that is a semidesert over much of its extent today. But further inland there are no permanent rivers. In the area east and south of Alice Springs (the geographical center of the Australian continent) lies the Great Artesian Basin, a vast desert area into which numerous stream channels flow, creating a subsurface water table that can be tapped by means of deep bores. In the heart of this area lies the Simpson Desert, a region of parallel, ruler-straight dunes of red sand. To the west of Alice Springs there is an area of approximately 1,300,000 square kilometers (500,000 sq. miles)' of uncoordinated drainage created by a vast pre-Cambrian shield forming a plateau about 300–450 meters (1,000–1,500 ft.) above sea level. This formation encloses the Western Desert, which on most maps appears as three deserts: the Victoria Desert, the Gibson Desert, and the Great Sandy Desert, from south to north respectively. As shown in Fig. 4, these are not bounded entities but intergrade with each other to form a desert continuum characterized not only by poor and undependable rainfall – the annual average everywhere is under ten inches – but also by a total absence of permanent streams or any kind of coherent drainage pattern that might include freshwater lakes and springs. The interior lakes shown on maps of Australia are all salt lakes. On those rare occasions when they contain water, that water is many times saltier than the ocean.

The north coast of Australia, from the Kimberley District on the west through Arnhem Land and eastward along the shoreline around the Gulf of Carpentaria to Cape York, experiences the greatest climatic extremes of any part of Australia. So much rain falls in the summer that there is widespread flooding along stream channels and on low ground, making movement extremely difficult at that time of year even for today's modern forms of transport. White Australians term this period "the Wet" and experience it predictably every year along with the winter dry season, during which much of the country acquires a parched, baked appearance. During this dry season one really notices the large bottle trees (*Brachychiton rupestris*) with their thick trunks adapted to retaining moisture throughout the long dry season. The coastlines and rivers of this tropical region abound in shellfish, turtles, fish (including barramundi), and even a unique sea mammal, the dugong.

While less extreme than the north, the temperate southeast and southwest of Australia also experience marked annual seasonal variation in temperature and rainfall. The Great Dividing Range and its outliers (including the mountains of Tasmania) provide Australia's only major area of uplands, in which altitude tends to accentuate the

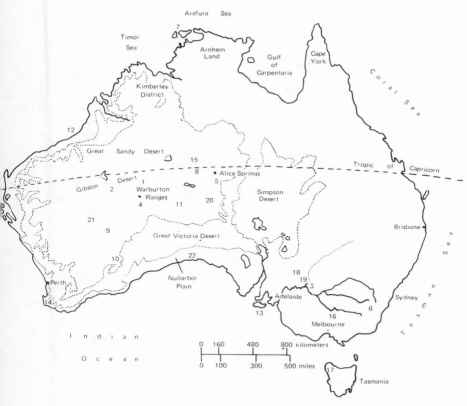

Fig. 4. Map of Australia showing principal localities mentioned in the text. Numbered locations are: (1) Tikatika and Clutterbuck Hills; (2) Pulykara and Mt. Madley; (3) Murray-Darling River System; (4) Puntutjarpa Rockshelter; (5) James Range East Rockshelter; (6) Australian Alps; (7) Melville and Bathurst Islands; (8) Papunya; (9) Laverton; (10) Cundeelee; (11) Wingellina Hills; (12) Eighty-Mile Beach; (13) Kangaroo Island; (14) Devil's Lair; (15) Yuendumu; (16) Mt. William Axe Quarry; (17) Rocky Cape; (18) Burke's Cave; (19) Lake Mungo; (20) Everard Range; (21) Wiluna; (22) Yalata.

extremes of the temperate climate. These uplands consist of long, rounded mountain ridges like the Snowy Mountains and the Southern Alps, capped by granite tors and ranging up to 1800–2100 meters (6,000–7,000 ft.) above sea level, occurring amidst broad tablelands like the Monaro, near Canberra, and the New England Tableland in northeastern New South Wales. Although these uplands are heavily forested in places, they also contain broad areas of grassy steppe. In Queensland these ranges, although lower in elevation, extend northward into the tropics and form the backbone of Cape York. Southwestern Australia lacks the high ranges and tablelands of the east but is heavily forested and enjoys an almost Mediterranean climate in places. The temperate region here is relatively small and forms a kind of coastal strip that tapers off rapidly into semi-desert as one travels inland or northward along the coast. Although the forests of this region are dominated by various eucalypts, none of the species found there occur naturally in the southeastern part of the continent. This anomaly suggests that the vegetations of southeastern and southwestern Australia have been reproductively isolated from each other long enough for these eucalypts to evolve into separate species (Pryor, 1976). The simplest explanation for this long-term isolation appears to be that the arid center of Australia and its southward extension, the Nullarbor Plain, are extremely ancient and have created a geographic boundary that has effectively blocked the interbreeding of these plant species (Darlington, 1965:99–101).

This interpretation might also be extended to the arid interior of Australia. In looking at the overall distribution of Australian flora, we find that Australia generally is characterized by relatively few genera, as compared with tropical Southeast Asia or other areas to the west of Wallace's Line, but that a remarkably large number of species may occur within a single genus. For example, botanists have identified around 600 species of eucalypts (Pryor, 1976:1–4). Many of these species evolved within localized portions of the continent, although some have extended their range into distant, interior areas. To return to the earlier bulls-eye image of Australian rainfall and floristic patterning, as one progresses from the better-favored areas along the coast toward the drier and less predictable interior, there is a fairly steady decline in the number of species within each plant genus (Gardner, 1944). When one reaches the most arid and non-seasonal parts of the interior, most of the Australian genera are still present, but each is represented by a relatively small number of species. Thus each zone of the bull's-eye might seem to have acted as a kind of filter, progressively eliminating species from the total list as one approaches the center. But it may also be that these species were once more widespread than they are today and that climatic deterioration, mainly in the form of increased aridity, has progressively eliminated them, leaving only the hardiest and most adaptable ones in the arid and semiarid areas. At present the latter argument appears stronger, since there are also many well-documented pockets of anomalous vegetation occurring in isolated areas throughout the Australian desert that can be interpreted as remnants of an earlier and wider distribution of these plant species. The most famous example of this phenomenon occurs at Palm Valley, Northern Territory, about 145 kilometers (90 miles) west of Alice Springs, where there is an ancient species of tropical palm that is not found elsewhere in the desert at all. In other, similarly isolated parts of the Central and Western Deserts, one also encounters *Xanthorrhea* plants (the so-called grass tree), a genus with a more coastal and temperate distribution in Australia. These and other anomalous plant occurrences in the arid regions of Australia all occur in small, localized areas that are protected in some way from the full rigors of the desert, and it appears that they have survived continuously in these isolated pockets since the onset of desert conditions.

Most of the unique characteristics of indigenous Australian fauna are well known. After becoming isolated to the east of Wallace's Line, the ancient mammals of Australia and New Guinea radiated into a wide variety of marsupials and their near-relatives, the monotremes, that ultimately evolved into historic and present-day species. As in other parts of the Old and New World, these mammals went through a phase that included many species of important megafauna such as *Diprotodon* (a rhinocerous-sized creature somewhat like a giant wombat), *Thylacoleo* (a marsupial carnivore with unique dentition), and *Macropus titan*[1] (a giant kangaroo) which became extinct near the end of the Pleistocene. The largest marsupial inhabiting the Australian continent today is the red kangaroo (*Megaleia rufa*), although by world standards these animals and their close relatives, the gray kangaroo and euro, are not large at all, with individual body weights only occasionally in excess of 45 kilograms (100 lb.). These animals are widely distributed over the Australian continent and have adapted to a wide variety of habitats, but they are not true herd animals and thus cannot be hunted efficiently by means of drives and surrounds in the manner of gregarious mammals, like the caribou and bison in other parts of the world. The same is generally true of the large Australian ground-dwelling birds, the emu and the cassowary (this latter species occurs only in tropical areas of northern Australia, but the emu is found widely). Big-game hunting, in the manner of Upper Paleolithic indigenes of the Old World or Paleo-Indians of the New World, would therefore not have been as productive for the earliest people in Australia, who were present there by at least 32,000 years ago, although some hunting of Pleistocene megafauna undoubtedly did take place in Australia. Thus from the earliest period of human occupation of Australia, there were pressures on these hunter–gatherers to exploit a wider range of local foods, including plants and marine resources, than might have been the case for their big-game hunting contemporaries in other parts of the world.

If we take a final look at the ecological bull's-eye of Australian rainfall and resources, we can see that the availability of water is the primary limiting factor for human settlement in which is by far the largest part of Australia, namely, the interior areas that lie beyond the reach of any permanent streams. With some minor exceptions, like the west edge of the Simpson Desert, where natural artesian springs occur, the principal sources of water are rain and rainfall catchments like rockholes, impermanent stream-beds, claypans, and small, localized water tables. Since rainfall in these areas is variable and unpredictable, so is the availability of water in these rainfall catchments. As the predictability and general availability of rainfall and/or catchments improve in certain parts of the desert – as, for example, in the northern edge of the desert where the seasonal monsoons are more reliable (although not especially prolific) or in the rocky ranges of the Central Desert where large and well shaded catchments abound – so do the prospects for human settlement. But all human settlement in arid Australia, both past and present, has entailed an element of risk. The degree of risk varies from the extreme conditions of the Western Desert to the slightly more benign qualities encountered in the Alice Springs area or in the northern Tanami Desert, as one approaches Arnhem Land; but everywhere in this region these conditions require that human settlers must estimate the degree of risk and pattern their economic activities accordingly. Archaeological and ethnographic evidence show that the Aborigines have been consistently better at making such estimates than Europeans. Whereas desert Aborigines have based their movements and activities upon estimates of the worst possible conditions they were likely to encounter, mainly with respect to water, many European settlers have looked at the country during years of good rain, when grazing conditions were optimal, and based their activities upon such ideal conditions. The result, in the case of European grazers, has often been complete decimation of their herds and ruin of their properties when droughts occur, and there are many cattle and sheep stations on the fringes of the Australian desert, like Carnegie Station in Western Australia, that have long histories of cyclical use and abandonment as each new owner finds out these hard truths for himself. In other, better watered areas of Australia, this constraint was less important, and it became possible for Aborigines and later for Europeans to expend greater efforts on optimizing the productivity of their respective economies instead of being as concerned as their desert counterparts with minimizing risks. Plus ça change . . .

The Australian desert adaptation
As noted earlier, the annual average amount of rainfall declines drastically as one approaches the arid center of Australia, and so do the reliability indexes that show when and where rains are likely to fall. The Aborigines residing in the Western Desert when my wife and I studied them in 1966–67 and 1969–70 collected thirty-eight

edible plant species, and they hunted and collected forty-seven named varieties of meat and fleshy food, most of which were small game like goanna lizards, mice, birds, grubs, as well as European-introduced rabbits and feral cats. Although we probably missed seeing some of the edible plants used by the Western Desert people, there is little doubt that their overall list of edible plant species is appreciably shorter than one finds even among other Australian Desert groups. Meggitt (1957) reports at least fifty-two edible plant species used by the Walbiri Aborigines, and O'Connell (pers. comm.) notes that the Alyawara Aborigines identify and consume at least eighty species of plants. I hesitate to offer any firm conclusions based upon negative evidence of this sort, but when compared with species lists from other deserts like the Kalahari or the Great Basin of North America, the Western Desert of Australia stands out as a place that is exceedingly poor in numbers of edible plant and animal species and in the actual amounts of those particular species as well. This relative poverty of resources is undoubtedly a product of a unique combination of harsh physical conditions and the peculiar evolutionary history of the Australian continent with respect to the isolation of its biota from the variability in other parts of the world. The Western Desert is the most extreme of Australian desert habitats in terms of stress and can be regarded as a baseline for comparison with other desert regions both within and outside Australia. In terms of water supplies and plant and animal resources, this is a physical environment that by any standard may be the most unreliable and impoverished in the world where people now live or are known to have lived directly off the land.

Given these conditions, we may regard the Western Desert as a "core" desert habitat – one that epitomizes the extreme tendencies already described for the ecology of Australia in general. In trying to understand how the Aborigines have adapted to this harsh region, it may be useful to apply some concepts about human adaptation presented by Bennett (1969:11–15) that are consistent with the ecosystemic approach discussed earlier. Bennett distinguishes between *adaptive behavior,* which involves short-term observations of problem solving or coping behavior by individuals and groups, and *adaptive processes,* which relates to adaptation as a long-term phenomenon involving the cumulative effects of such adaptive strategies, whether successful or not, on societies over long periods of time. This distinction parallels similar ones made in the biological sciences between adaptive mechanisms, usually genetic in nature, that enable individuals and groups within a species to maintain themselves from day to day, and the effects of natural selection on these mechanisms within and between species over the long run. Archaeologists, like evolutionary biologists, are concerned with adaptations in both the short- and long-term sense and must deal effectively with both. The importance of behavior observed on any single day at Tikatika, for example, can only be understood in relation to an overall model of the nature of adaptation in the Western Desert as observed ethnographically for longer periods of time and in the context of an even longer sequence of human occupancy of this region. The limiting factor of water and its close correlate, the meagre variety and amount of wild edibles, is the principal selective constraint in this particular habitat, and its effects must be viewed both in the short- and long-terms proposed by Bennett.

Adaptive behavior

Table 2 presents the staple foods upon which nomadic Western Desert Aborigines observed in this study were subsisting, and Tables 3 and 6 provide additional information about Western Desert Aborigine food-getting. The following general statements about subsistence behavior are made largely with reference to these tables:

1.   The diet is primarily vegetarian. Women and girls forage for a total of seven staple plant species (here defined as any food that constitutes at least 30 percent of the total diet by weight at the time it is collected) and thus provide the bulk of the diet. Observations made during this study, while not continuous and containing some important gaps (see especially those noted in Table 2 under the drought year of 1969–70), show that at least 90 percent of the time females provide about 95 percent of the food available to the group as a whole. Children under the age of ten contribute a small but significant amount of food to this total, although their contribution is intermittent and somewhat difficult to monitor.

2.   Men hunt constantly but with generally poor success. Both they and the women collect small game, which provide the only protein available most of the time. Only on relatively rare occasions of sustained and heavy localized rainfall in areas of predominantly mulga scrub cover does game become abundant enough for the mens' hunting efforts to provide the bulk of the diet, and these instances are of short duration. In a sense, it is the dependable efforts of the women in gathering that free the men for more chancy hunting activities. In terms of amounts of food obtained, we could easily refer to the Western Desert people as gatherers-and-hunters, since the bulk of their diet on most occasions consists of plant foods. Yet from the point of view of time expended, hunting ranks as a major subsistence activity.

Table 2. *Staple food procurement systems of the Western Desert Aborigines of Australia*

Wet year (1966–7)

Procurement Systems	Food staples	J	F	M	A	M	J	J	A	S	O	N	D
Ground and tree fruits	Kampuṟarpa (fresh) *(Solanum centrale)*						▓	▓	▓				
	Kampuṟarpa (sun dried) *(Solanum centrale)*	▓	▓	▓									
	Ngaṟu *(Solanum chippendalei)*	▓	▓	▓									
	Yawalyuru *(Canthium latifolium)*			▓	▓	▓							
	Wayaṉu – "quandong" (fresh) *(Santalum acuminatum)*								▓	▓	▓		
	Yili – "wild fig" *(Ficus sp.)*										▓	▓	▓
Edible seed	Wanguṉu *(Erograstis eriopoda)*					▓	▓	▓					
	Kalpaṟi *(Chenopodium rhadino-stachyum)*					▓	▓	▓					
Large game	mainly large macropods (kangaroo, euro, wallaby), emu	▓											▓

Drought year (1969–70)

Procurement Systems	Food Staples	J	F	M	A	M	J	J	A	S	O	N	D
Ground and tree fruits	Ngaṟu *(Solanum chippendalei)*	▓										▓	▓
	Yili – "wild fig" *(Ficus sp.)*	▓			▓	▓	▓			▓	▓	▓	
	Wayaṉu – "quandong" (sun dried) *(Santalum acuminatum)*			▓	▓	▓	▓						

Inadequate opportunity to observe   Inadequate opportunity to observe

Table 3. *Distance and frequencies of moves to new or different campsites by desert-dwelling Aborigines in the Tikatika–Clutterbuck Hills areas (1966–7) and in the Pulykara–Mt. Madley area (1970)*

Period	Group size	Number of moves	Total distance covered in kilometers (miles)
Nov. 18/66– Feb. 1/67	13	6	185 (115)
Feb. 8/67– April 11/67	12–13	8	415 (258)
Mar. 15/70– April 27/70	10–11	3	97 (60)

Table 4. *Estimated weights of staple plant foods taken daily by desert-dwelling Aborigines on seventy-three days from July 1966 to April 1967 (11 ± 3 persons) and seventeen days from April 1969 to July 1970 (9 ± 2 persons)*

Name of staple plant species	Amount (kg.) obtained per person[a]	
Kampuṟarpa *(Solanum centrale)*	fresh	0.61
	sun-dried	1.23
Ngaṟu *(Solanum chippendalei)*		0.41
Yawalyuru *(Canthium latifolium)*		0.82
Yili–"wild fig" *(Ficus sp.)*		0.72
Wayaṇu–"quandong"	fresh	0.64
(Santalum acuminatum)	sun-dried	1.00

[a]Based on overall average of ten persons in camp each day.

3.   The food-quest does not require more than a maximum of six to seven hours of work for each woman each day, and generally it requires less. Even during periods of drought, two or three hours' collecting by the women can provide sufficient food for the group for that day. Much more time is expended by the men in their hunting, for much poorer returns. On the other hand, nearly everyone forages and/or hunts every single day. The principal exceptions to this general pattern are the aged, who still try to forage when they can, and most women and girls on those occasions when hunting is providing most of the food.

4.   On most occasions there is ample leisure time for people to use in resting, gossiping, making tools, and other

Table 5. *Game animals caught by desert-dwelling Aborigines on seventy-three days from July 1966 to April 1967 (11±3 persons) and seventeen days from April 1969 to July 1970 (9±2 persons)*

Name of animal	Number of animals recorded	Total weight (kg.) of animals recorded	Average amount of meat (gr.) per person/day[a]
Sandplains goanna			
(*Varanus gouldii*)	182	229.3	2.5
Perentie lizard (*V. giganteus*)	10	27.5	0.3
Blue tongue (*Tiliqua scincoides*)			
and other small lizards	200+	108.0+	1.2+
European rabbit	31	46.0	0.5
Mouse[b]	many	75.0+	0.8+
Kangaroo (*Megaleia rufa*)			
and other macropods	3	123.8	1.4
Emu (*Dromaius novaehollandiae*)	0	0	—
Feral cat	21	113.4	1.3
Australian bustard (*Eupodotis*			
australis)	18[c]	41.2	0.5
Carpet snake (*Morelia spilotes*)	1	3.7	negligible
Peregrine falcon			
(*Falco peregrinus*)	2	2.0	negligible
Wild dingoes (*Canis familiaris*)	0	0	—
Total		773.8	

[a] Based on an overall average of ten persons in camp each day. [b] Mouse hunting observed only in April 1967. [c] Including three chicks.

activities. To a large extent, of course, this represents a kind of enforced leisure, since it is hard to imagine what advantage these people would gain from industriously gathering, processing, and storing large amounts of plant staples that are often available in a sort of de facto storage in the wild cause by natural dessication. Perhaps hunting is the only primary subsistence activity in which greater efforts might yield greater returns, although the data in Tables 5 and 7 show that in the long run a disproportionate amount of time is expended in this activity in relation to whatever game is captured.

5.   As can be seen in Table 2, there are times when the same staples may become available at widely differing times of year. Note, for example, how wild figs were available in October–November in the wet year of 1966, and in November–December and April–May in the drought year of 1969–70. This variation arises from localized variations in rainfall or drought that can result in staples ripening at

Table 6. *Game animals caught by Western Desert Aborigines at locations within 97 kilometers (60 miles) of Warburton Ranges Mission on thirty-five days from August 1966 to May 1967 (40±5 persons) and on sixteen days from November 1969 to July 1970 (40±5 persons)*

Name of animal	Number of animals recorded	Total weight (kg.) of animals recorded	Average amount of meat (gr.) per person/day[a]
Sandplains goanna *(Varanus gouldii)*	34	42.8	0.2
Perentie lizard *(V. giganteus)*	2	5.5	negligible
Blue tongue *(Tiliqua scincoides)* and other small lizards	100+	54.0+	0.3+
European rabbit	153	227.2	1.1
Mouse[b]	many	100.0+	0.5+
Kangaroo *(Megaleia rufa)* and other macropods	16	540.0	2.8
Emu *(Dromaius novaehollandiae)*	4	108.0	0.5
Feral cat	8	43.2	0.2
Australian bustard *(Eupodotis australis)*	4	10.4	0.1
Wild dingoes *(Canis familiaris)*[c]	14	—	—
Spoonbill *(Platalea regia)*	1	negligible	—
Pelican *(Pelecanus conspicillatus)*	1	negligible	—
Total		1131.1	

[a] Based on overall average of forty persons in camp each day. Does not include maximal grouping at Waṇampi Well (max. of 107 persons) during mid-December 1966. [b] Mouse hunting observed only in April–May 1967. [c] Not eaten, taken for bounty only.

different localities. There is no annual seasonal pattern of food collecting, since in general there are no predictable seasons in the desert when edible plants may be expected to ripen.

6.   Although the number of edible plant species is reduced during drought years, the actual quantities of these drought-staples are generally greater than is the case for the same plants during wet years. In the case of quandong *(Santalum acuminatum)* this is the result of natural preservation of the dessicated fruits while the weather remains dry, but for other drought staples it seems to be a case of larger yields stimulated by the prolonged dry weather. Thus foraging in drought years may not be as hard as one might at first suppose. It must be remembered, however, that no anthropologist has ever studied

Wayaṇu (*Santalum acuminatum*) being collected by a Western
Desert Aborigine child near Mt. Madley, Western Australia, in
April 1970. This staple food plant is especially important to the
Aborigines during droughts, when it remains available on the
ground in a naturally dessicated, sun-dried condition for long
periods.

nomadic Aborigines at first hand living under conditions of extreme drought (of the order of ten to twelve years' duration), and the strategies for dealing with such extreme occurrences are, as yet, little known. The period 1969–70 was the second year of a three-year drought in the Western Desert, which, for that region, is hardly extreme at all.

7.   The largest groups, usually numbering between 100 and 150 individuals, come together on the rare occasions when hunting is good. Mid-December 1966 to mid-January 1967 was one such occasion in an area to the east of the Warburton Ranges Mission, although conditions remained dry in other areas like Tikatika and the Clutterbuck Hills at that time. This is when ceremonies are most likely to occur, and novices are saved up for initiation until rainfall and localized hunting conditions will permit such a "critical mass" of people to camp together. Such groupings are always the result of natural rather than manmade surpluses of food, even though the desert Aborigines possess the technology to prepare and store many of their plant staples. There is evidence to suggest that these food-storage practices may be oriented primarily toward emergency situations such as times of extremely prolonged drought, but this is still somewhat conjectural.

8.   As drought conditions worsen and hunting becomes more difficult, groups tend to fragment and move to areas where they can base their activities close to one or more relatively dependable water sources. The signal for such a fragmentation of maximal population aggregates usually takes the form of reduced intake of meat, to where it falls below an average of about 0.56 kilograms (1¼ lb.) per person per day in camp, with consequent grumbling and discussion about the possibility of better hunting elsewhere.[2] While no water sources are totally reliable or permanent, some are better than others; and it is these that one finds in use by minimal groups of from ten to thirty individuals during drought periods. Tikatika in November 1966 to April 1967 was just such a case, although modified somewhat by the previous involvement of these people with the Warburton Ranges Mission and Laverton settlements.

9.   Aborigines must move frequently and travel long distances in order to maintain themselves. Journeys of as much as 400–500 kilometers (250–300 miles) are not un-

usual, particularly in times of drought. The people observed at Tikatika moved nine times within a period of
three months, living in a different camp each time and
foraging over an area of almost 2,600 square kilometers
(1,000 sq. miles) during that period, and other minimal
groups observed during droughts moved with similar
frequency and over comparable areas (see Table 3). This
is one of the most extreme examples of nomadism reported for any known hunting-and-gathering society in
the world. Along with this, there is evidence for extremely low population densities prior to European contact, of the order of one person per 90–100 square kilometers (35–40 sq. miles). Actual concentrations of population were much greater than this average figure would
indicate, but one must also remember that the desert is
even more depopulated today now that most Aborigines
have been resettled in close proximity to European missions, stations, and towns.
10.   A single habitation campsite may be reoccupied
more than once in the course of a single year as different staples are exploited in the same area; or, conversely,
a camp may not be revisited for several years in succession if no rains happen to fill nearby waterholes during
that period.

The grouping of food staples into units called "procurement systems" in Table 2 reflects a modified usage of Flannery's (1968) approach. These groupings present the universe of important edible
resources in this region from the point of view of how human beings
organize their movements, technology, and social groups in order to
harvest them effectively. Thus, various classes of primary resources
may be grouped with regard to their commonalities according to
how they are obtained by a human population. These commonalities
provide a basis for observing interactions between aspects of human
behavior and particular ecological variables, leading finally to a descriptive model of the total adaptive system operating aboriginally in
the "core" desert region of Australia.
   The Western Desert Aborigines present a picture of opportunistic
movement, based upon subjective assessments of the uncertainties of
food and water resources, that is borne out by their behavior in
specific situations on the ground. It can truly be said of the desert
Aborigines that they "chase rain" in the sense that a primary determinant in planning any move is the observed occurrence of falls of
rain, correlated with (1) known occurrences of water catchments;
and (2) the further correlation of these catchments with known oc-

currences of plant staples nearby. Rain can be seen falling in the desert for distances of up to, and in some cases exceeding, 80 kilometers (50 miles), and these falls are observed and related by the Aborigines to visible landmarks (often localities of totemic or sacred significance) that lie at or near the waterholes.

In these cases, opportunism based upon actual occurrences of rain is combined with traditional geographical knowledge of the exact location of water catchments in order to minimize uncertainties. For example, a move into an area where rain has been seen falling and where staple food plants are known to abound, but where few good rain catchments exist, is always a tempting but high-risk proposition. There have been cases reported as recently as 1964 of families becoming trapped and perishing in such areas, where there may be plenty of food but no water. On the whole, Aborigines tend to avoid such areas except when the rains are so extensive that even the smallest and most widely scattered catchments can be expected to be full. To avoid the dilemma of arriving at a key water source after several days' travel only to find that the rains – seen at a distance – just missed the catchment and failed to fill it, members of the group sometimes fan out while on the move and plan to approach the water source by several different routes, visiting other potential water sources on the way. In such cases, whoever finds water lets the others know by means of a prearranged smoke signal, and they come across to join him. People will generally avoid moving in a direct line toward the most reliable water source, preferring instead to forage in the vicinity of smaller waterholes first, since these are likely to dry out first, and reserving the food near the better waterholes for later when these other options are closed. Groups traveling during droughts sometimes do a complete circuit of the country around a more or less reliable waterhole like Tikatika before settling there, using ephemeral waterholes like Tjalputjalpu and others as temporary foraging bases while the water in them lasts.

None of the three staple food procurement systems presented in Table 2 requires a high level of technological specialization or cooperative social organization. By taking a task-oriented view of Aboriginal tools and work groups, we can see how they support the opportunistic strategies these people use to adapt to the conditions of the Western Desert habitat. Aboriginal nomadism puts a premium on portability in material culture. Since these people lack any kind of horse or dog traction to assist them, they cannot carry a large array of tools with them in their travels, especially if these tools are bulky or heavy. The requirements of portability and utility under "core" desert conditions are solved in three ways. (1) They use *multipurpose tools* that are lightweight and easy to carry, such as the spearthrower, which serves not only for throwing spears but also for starting fires,

Ethnographic Western Desert Aborigine spearthrowers. These represent an important class of multipurpose tool; they are also used to start fires, as mixing trays for tobacco and pigments, as percussion instruments at dances, and the stone adze flake hafted to the handle serves as a woodworking implement. The incised decorations on two of these items serve a maplike function with respect to sacred landmarks. (Photo courtesy of the American Museum of Natural History, New York.)

woodworking, mixing tobacco and pigments, and a variety of other tasks (Gould, 1970). (2) They use tools (mainly of stone) that can be left where they are needed and reused whenever that particular place is visited – in other words, *appliances*. Grinding slabs and stones are the most common class of appliances in the Western Desert, where they are used to process all edible grass seeds (Procurement

This double-basin seedgrinder was found on the surface at the James Range East Rockshelter site and is a good example of an appliance among the Central Desert Aborigines. (The scale in this photograph is 15 centimeters.)

System No. 2 shown in Table 2) and sun-dried kampuṟarpa as well. These items become more or less permanent fixtures of the camps where they are kept, although considerable initial effort may be needed to transport a large grinding-slab from its quarry or source to the camp where it will be used. Unbroken specimens we have weighed in the desert ranged from 5 kilograms (11 lb.) to slightly over 18.5 kilograms (41 lb.; this latter example was at Tikatika, where the nearest source of suitable stone is the Clutterbuck Hills, almost 65 kilometers distant). (3) They take the knowledge of tool-making with them and apply this knowledge when the need arises to make necessary tools from raw materials immediately at hand. I term these *instant tools,* and in most cases they are discarded immediately after use. Thus a naturally sharp stone may be picked up and used to slit a kangaroo's belly in order to remove the intestines, or a twist of grass may be fashioned on the spot as an impromptu pad to cushion a heavy load carried on one's head. Instant tools are the most varied and pervasive part of Aborigine technology, yet they also require minimal alternation of the natural material and are discarded whenever and wherever their use-life is over – often far

This impromptu circlet of wanguṇu grass (*Eragrostis eriopoda*) was used by one of the women at Tikatika to cushion her load of harvested plant foods on her return to camp, and it is a good example of an instant tool. The picture was taken immediately after she discarded the item. Instant tools like this are a pervasive part of Australian Desert Aborigine technology.

from any kind of habitation base camp. So a very large proportion of Aboriginal technology is as ephemeral to the archaeologist as the water sources these Aborigines depend upon. None of the tools in any of these three categories requires more than the efforts of a single individual to make, use, or maintain them.

The quantitative definition of a staple food given earlier is not altogether adequate for describing the relationship between natural food resources and human adaptive responses in the Western Desert. Alternatively, we can view staple foods in behavioral terms. All of the food staples listed in Table 2 are harvested in bulk quantities and transported back to camp for further processing and for division and sharing among kin. This is in contrast to supplemental foods that are collected in small quantities. These latter are usually eaten as snacks, on the run, while people are on the move in search of large game or staple food plants. Thus behavioral observations can define these categories of staple versus supplemental foods as adequately as can quantitative measurements of food amounts or calories obtained. But, more importantly, looking at procurement behavior also reveals variation that quantitative considerations alone

A Western Desert Aborigine hunting in burned-over sandhill country near Mt. Madley, Western Australia. The feral cat he is carrying is the only game he captured that day, despite many hours of effort.

might cause us to overlook. There is a low-level but steady intake of small game, mainly consisting of goanna lizards (*Varanus gouldii*, hunted mainly in the sandhill country, and *V. giganteus*, more commonly found in rocky country), "bush turkeys" (*Ardeotis australis*), various small marsupials and birds, and feral cats and rabbits (introduced by Europeans and now widespread throughout the desert). Like the staples mentioned in Table 2, these small animals are always transported back to camp for further division and sharing, despite the relatively small contribution to the overall bulk of the Aboriginal diet – on an average, less than 9 percent of the daily diet by weight. Rarely does a day go by that one does not see at least a few of the above-mentioned animals brought into camp for general consumption by the whole group. Although individual portions tend to be small – sometimes, as at Tikatika, no more than a single mouthful – everyone in camp gets a share, just as they do with the staples. Given the fluctuating and undependable yields from hunting large macropods and emus, small game is more important as a source of essential protein, from day to day, than large game. Unlike staple foods, small game is collected by everyone, without regard for the sexual

Roasting a feral cat in the coals of a small hearth at Tikatika. Like lizards and other small game, feral cats are an important source of protein for both desert-dwelling Aborigines and people living close to European settlements.

division of labor that is otherwise such a conspicuous part of staple procurement. Even children contribute significantly by digging up small lizards and grubs. Meat foods of any kind, including small game, are consistently rated as tastier than plant foods, which, as this observer has good reason to know, are rather uninteresting to the palate. So even small amounts of meat and fleshy food are welcomed for the variety they give to the diet. According to criteria of nutrition and flavor enhancement, one could regard small game as a fourth Aboriginal procurement system, even though the total amounts of food these represent are not great.

In contrast to the situation on other continents, man is the only large predator in the Australian landscape. The absence of gregarious mammals generally in Australia may have something to do with this unique condition, since the evolution of predators presumably bears a relationship to the presence of prey that can be hunted effectively. For the Australian Aborigine there are both benefits and costs in this situation. The principal benefit is that he does not have to defend himself against other predators. The principal cost is that there are no herds for him to exploit. At no time in the prehistoric past of Australia or in the ethnographic present can we see any evidence of man as a "superpredator" of big game along the lines suggested by Martin (1967) for European Upper Paleolithic hunters or Paleo-Indians in America.

Another unusual feature of Aboriginal hunting in the Australian desert is the total absence of traps and snares in the hunting technology. It is possible that traps and snares may not have been efficient for hunting indigenous small marsupials, birds, and lizards. Perhaps more important is the fact that desert Aborigines move their base camps frequently and unpredictably, so, as O'Connell (pers. comm.) has suggested, "Why fool with making traps and setting them up if you can't be certain you will be back the next day?" But it is also clear from existing observations that the desert Aborigines expend extraordinary amounts of time in their pursuit of game, both large and small. In taking small mammals and lizards, the animals are tracked to their burrows and dug out of the ground. European-introduced rabbits are still obtained in this way even when simple and cheap mechanical traps are available that would accomplish the task with far less effort. A woman may dig continuously for three or four hours to obtain a single rabbit or rabbit-eared bandicoot. But, given Aboriginal skills in tracking and in following out animal burrows, this method of hunting small animals is almost completely reliable. In fact, 98 percent of observed hunts of this kind were successful. So, from a behavioral point of view, it looks as if reliability in terms of the catch outweighs effort. It is vitally important to the Aborigines to maintain a steady, if somewhat low-level, supply of protein, and to this end low-risk but time-consuming techniques are consistently applied.

Tables 4 and 5 permit one to compare relative intakes of meat and plant foods and to relate these in a general way to the time spent by desert-dwelling Aborigines in obtaining these basic resources. These tables must, however, be viewed with some caution. For one thing, they represent only limited amounts of observation time (stated as "observation days" when these variables were monitored directly). For another, the actual quantification is open to dispute, especially with regard to the figures presented on hours of work in Table 7. There is an unavoidable element of uncertainty built into these particular figures by the fact that Aborigines rarely ever perform a single task to the continuous and utter exclusion of other activities. For example, a group of men on a hunt may take some time on their trip to venerate a sacred site or collect raw materials for toolmaking. These figures are approximations that represent my best effort to eliminate such "extraneous" activities from the totals, and I would not wish to attribute a high degree of reliability to them. So, too, the "Index of subsistence effort" – a useful idea proposed by Lee (1969:86) – must be viewed as an approximation in this case. The indexes for weeks II and III compare favorably with Lee's !Kung data and show that the Western Desert Aborigines probably possess even greater amounts of leisure time than the !Kung.

Table 6 was included to provide a rough comparison between the hunting effectiveness of desert-dwelling Aborigines versus Aborigines living in detached base camps within a 97-kilometer (60-mile) radius of the Warburton Ranges Mission. Unlike the desert dwellers, these latter people received rations (mainly flour, tea, and sugar) periodically by truck from the Mission, and some of them possessed rifles or shotguns. Moreover, the countryside around the Mission, even as far out as these camps, was subject to heavy foraging pressure by the abnormally large concentration of Aborigines there, so hunting of small animals tended to be less productive than farther out in the desert. While the average amount of meat per person per day was not appreciably different in such cases, the relative importance of large animals (macropods and emus) as well as rabbits in the diet was greater, while lizards and most other small game declined in importance.

While men often hunt in small groups (the largest observed was eleven, but groups of three or four are more common), there is little in the way of planned, cooperative effort. Most hunting is done by stealth, from behind simple brush blinds, rock crevices, or tree platforms close to a water source. In the Barrow Range, about 80 kilometers (50 miles) east of the Warburton Mission, the Aborigines are known to have used permanently constructed rock walls close to waterholes for their hunting blinds. The Aborigines often hunt this way at night, since most marsupial game is nocturnal. Dogs are not used in hunting at all, since their presence in or near the blind would frighten game away, and there is little hunting by means of direct pursuit unless an ideal opportunity presents itself or there is a wounded animal to be run down. If a hunter can see a kangaroo before it recognizes him, he may be able to stalk it from a considerable distance. But once alerted, large macropods are virtually impossible to catch owing to their speed and bobbing motion. Sometimes, however, groups of men trap emus in natural defiles where there is water to attract the animals. While one or two men try to spear the birds from blinds close to the waterhole, the others position themselves near the entrance to the defile hoping to block the birds' escape and get in a good throw with a spear. Today, of course, rifles are used, but the tactics are the same. There is no real organization to hunts like this – just an informal divison of tasks and a general melee when the animals race out of the defile entrance. Also, there

Table 7. Work diary for desert-dwelling Aborigines for four selected weeks[a]

Week	Date	Locality	Adults	Children	Person-days of consumption	Person-hours of work		Index of subsistence effort[b]
						Man-hours of work	Woman-hours of work	
I.	July 18/66	Tikatika–	6	5	11	8		.03
	19	Clutterbuck	6	5	11	2		.01
	20	Hills area	6	5	11	2		.01
	21		6	5	11	5		.02
	22		6	5	11	4		.02
	23		6	5	11	2		.01
	24		6	5	11	2		.01
II.	Dec. 27/66	Tikatika–	9	4	13	14	38	.17
	28	Clutterbuck	9	4	13	20	40	.19
	30	Hills area	9	4	13	22	30	.17
	31		9	4	13	12	32	.14
	Jan. 1/67		9	4	13	26	38	.21
	2		9	4	13	16	40	.18
	Feb. 25/67	Tikatika–	6	7	13	24	38	.20
	26	Clutterbuck	6	7	13	25	36	.20
	27		6	7	13	12	41	.17

III.							
28	Hills area	6	7	13	21	32	.17
Mar. 1/67		5	7	12	6	35	.14
2		5	7	12	21	40	.21
3		6	7	13	16	39	.18
Apr. 20/70		9	2	11	26	28	.21
21	Pulykara–	9	2	11	26	10	.14
22	Mt. Madley	9	2	11	24	6	.11
23	area	9	2	11	26	6	.12
IV. 24		9	2	11	30	2	.12
25		8	2	10	26	6	.13
26		9		11	28	4	.12

Average index of subsistence effort for weeks II and III = .17

[a] During weeks I and IV a significant part of the Aboriginal diet came from food that we contributed. In week IV this totaled 11.3 kilograms (25 lb.) of flour. So weeks I and IV are included here for the sake of completeness (i.e., they also affect the totals for foods collected as shown in Tables 2–4).

[b] This index is based on Lee (1969:86), where S = (person-days of work × 100)/(person-days of consumption) (i.e., the average for S during weeks II and III = .17, or 17 days of work per 100 days of consumption, or 1 work day produced food for 5.9 consumption days).

are accounts of Western Desert Aborigines using fire drives to flush game of all kinds, and such hunts generally involved several men (Finlayson, 1935). In 1934 a large hunt was observed in the Warburton Ranges area that suggests a higher degree of cooperation than one normally finds in desert Aborigine hunting. The Warburton area contains numerous small pointed and flat-topped knolls, many of them less than 30 meters (100 ft.) high. Aborigines, including both men and women, surrounded the base of each knoll completely, then walked together toward the top while shouting and beating the bushes with sticks. Game fleeing to the top was trapped, where the men administered the coup de grace (H. Lupton, pers. comm.). Other early observers like Helms (1896:256, 295), Basedow (1925:143–4), and Finlayson (1935:62) reported seeing brush fences that suggest some form of communal hunting. But all large game in the Australian desert is basically solitary and cannot be hunted effectively en masse. Even when one sees a "mob" of kangaroos or emus, it tends to disperse when pursued. So while there is some evidence for communal or cooperative hunting in the Western Desert, its role aboriginally would have been limited in terms of the diet and only an occasional occurrence. In the Western Desert there is little evidence for a special fourth category of extractive technology involving an expanded social context that I shall term *facilities*. My use of this term should not be confused with an earlier and quite different definition by Binford (1968:272). A facility is defined here as an artifact or a class of artifacts used to procure basic resources that is built, used, and in some cases maintained by a task group consisting of personnel above the level of the individual family. Perhaps the most impressive facilities of this sort occurred in the form of large salmon-fishing weirs and platforms as well as ocean-going canoes for sea mammal hunting among certain Indians of the northwest coast of America, but sophisticated and effective fishtraps have been reported ethnographically from Arnhem Land (Thomson, 1939b), and massive fishnets were reported historically from the Murray-Darling River system (Allen, 1972:47) in Australia as well.

Thus all of the Aboriginal staple food procurement in the Western Desert, as well as the hunting of large and small game, is carried out by individuals or small groups of relatives. Task groups are fluid in size and composition and are subject as much to personal preferences and sentiment as they are to the obligations of kinship. Co-wives, if they get along well together, will forage for staples and look after each other's children. But co-wives who are antagonistic may forage with other women with whom they are friendlier, even if they are more distantly related. Brothers and classificatory brothers tend to hunt together, as do fathers and sons, but only if there are friendly relations between them. Interpersonal relationships with respect to food procurement are essentially egalitarian, with none of the seniority of age and knowledge that characterizes Aboriginal sacred matters. Task groups are always small. Even when a relatively large number of men go out from camp together to hunt, they do not stay together as a single group but disperse into smaller groups to hunt in different localities and rendezvous later (usually in response to a prearranged smoke signal). It is unusual to find a food procurement task group of any kind exceeding five or six individuals.

While it is hard to classify these kinds of behavior strictly under the heading of technology, the use of fire, dogs, and geographical knowledge all bear a direct relationship to the business of making a living from day to day in the Western Desert. Fire is without doubt the most versatile tool possessed not only by the Aborigines but by hunters – gatherers in general. In the Western Desert fire is used to perform a wide variety of domestic tasks including such obvious functions as cooking, warmth, and illumination. More interesting, though, is the widespread use of fire for more specialized tasks in hunting and for such purposes as signaling. Game, for example, is often flushed into the open by lighting fires, and smoky fires are sometimes used to chase ground-living animals out of their burrows. From an ecological point of view, the most important aspect of the Aboriginal use of fire is that, regardless of the specific purpose of a particular fire, fires are always allowed to burn themselves out and are never extinguished. One could easily gain an impression of these people as "native pyromaniacs" since the effect of this behavior is often to let fires burn on for hours or days until large areas are affected. On one occasion near the Clutterbuck Hills, I watched a group of five boys catch three large feral cats, totaling about 8.1 kilograms (18 lb.) in weight, in a single hunt. During this hunt they burned a total of over 23 square kilometers (9 sq. miles) of country – in other words, much more than was required for the hunt itself; and such behavior is commonplace.

The climax vegetation over most of the Western Desert is spinifex of a variety that reproduces by seed-dispersal. It dominates the biotic landscape. Since spinifex is of only limited economic value to the Aborigines, large areas of climax spinifex are essentially sterile from their point of view. However, when large areas of spinifex are burned off, recolonization by other desert plants begins as soon as there are rains in the area, and a succession of plants appears leading ultimately back to climax spinifex. Several species of edible, staple plants are conspicuous in these successions, particularly the *Solanaciae*. I have observed several cases of Aborigines revisiting burned-over areas of spinifex following rains as much as a year or eighteen months after the burning to harvest large amounts of edible ground fruits. While the Aborigines seem generally aware that these burned-over areas are good places to forage after rains, they never expressed any awareness themselves of the relationship between burning of spinifex and the enhancement of their basic food resources. Questions of this kind always brought the reply that the burning was for some particular purpose like signaling or chasing game. But regardless of whether or not the Aborigines are conscious of the ecological consequences of their behavior with fire, there is little doubt that fire serves a major role in building up their food supply.

There is no direct evidence to show that Western Desert Aborigines aim their fires in particular directions.[3] Yet despite the apparent casualness of their use of fire, especially in allowing fires to burn unchecked, I have never encountered an occasion when a fire actually invaded an area that was already producing wild food crops. Does this mean that the Aborigines were aiming their fires away from areas that currently contained edible wild plants? No conscious expression of this idea was ever given by the Aborigines I observed, although one could infer this idea from their behavior. In addition to enhancing their future food supply, these people used fire in such a way as to ensure that there would be no interference with their already-existing supplies.

A dog's life among the Aborigines is not particularly joyous, though it can have its better moments. Unlike most hunter–gatherers we know about, the Western Desert Aborigines never use their dogs for hunting. Since man and animals generally use the same limited water sources in the Western Desert, most hunting is done by stealth, from concealment behind natural or artificial blinds rather than by pursuit across open country. Under these conditions, dogs are a definite drawback, since their noises will frighten game away. While men are out hunting, the women take the dogs with them, mainly to keep them out of the way. The one exception I saw to this was a dog that was allowed to accompany its male owner on hunts but was trained not to follow the hunter too closely.

People sometimes show great affection toward their dogs, although this rarely extends to feeding them. Most camp dogs subsist on scraps and offal. Puppies are fed, however, and are sometimes even nursed by the women. In some cases dogs are shown special consideration, as, for example, when the bones of the perentie lizard (*Varanus giganteus*) are stripped of their meat after roasting and placed in the branches of trees, since, unlike *V. gouldii*, this lizard's bones are brittle and shatter into splinters which would choke a dog if it were to eat them. The bones of this animal are placed out of the reach of the dogs for their own protection. What we appear to have are emaciated adult dogs that are strongly imprinted by their association with human beings and thus are reluctant to go wild, even though those relatively few dogs that have gone wild seem much

In order to prevent their dogs from choking on shattered bone
splinters of *Varanus giganteus*, the bones of this large perentie
lizard are stripped of their meat by the Western Desert Aborigines and place in a tree, high out of reach. This scene is adjacent to a habitation base-camp at Taltiwara, near the Alfred
and Marie Range, April 1967.

better fed and in better condition than their semidomesticated doggie counterparts. From both the human and the canine points of
view, the relationship between dogs and man in the Western Desert
is anomalous. Neither party expects very much, and the mutual
benefits are minimal.

In all of this research I have yet to see or hear of an Aborigine who was lost, this despite the relatively featureless terrain covering much of the region. There is no formal body of geographical knowledge as such; rather, such knowledge is embedded in various aspects of the sacred life, in the form of associations of totemic mythical beings to specific landmarks, including water sources. Names and locations of these landmarks are memorized by novices as part of their instruction into the sacred life. Tindale (pers. comm.) and others have even suggested that physical ordeals like circumcision, subincision, chest-scarification, and others act as mnemonic devices to ensure that this vital geographic knowledge is remembered and retained by succeeding generations of young men before they marry and raise families. Enough has been observed and written about the sacred life to indicate that, while some innovation is possible, this is perhaps the most conservative aspect of traditional Aboriginal behavior.

Knowledge of the desert landscape requires total memorization because it is not organized along the lines of rules or grammatical principles. One cannot learn a basic system and then deduce the locations of water sources by means of the system. Rather, one must know the specific location of each water source and relevant landmarks in any given area of the desert by heart and be ready to correlate this knowledge with occurrences of actual falls of rain and ripening of food plants in that area. Considering the basic importance of such specific geographic knowledge in the day-to-day business of making a living, it is not surprising to see all the ritual elaboration and many years of intermittent training required to impart and maintain it intact.

Perhaps the most complex social behavior involved with overcoming uncertainties in the resource-base arises in the area of kin-based sharing of food and access to resources. Most discussions about Aboriginal kinship center on marriage, but they also make clear the obligatory nature and importance of sharing food with one's in-laws and other classes of affinal kin (Berndt and Berndt, 1964:82). In other words, food-sharing and sharing of access to basic resources is not limited to one's immediate family but ramifies widely. Second cross-cousin marriage is preferred among most Western Desert Aborigines (similar to the Aranda system described by Elkin, 1964:72–84), which means that a man is expected, in most areas, to marry a woman related to him as his mother's mother's brother's daughter's daughter. Whenever possible, marriages are arranged along these lines, and this system is correlated with and supported by a system of eight named categories of kin, the subsection system. One may seek a spouse from only one of these subsections – the one containing one's second cross-cousins. The cumulative effect of these rules is to produce a shortage of potential marriage partners nearby to where one normally lives and forages, since there will be very few people standing in this relationship in any local group, and most of these will already be married or betrothed. Thus one is compelled by the nature of the system to look farther afield for a marriage partner, often hundreds of miles away. But a long-distance marriage of this sort can be viewed as adaptive, since it furnished obligatory kin-sharing ties between people in widely distant areas. A drought or food shortage in one area can be overcome by moving into a better-favored region where one can share food and access to local resources with one's in-laws. Since the Aborigines are polygynous, multiple long-distance marriages may be arranged in several directions, and what one sees, in fact, throughout the Western Desert are widely ramified and interconnected kin-sharing networks that serve to mitigate the uncertainties of rainfall and food. Such obligatory kin-based sharing has been widely observed among hunter–gatherer societies, although nowhere does it appear to be more elaborate or extensive than among the Western Desert people, where the uncertainties and risks in the physical environment are the greatest and where the limiting factor of water presses most directly.

In terms of everyday behavior, what occurs is a constant "giving away" of any extra meat or plant foods or goods like spears, hairstring, and other items to one's relatives whenever the opportunity arises. Security in this case rests in having as many kin as possible who are obliged to share what they have with you whenever you and your family have real need. Individual accumulation of surpluses of food and other goods in anticipation of future shortages would negate this sharing ethic and engender a revulsion more extreme than any connected with Western notions of hoarding in times of scarcity. In short, the Western Desert people do not traditionally conform to any kind of "money in the bank" conceptions of how to deal with scarcity, and personal or family aggrandizement of food or goods does not occur.

While all kinds of food are shared regularly among kin, the division of meat with respect to large game involves the greatest formality in terms of rules and reveals several important principles. When a group of men hunts a kangaroo or other large animal, it is the man who kills the animal who is the last to share, and his share sometimes amounts to only the innards. A kangaroo is divided into a fixed number of named portions, nine in all, immediately after roasting and not far from where the animal was killed. The desert Aborigines do not possess any techniques for storing meat, so it must be shared as widely as possible and eaten before it rots. Certain classes of the hunter's kin, such as his father-in-law and brothers-in-law, have first choice from among the portions, which are laid out on a bed of mulga boughs or eucalyptus leaves. They are followed in order by other classes of kin, like elder brothers and younger brothers, and, last of all, by the hunter himself. These shares are transported back to camp and divided, in turn, by each sharer among his own parents, wives, and children.

Since the hunter is himself related to the other men he hunts with, he will, in the long run, be entitled to a share in someone else's kill by virtue of these same rules. This means that, ultimately, meat is available on a more or less equal basis to all who hunt, and, through them, to the rest of the group. Thus, regardless of the number or size of animals killed, a remarkably even distribution of meat takes place. But this arrangement does more than simply distribute the catch. It also doubles the rewards to the hunter by giving him both social prestige as a good kinsman and meat, when, according to these rules, he takes his share from someone else's catch. The Western Desert Aborigines have evolved a system that compels people to share food, even when such sharing might not be strictly necessary, in order to assure that when such sharing is needed in an emergency – such as during drought or localized shortages of game – the relationships that require sharing between kin are strong. In short, food-sharing relationships among these people are too important to be left to whim or sentiment.

Adaptive processes
Having examined various adaptive strategies that characterize the day-to-day business of the Aborigines' quest for food, water, and other basic resources in the Western Desert, we can now consider the overall adaptive system of which these strategies are components. What is the cumulative pattern or "trajectory" of these strategies? An adaptive model is essential as a framework for making predictive statements about residue behavior in the Australian desert, as it is in any place where one attempts to do living archaeology.

The Western Desert Aborigines lack any kind of annual seasonal round, and this is seen as a function of the absence of seasonality in the patterning of rainfall in the "core" desert regions of Australia. About the only generalization one can offer about annual seasonality in relation to rainfall is the statement that any substantial rains that might occur will do so during the Australian summer, the time of year when evaporation is the highest. There is annual seasonality in temperature, but this has only secondary importance with respect to Aboriginal adaptive strategies. The desert Aborigines have adapted by combining their traditional knowledge of the local geography with their observations of actual falls of rain and occurrences of edible staples, an essentially random matter requiring an opportunistic response. All subsistence decisions and behavior occurring within this framework tend to minimize uncertainty, even at the possible expense of increased yields of food in certain areas where reliable waterholes do not exist. Movement by groups is frequent and far-ranging and is basically random with respect to areas that do contain usable water sources. Groups also fluctuate in size in direct response to the local availability of rainwater. As long as one knows the location of key water and food resources in the desert and can correlate this knowledge with the actual occurrence of rains and act accordingly, life there is fairly comfortable. But virtually no other options exist, and a hunting-and-gathering life based on any other approach, including a seasonal one, would surely fail.

Thus what we are seeing in the Western Desert is a risk-minimizing adaptive system, in which technological, economic, and social behavior can be viewed as responding to and interacting with other ecological variables. Nowhere within the total system is this more apparent than in the Aboriginal use of fire, which clearly involves feedback effects by man upon the desert flora. This is not to say that all aspects of Aboriginal behavior are determined by ecological requirements. It would be difficult indeed to demonstrate that most of the stylistic complexities of Aboriginal mythology and ritual or the subtleties of belief concerning the sacred life are determined by environmental considerations. But, keeping in mind the earlier strictures about neutral determinism, it can be proposed that these ideational and symbolic elaborations do not violate the ecological requirements to any extreme degree. In an ecological sense, my burden here is simply to show to what extent various characteristic kinds of Aborigine behavior conform to the requirements of life in a "core" desert. In particular, I have argued that ramified kin-sharing networks are an adaptive mechanism for minimizing risks in this risky habitat, and that elaborations of this pattern (i.e., second cross-cousin marriage, the eight subsection system, division and sharing of meat, memorization of sacred landmarks, etc.) are indirectly supportive of, or at least consistent with, this risk-minimizing mode of adaptation. In the Western Desert of Australia, we can observe an extreme case of human behavioral responses to particular ecological stresses and requirements, most notably the limiting factor of water and related problems of food procurement. Furthermore, there is archaeological evidence from the Puntutjarpa Rockshelter site near Warburton to show that this risk-minimizing mode of adaptation is of long standing in the Western Desert, extending back at least the last 10,000 years under climatic and biotic conditions that did not differ greatly from present-day conditions (Gould, 1977).

4

Other adaptive models in Aboriginal Australia

It is easy to gain an impression that the Aranda, Pitjantjatjara, and other desert people are somehow typical of Australian Aborigines in general. It was in the Australian deserts that the traditional way of life continued, largely unaffected by European intrusion, until recently enough so that it could be observed by anthropologists, with the result that the ethnographic literature on the Aborigines has always been somewhat overbalanced in favor of desert dwellers. This is an unfortunate impression, since it has, at times, led scholars – particularly in Europe – to look to the desert Aborigines (and by implication, all Aborigines) as examples of arrested development in human cultural evolution. Tylor (1899:ix) argued that because of the Aborigines, by which he included the Tasmanians and other peoples of Australia, "Man of the Lower Stone Age ceases to be a creature of philosophic inference, but becomes a known reality." This view was echoed by Fraser (1898: 281; 1913, I:87–126; 1923: 55) and Sollas (1915), who saw in the Australian Aborigine a perfect analogue for the *uhrgeschichte* of the human species. In the light of what was happening in late nineteenth century anthropology in Europe, this reaction to the Aborigines was understandable. Remains of Neanderthal Man were being uncovered at an ever-increasing rate, posing inevitable questions of how these apparently pre-*sapiens* form of early man lived. When Spencer and Gillen published their early accounts of the Central Desert Aborigines of Australia (1899, 1904), these people seemed to many scholars to be living representatives of the early Stone Age and worthy of study on that account. The already excellent literature on Aborigines living in other, better favored parts of Australia, such as Howitt's studies of the Kurnai and other groups of southeastern Australia (1904) and Brough-Smyth's review of the Aborigines of Victoria (1878), was largely ignored overseas at that time. Greater recognition of these early accounts of Aboriginal life in southeastern Australia at that time might have helped to counterbalance the desert-centric impression of Aborigines that grew up then and the assumptions that flowed from it.

In some ways the desert Aborigines of Australia can be viewed as atypical because, prior to European contact, by far the largest numbers of people in Australia lived in the tropical and temperate coastal regions. These areas contained the most sedentary and dense human populations in Aboriginal Australia. Of course, many of these areas were also deemed attractive for European settlement, with the result that the Aboriginal populations living in them were the first to be displaced, massacred, or otherwise decimated. Even in the tropical areas where European settlement was less disastrous for Aborigines, the study of economic, ecological, and technological aspects of Aboriginal life were neglected for many years – the most conspicuous exceptions being work by such "mavericks" as Donald Thomson and Norman Tindale, who were clearly outside the mainstream of academic Australian anthropology at that time. Because the Aborigines of coastal Australia and adjacent regions were, to varying degrees, affected by early European contact, some measure of reconstruction has always been needed to study their economic and ecological adaptations. In some cases, as with the Tasmanian Aborigines, the need for reconstruction is total, since the traditional Aborigines there were completely extinct by 1876. In other areas, like Arnhem Land, there have been changes to the traditional life that must be considered, although the indigenous population has survived.

Despite the heavy element of reconstruction that must sometimes be used, Australian scholars are finding that there is much valuable information to be gained from studying these groups. In fact, some of the most intriguing and unusual adaptations in the world occurred in these areas outside the arid portions of Australia. They are worthy of note in their own right, and they also can be valuable for comparison with what we already know about desert adaptations in Australia. For living archaeology, they provide a broader view of the range of adaptive models possible not only in Australia but for world prehistory in general. Above all, they can be compared with desert adaptations to provide an adaptive model that can generate propositions about risk-minimizing behavior in human societies generally.

The shell game

One consequence of the recent outstation movement on Australian Aboriginal Reserves (documented for the Western Desert by Coombs, 1977, and for coastal Arnhem Land by Meehan, 1977a) has been the reestablishment of at least partial dependence on wild foods by some Aborigines who have chosen to leave the missions and other centers where Aborigines have been concentrated for many years. One such group is the Anbara, a subgroup of Gidjingali-speaking Aborigines who have left the Maningrida settlement in Arnhem Land and spend a substantial part of their lives living on the coast near the mouth of the Blyth River. While these people depend upon Europeans for some food as well as for medical and educational services, they remain largely traditional in their social organization and derive all of their meat and fleshy foods from hunting and gathering within their own territory, including the sea and coastline. This group was studied by Betty Meehan in 1972–73, with special attention to patterns of shellfish procurement, consumption, and discard (Meehan, 1975; 1977a, 1977b).

Archaeologists have long speculated on the nature and composition of shellmounds, which appear as prehistoric sites on post-Pleistocene shorelines in most parts of the world. Various attempts have been made by archaeologists to infer the elapsed time represented by these midden accumulations (Nelson, 1909), to estimate prehistoric population size (Ascher, 1959), and to estimate the dietary content of the food represented by these remains (Shawcross, 1967), but these remain purely archaeological estimates, augmented in the case of Shawcross's study by a detailed consideration of the dietary potential of the fisheries and other marine resources adjacent to the archaeological site being analyzed. Bailey (1975) presents a comprehensive review of various attempts to interpret shellmound remains in general, with particular reference to Australian middens. Earlier attempts to study ethnographic patterning of shellfish remains of the Andaman Islanders (Cipriani, 1966) and coastal inhabitants of South Africa (Bigalke, 1973), although clearly a step in the right direction, were not as detailed or comprehensive as the Anbara study by Meehan, which represents the first major assault by living archaeology upon the problem of shell-midden formation behavior.

In monitoring shellfish procurement, Meehan noted that the Anbara collected shellfish on 194 of the 334 days she observed their food quest. Although shellfish gathering was as important during the dry season months as it was in the "wet," Meehan noted that most shellfish collecting coincided with the time during the wet season when rain fell most heavily and regularly. On these 194 days, the Anbara Meehan observed collected at least 6,700 kilograms (14,740 lb.) of shellfish, mainly of five species, with the most important being *Tapes hiantina* (accounting for 61 percent of the total collected, by weight). Although many of these species were available on most occasions when the women went out collecting, there was a marked tendency to harvest only one species on any particular shellfish-gathering expedition. The main exception to this strategy occurred after heavy seas had deposited debris on shore, making it easier to collect all the species that had washed up together. Even when this happened, however, the Anbara women kept each species of shellfish they collected in a separate container.

From such observations, Meehan (1975:118) concluded that there was ". . . a carefully planned strategy on the part of the Anbara, rather than a random collection of edible shell fish."

Although the Anbara focused their attention upon a narrow range of a few preferred species, they did not carry this tendency to its ultimate or logical conclusion, namely, exclusive reliance upon a few species that were most abundant or easiest to collect. Some species that made a miniscule quantitative contribution to the diet were nevertheless harvested whenever suitable conditions prevailed. An example of this was *Melo amphora,* a large shellfish available during periods of extreme low tide arising from the right combination of wind, tide, and weather. Variety was as important to the Anbara in their diet as it was among the Western Desert people.

Women were generally reluctant to discuss their shellfish-collecting plans in camp, because they feared the small children might overhear and want to come. Children were usually left in camp with relatives, especially since the women would try to remain out as long as possible even after the tide was rising, when the collecting was good. The stated reason that was usually given for finally leaving the shellfish beds was fear of sharks, which cruise in large numbers off the main beaches. Camp dogs were encouraged to accompany the shellfish collectors, since their noise and splashing about was thought by the Anbara to frighten away sharks. Most major collecting expeditions for shellfish were made up of mature women who regarded this as their primary food-getting activity for the day. However, shellfish were also collected along with other edible plants and animals and were sometimes eaten as snacks by old women and children while the serious foragers were away from camp.

Most shellfish collecting was done by the women and girls. Females accounted for 85 percent of the total weight of *T. hiantina* gathered during the year. When men did shellfish collecting, however, their efforts in terms of distances traveled from camp and weights collected were measurably greater than those of the women. As among the Western Desert people, very small children were often encouraged to help with the collecting and were made much of when they picked up a few shells. Certain women could be identified as "serious" shellfish collectors in that they devoted a significant amount of their time to gathering *T. hiantina,* and prolonged observation revealed some of the special skills that went into harvesting this species. Women generally foraged along the outer edges of beds exposed by Spring tides, since the shellfish collected under those conditions tended to be larger than average. But for the most part the Anbara preferred to gather large amounts of shellfish rather than to concentrate of collecting big shellfish.

Meehan argues from her observations that:

> The importance of shellfish gathering by women and girls
> in Gidjingali society, rested not so much on the weights
> they collected . . . but in the frequency with which they
> produced shellfish during periods when it was most
> needed . . . In the diet of the Gidjingali, or for that mat-
> ter, of any hunting group, it is the amount of protein
> (animal or vegetable) that each person gets each day that
> really regulates the health of its members, not the massive
> quantities that are brought in irregularly . . . [1975:197]

Like the Western Desert Aborigines, the Anbara have no technology
for storing meat or fleshy foods, making it all the more important to
maintain a steady minimum intake of fresh protein. Meehan calculates that each person in the group she studied received an average
of 0.6 kilogram of shellfish every day of the year, or 1.1 kilograms
for each day that shellfish were collected. This was equivalent to 0.03
kilogram of protein each day or 0.05 kilogram on each shellfish
collecting day. Although shellfish contributed only 0.3 percent to 14
percent of the total calories available to each person at the times
when caloric intakes were sampled, the nutritional (i.e., protein) contribution of shellfish was significant. Shellfish collecting was especially important at those times when other protein resources like fish
were scarce. Meehan concludes:

> [Shellfish] collection was not regulated by the skill of the
> gatherers, nor by the intricacies of the behaviour of the
> prey. If absolutely necessary, some kinds of shellfish could
> have been collected every day of the year. They were
> there for the taking, like food on the supermarket shelf
> with which they were sometimes compared. Once gather-
> ers were actually on the beds, it was simply a matter of
> mining in the shell-producing areas. Women could, within
> certain limits, designate the amount of shellfish they
> wanted to collect; the more effort they put into the pro-
> cess, the more they reaped from it. [1975:228]

While the Western Desert Aborigines lack anything on their menu
that equates exactly with shellfish, which are a sessile and abundant
source of protein, the role of hunting small game in their adaptation
is similar to the role of shellfish collecting for the Anbara. In each
case, the hunting of large game (and for the Anbara, fishing as well)
is inadequate to provide the day-to-day minimum amount of protein
needed by the group, and small game and shellfish, respectively,
assume a dietary importance that is not commensurate with their
contribution to the diet by weight or calories. In each case, the behavior directed toward these "protein staples" is essentially the same,

involving some kind of transport of the food back to camp for final sharing and consumption by the members of the group. The Western Desert Aborigines would not know what a fish was if they saw one (we tried showing them pictures of fish, shellfish, and various crustaceans during our fieldwork, but there was no recognition by them at all) and rely completely upon terrestrial resources, while marine resources furnish 68 percent of the total protein intake for the Anbara. Yet despite these fundamentally different economic orientations, the roles of small game hunting and shellfish collection, along with the predominance of women in both activities, in relation to ecological requirements in these two societies are essentially the same.

The Anbara "ethic of generosity" (Hiatt, 1965: 103; Meehan, 1975: 82) was also essentially the same as that of the Western Desert people, to the extent that, as Meehan discovered, "One of the major problems of our fieldwork was that according to Gidjingali custom, anyone making any inquiry about food was tacitly making a request to be given some" (1975: 82). Despite the higher degree of annual seasonal predictability of resources along the Arnhem Land coast than in the Western Desert, some signs of stress are apparent that might encourage such a sharing ethic. Meehan describes a "molluscan eco-disaster" that occurred at the mouth of the Blyth River in 1973-4 when an influx of fresh water from exceptionally heavy monsoonal rains wiped out entire shellbeds of *T. hiantina*. Fewer of these shellfish were eaten during the 1973-4 wet season than in the preceding year, and there was a greater dependence upon mangrove-dwelling species like *Crassostrea amasa* and *Batissa violaca,* which are more tolerant of fresh water. Other foods, like fish and wild yams, also were more important during this period.

The events of 1973-4 showed that the amounts and locations of essential shellfish resources could fluctuate much more than the 1972-3 observations had suggested. Perhaps the tendency of the Anbara to seek variety in their shellfish diet even when it would be easier to concentrate on one or a few species to the exclusion of all others is, in fact, an adaptive mechanism to ensure that alternative sources of protein will be available during emergencies of this kind. Anything that affects a basic dietary resource to this extent can be viewed as a potential limiting factor, and the low-level but persistent efforts by the Anbara to vary their shellfish diet even under optimal conditions for harvesting the primary species could be an adaptive response to overcome such stress imposed by this limiting factor. If the reader will forgive my piling one supposition on top of another, we could go farther and even suggest that such adaptive behavior, in Bennett's sense of this term, would give rise to the low-level but persistent presence of a wide variety of shellfish species in the shell-midden refuse, over and above the primary species like *T. hiantina,* over long periods of time. Thus one could interpret this variety, both in living Anbara society and in the shellfish refuse in Arnhem Land, as the signature of adaptive behavior that leads to a long-term pattern arising from strategies to cope with infrequent but nevertheless severe stress such as occurred in 1973–4.

Facilities management

In American today there is a widespread tendency to assign elegant-sounding titles to rather mundane activities. New York City garbage collectors are officially referred to as "Uniformed Sanitation Workers." At the Kaiser Medical Center in Honolulu there is a sign over the entrance to the emergency clinic that says "Wound Management." And at the University of Hawaii there is a department called "Facilities Management." Upon examination, this department turns out to consist of a few big Hawaiian guys who move furniture and sometimes fix the plumbing.

Yet the term "facilities management," pompous as it may sound, could have some value for the study of living archaeology in Australia and elsewhere. Facilities are exactly what many Aborigines in certain parts of Australia were managing in their food-getting activities, and they appear to have done this efficiently and on an impressive scale. In Chapter 3 I defined a "facility" as an artifact or class of artifacts used to procure basic resources that is built, used, and maintained by a task group consisting of personnel above the level of the individual family. Although facilities, thus defined, do not occur among the desert Aborigines, they are reported from other areas of Australia, mainly in ethnohistorical sources. Recent studies by Harry Allen (1972, 1974) have revealed the extensive use of facilities by historic Aborigines living in the Darling River Basin, an area of approximately 233,000 square kilometers (90,000 sq. miles) in southeastern Australia to the west of the Great Dividing Range. Today this is a flat, semiarid region with chains of dry lakes that were once part of the Murray-Darling drainage system. It is covered with wide stretches of mallee and *Acacia* shrub woodland, with extensive areas of open steppe and savannah grassland. Today this area is much affected by overgrazing, but during the Pleistocene it was well watered and supported an extensive fauna consisting of at least sixty species, fifteen of which became extinct by around 15,000 years ago (Allen, 1972: 18). The fossil-bearing localities at Lake Menindee and other Darling Basin sites contain some of the best evidence available on the Pleistocene fauna of Australia.

The earliest European explorers to visit this region in the early nineteenth century were wrong in their idea that father inland there was a great shallow sea. Oxley's original "unfortunate guess" about this supposed inland sea prompted later explorers like Sturt to set out during periods of drought in order to avoid this hypothetical body of water (Allen, 1972: 72). So their observations of the Aborigines in this region were limited to a view of people living under drought conditions, while the explorers themselves were tied to the flowing rivercourses for their own water. This meant that their observations were heavily biased toward people living along the rivers and tended to ignore people who may have been foraging in the dry hinterland. Thus our best historic evidence of Aboriginal life for this region comes from groups that inhabited areas of river frontage, mainly the Bagundji and their neighbors. These people spoke essentially the same language and shared many characteristics of kinship and social organization, and Allen estimates that 30–50 percent of the food eaten by these people came from or was directly associated with the Darling River. Mitchell, one of the earliest explorers to visit this area, noted that: ". . . these tribes inhabiting the banks of the Darling may be considered Ichthyophagi, in the strictest sense . . ." (1838,I: 268).

The Bagundji subsisted largely on fish (mainly Murray cod and silver perch), freshwater mussels, crayfish, turtles, and aquatic birds and plants. Early eyewitness accounts describe the use of fishing nets over 90 meters (100 yd.) long, with weights made of calcined clay and floats of reed bundles (Allen, 1972: 47). Sturt (1833,I: 90–2) described such a net in use, and he also observed large weirs and scaffolds constructed by the Aborigines, although not in use at the time of his visit (1833,I: 41). Eyre saw individual hauls of codfish totaling between 135 and 225 kilograms (300 and 500 lb.) along with substantial amounts of turtles and catfish being taken with nets of this kind. Eyre (1845,II: 283–6) also reported seeing large nets hung across waterways from trees or large poles to capture ducks. Men and women worked together to set these big nets, although they were tended mainly by women. Nets and weirs were effective only at certain seasons, mainly in the spring and summer when there was a large volume of water flowing through the Darling River system, bringing increased runs of fish. The October flood was especially good, most notably at places like the "Brewarrina Fishery," a series of stone fish traps on the upper Darling (Mathews, 1903: 152). In contrast, the winter was generally a period of dependence upon nonriverine sources of food of lower overall productivity. Emus, kangaroos, and wallabies were hunted at this time, but plant foods like edible grasses and *Acacia* seeds made up at least one-third of the total diet (Allen, 1972: 75; 1974). The principal species of edible grass was native millett (*Panicum decompositum*), which produces edible seeds in December–April. Since the Darling River area receives less rain annually than most of the Central Desert of Australia, Allen argued, "It was the river that made the Bagundji country a far better habitat than Walbiri [a well documented Central Desert group] country and changed the entire Aboriginal response to the climate." (Allen, 1972: 94) Lawrence (1968: 94) further concludes:

> The reports of the explorers are particularly valuable because they show that the methods used in fishing changed with the season and the condition of the river, and the efficiency of each method in relation to the amount of food available, presumably determined the population which could be supported at any one instance.

We have little direct evidence about the task groups that made and used these nets and weirs, although their size and complexity of use makes it improbable that any single nuclear family could have operated them effectively. Duck hunting by means of large nets was reported as a communal activity (Eyre, 1845,II: 283–6), and it seems reasonable to assume, at least for the purpose of discussion, that cod- and perch-fishing with large nets and weirs was similarly communal. While the nature of the social organization for these communal Bagundju food-getting enterprises remains conjectural, it does appear that a certain "critical mass" of labor was needed to carry out procurement tasks connected with these large nets and weirs. Large scale seasonal harvesting of fish and waterfowl in this manner necessarily presupposes a work force of sufficient size to build, use, and maintain the facility in question.

If, for example, ten fishermen stand in a river with their spears, they may catch ten fish apiece during a peak run and consider it a good day's catch. But if those same ten men work together to construct a weir or net that will effectively trap most or even all of the fish coming upstream, then the total catch may be multiplied a thousandfold. Instead of catching 100 fish in a day, those ten men could easily catch 100,000, with the actual amounts depending, of course, upon the habits of the fish, condition of the river, and so forth. The opposite side of this equation is that it may take a minimum of ten men to construct and operate the weir or net with any degree of efficiency at all. Given any fewer men, the only option is to fish on an individual basis, with consequently reduced yields. So what we have is one of those "better tautologies" referred to earlier, which posits a necessary relationship between the size of the task group and the artifact or structure needed to accomplish the task with enough efficiency to support a group of that size. It is unfortunate that the Bagundji evidence does not permit us to calculate the size of the task group required for each kind of facility they used, but the documented existence of these artifacts and structures among the Bagundji argues for the existence of task groups big enough to reasonably account for their presence. Other documented cases from Australia, like that described from Arnhem Land by Thomson (1939a), further support the idea that at least some Australian Aborigines did, in fact, develop true facilities as part of a specialized and seasonal kind of food procurement system.

Moth-hunters and macrozamia collectors

When we turn our attention to the uplands of the Great Dividing Range of Australia, we are dealing again with another part of Australia where living archaeology among Aborigines, in the strictest sense, is not possible. This is one of those areas where the indigenous populations were long ago displaced by European intrusion, so one cannot actually observe Aborigines there living off the land. Here, too, a heavy element of historical and ethnographic reconstruction is needed. Fortunately, the ethnohistorical sources contain useful first-hand accounts by early explorers and settlers that can be combined with current knowledge about climatic, edaphic, and biotic conditions in the Australian uplands. Recent research into Aboriginal adaptations to the uplands of Australia have revealed behavior that, although extraordinary in its own right, also sheds light on the adaptive behavior of the desert people and, indeed, Australian Aborigines in general.

Imagine great clouds of moths moving through the warm air of the antipodean summer to converge on the granite tors atop the summit ridges of Australia's highest mountains. Individually, these small brown moths (*Agrotis infusa*), called "Bogong" by the Aborigines of the Monaro Tableland and adjacent areas, are not impressive, but in the aggregate they are a mighty mass. Millions of these moths swarm to the alpine peaks to aestivate in the cracks and crannies of these rock formations. An early European visitor in this region, Robert Vyner, climbed up to one of the these moth-aestivation centers at what was probably Numbananga Peak, near the Tumut Valley, in 1865 and described what he saw:

> The moths were found in vast assemblages sheltered within the deep fissures, and between the huge masses of rocks, which there form recesses, and might almost be considered as caves. On both sides of the chasms the face of the stone was literally covered with these insects, packed closely side by side, over head and under, presenting a dark surface of a scale-like pattern . . . so numerous were these moths that six bushels of them could easily have been gathered by the party at this one peak; so abundant were the remains of the former occupants that a stick was thrust into the debris on the floor to a depth of four feet. [Flood, 1973: 74]

Such occurrences of Bogong moths are known in recent times as well, although their numbers and movements have been adversely affected by the introduction of pesticides into the agricultural districts of eastern Australia.

Recent studies by Josephine Flood (1973, 1976) reveal the full extent of human reliance upon this unique resource prior to European settlement in this region. In general, the uplands were not an especially attractive zone for Aboriginal settlement. The uppermost areas, 1,500–2,100 meters elevation (5,000–7,000 ft.) were glaciated during the late Pleistocene and remained alpine or subalpine in character during post-Pleistocene times following the retreat of these montane galciers. Treeline today occurs at around 1,800 meters (6,000 ft.) and the winter snowline at between 1,500 and 1,650 meters (5,000 and 5,500 ft.). Although not rugged by mountaineering standards in other parts of the world, the winter snowmass of this region is massive and encompasses an area of about 2,600 square kilometers (1,000 sq. miles). Below these alpine and subalpine habitats, the country is rugged and heavily forested, with deeply cut river gorges and steep slopes. At elevations of around 600–900 meters (2,000–3,000 ft.) one encounters tablelands that, like the Monaro, are often cold, dry, and treeless steppe. Early explorers' accounts and archaeological surveys support the view that in this area, "There seems . . . to be a correlation between lack of population and increased altitude, which may in fact relate to reduced food resources in the higher zones" (Flood, 1973: 49).

Yet despite the apparently poor resources of these high-altitude habitats, Aborigines converged upon this region in large numbers during the summer to harvest and feast upon the moths. Aborigine moth feasts are reported for the Bogong Range, Tumut Valley, Mt. Kosciusko, the Brindabella and Tidbinbilla Mountains, and the Victorian Alps; in other words, all the highest ranges in Australia and covering the entire area of what are usually referred to as the Australian Alps. Sometimes these moth flights were blown off course and failed to arrive, and the precise timing of their arrival at the aestivation centers was somewhat variable, but on the whole this was a predictable, seasonal resource. The fat content of the moths' abdomens exceeds 61 percent of their dry body weight for males and 51 percent for females (Flood, 1973: 89), and the Aborigines are reported in some cases to have pounded the moths into cakes of fat and sometimes preserved the fat by smoking. Richard Helms, the same early observer who saw brush traps in use for wallaby hunting in the Barrow Range in the Western Desert, has provided the most detailed ethnographic account of Aborigine moth hunts, and this account is worth quoting at length:

As early as October, as soon as the snow had melted on the lower ranges, small parties of natives would start during fine weather for some of the frost-riven rocks and procure "Bugongs" for food. A great gathering usually took place about Christmas on the highest ranges, when sometimes about 500 to 700 aborigines belonging to different friendly tribes would assemble almost solely for the purpose of feasting upon roasted moths. Sometimes these natives had to come great distances to enjoy this food, which was not only much appreciated by them but must have been very nutritious, because their condition was generally improved by it and when they returned from the mountains their skins looked glossy and most of them were quite fat. Their method of catching the insects was both simple and effective. With a burning or smouldering bush in the hand the rents in the rocks were entered as far as possible, when the heat and smoke would stifle the thickly congregated moths, that occupied nearly every crack, and make them tumble to the bottom of the cleft. Here an outstretched kangaroo skin or a fine net made of kurrajong fibre would receive most of the stupefied and half singed insects, which were then roasted on hot ashes . . . The taste of the roasted bodies of the "Bugongs" is, according to some Europeans who tried them, sweetish and nutlike and rather pleasant eating. [Helms, 1895: 394–5]

Presumably these moths were roasted when they were to be consumed immediately, whereas pounded and/or smoked cakes of moth fat were saved for later consumption and even transported to other areas. Large aggregations of Aborigines of the sort described by Helms afforded opportunities for trade, ceremonies, and marriage arrangements (Flood, 1973:74, 77A–B).

Archaeological studies by Flood have uncovered what appear to be large campsites at central points that give ready access to the actual moth-collection centers. These are usually found at a lower elevation, where the Aboriginal inhabitants could live in greater comfort than would be possible up on the exposed ridges. Small campsites have been found up to the treeline as well, and at some large and small campsites Flood has found smooth river pebbles that may have been used as pestles to grind or pound the moths into a fatty paste. Flood interprets moth hunting as part of a wider cycle of transhumant Aboriginal exploitation of resources contained in different altitudinal zones, with people migrating from the lowlands to the uplands during summer. She views moth hunting as the primary attraction for these movements, since the uplands were otherwise rather poor in food resources.

It is uncertain, however, whether Bogong moths were more important to the Aborigines in terms of caloric intake or nutrition (especially protein). A recent examination of the chemistry of Bogong moth fat has shown that the protein value of this substance is low, suggesting that Flood's original claim that Bogong moths provided essential protein for the Aboriginal diet during the summer is incorrect (Chapman, 1977: 34). A reasonable variety of edible marsupials and birds occur naturally in the uplands and could have been hunted as a source of protein. It is worth keeping in mind, however, that the native mammals of the uplands, like all Australian marsupials, are nongregarious and could not be hunted effectively en masse. While solitary hunting during the summer may have been adequate to maintain the steady supply of protein needed by the human population, the early European accounts all suggest that the Bogong harvest provided the bulk of the diet for these Aborigines during most summers. No estimates have yet been made for the caloric value of Bogong fat, but it was uncoubtedly high enough to make this fat a staple food source when collected in the prodigious amounts that are implied in the historic accounts.

The fact that Bogong fat is low in protein does not, in itself, make the large social groups that came together during Bogong harvests anomalous, since Bogongs appear to have been a staple food that was adequate to support large gatherings of people. What is anomalous, however, is the fact that no facilities of any sort were required for harvesting Bogongs. This was a procurement activity that could just as easily have been carried out by individuals or by individual families. It did not require any special cooperative efforts, nor any special apparatus beyond lighted torches and skin cloaks or net for carrying away the harvest. Thus there was no intrinsic or necessary relationship between the resource being harvested and the large number of people who assembled together each summer during the harvest. No "critical mass" of personnel was required for this kind of harvesting, and the abundance of this resource merely permitted rather than necessitated the social gatherings that took place.

The same sort of anomaly arises when we consider resource procurement in other parts of the Australian uplands. The well known practice of many southern Queensland Aborigines of harvesting edible nuts of the Bunya pine (*Araucaria bidwillii*) gave rise to similar large social groups. As one early observer noted of Bunya pine nuts:

> They are plentiful once in three years, and when the ripening season arrives, which is generally in the month of

January, the aboriginals assemble in large numbers from
a great distance around, and feast upon them. [Maiden,
1889: 7]

There was no necessity in this case for large groups to carry out the
harvesting efficiently, and no use of special facilities either. Bunya
pine nuts harvest occurred less frequently than Bogong moth harvest, but they had the same effect of permitting large groups of
Aborigines to congregate whenever they took place. More recently,
studies by John Beaton and by David Harris have shown the extent
to which cycads, especially *Cycas media* and *Macrozamia sp.*, operate in
this same way.

Cycads are an ancient variety of plant whose ancestry can be
traced back to the late Paleozoic, about 200 million years ago. Although they often look like palms or ferns, they are unique in producing large, pineapplelike reproductive structures called stroboli in
all genera except *Cycas*. The "seeds" of these plants are thus large
and often conspicuous by their shape and/or color. Cycad stroboli
eaten in their natural state, directly off the plant, are all intensely
toxic to animals as well as to human beings. As Beaton (1977: 141)
points out, "A listing of the early records of cycad poisoning of
Europeans in Australia is not far short of a 'Who's Who' of Australian discovery and exploration." The most immediate form of poisoning is ataxia, often referred to in the Australian outback as "rick-
etts" or "zamia staggers" because of its effects on herds of livestock.
This acute form of toxicity, while severe, is usually only temporary
for human beings unless they persist in ingesting untreated cycad
material, in which case it can be fatal. More insidious, however, is the
chronic form of cycad toxicity which leads ultimately to cancer. Cycads possess a uniquely structured biochemical compound that was
discovered in 1949. It was not expected to occur in living organisms
and had almost no precedent among synthesized compounds. This
toxin is not only the source of acute cycad poisoning but is also one
of the most potent carcinogens in the world. The suggestion now
(Beaton, 1977) is that the survival of cycads from precontinental
drift times, when there were large vegetarian reptiles around in
large numbers, may have been due in part to this toxicity.

Cycads are widely used as food plants in Africa, Mexico, India,
Japan, Fiji, and the Marianas as well as in Australia, but their use is
best documented in Australia. Beaton (1977: 162) notes that in some
societies, especially in the western Pacific, cycads are used as an
emergency or "starvation" food, since these islands have a low floristic and faunal variety and are vulnerable to losses from typhoons
and tidal waves. But in Australia, as in most places where they are
eaten, cycads often served as a staple food at least at the time of year

when they were consumed. One of the best published descriptions of the role and importance of cycads as a dry-season staple food in tropical Australia comes from Thomson's account of their use by the Aborigines of eastern Arnhem Land:

> Vast quantities of *ŋätu* [*Cycas media*] are gathered in the course of the year. It has the merit that, unlike most other foods of the aborigines which must be eaten immediately after preparation, it can be kept for some days or weeks. The fact that it is abundant gives *ŋätu* a special value in native economy, for it enables the women to maintain an adequate food supply on ceremonial occasions when hundreds of people are gathered in one camp for weeks or months at a time, who could not otherwise by supported for such periods on local resources. *ŋätu* is also the principal food eaten in Arnhem Land on ritual occasions. [1949: 22–3]

Yet Thomson goes on to note that:

> Although . . . *ŋätu* can be kept, after preparation, for several days, the natives of Arnhem Land, in common with other Australian aborigines, do not store food, but are dependent for their subsistence on the result of each day's hunting. [1949: 23]

In Thomson's description, which applies widely throughout tropical Australia, we once again encounter the odd paradox of a storable staple that is not stored. We shall return to "Thomson's Paradox" anon.

Cycad kernels produce prodigious amounts of starch, and many species of *Cycas* and *Macrozamia* produce prodigious amounts of kernels. Experiments in north Queensland with *Cycas media* showed yields of 13 kilograms (28.6 lb.) of kernels in a 200 square meter (40 sq. yards) plot. *Macrozamia communis,* while less dense in its growth than *C. media,* can produce at least 70 kilograms (154 lb.) of usable kernel-flesh in a 2,500 square meter (500 sq. yard) plot (Beaton, 1977: Table 49). Cycads tend to produce in late dry seasons, when other food plants are less abundant. In terms of calories and nutrition, *C. media* is an exceptionally rich source of carbohydrate and provides significant amounts of calories, although available analyses disagree on the exact caloric values (compare, for example, estimates in Fysh, Hodges, and Siggins, 1960:138, with those in Harris, 1977:428). Harris (1977:428) notes, in particular, the exceptionally low shell: kernel ratio (1.0:1.3) of *C. media,* which, when combined with its high nutrient status and prodigious yields per unit area, leads one to view this resource on a par with some cultivated crops.

Harris calculates that, on the average, a single seed-bearing plant of *C. media* will produce approximately 1,625 kilocalories of food energy, and he concludes:

> Cycads were a plant food resource of major importance to Aboriginal populations in the open-country woodlands of the Peninsula [i.e., Cape York] . . . To a seasonally mobile human population they offer a highly productive, quite nutritious, easily harvested resource, the seasonal and spatial availability of which can be predicted, and the productivity of which can be enhanced by the judicious deployment of fire to clear competing vegetation. [1977: 428–9]

Cycads were harvested as staple foods on Groote Eylandt (Tindale, 1925), and on Cape York (Lawrence, 1968: 208) as well, often in the context of large gatherings of Aboriginal populations. Although the productivity of cycads may have varied from year to year within local populations, they were generally regarded as a reliable and abundant seasonal food resource.

Of course, as Beaton (pers. comm.) points out:

> All the advantages for man of cycad productivity are threatened by one undeniable fact – the extraordinary toxicity of MAM [the biochemical compound responsible for these toxic effects]. This fact is clearly recognized by users of cycads who have applied at least two technologies, leaching and fermenting in order to take advantage of the cycad's bounty.

In Australia the sequences of preparation to remove the toxins from cycad material are essentially the same, although with many variations in each step. One approach involves dissecting the kernel and leaching out the toxins with water, followed by baking or roasting of the leached material. The other is a chemical or "fermentation" process in which the dissected kernels are placed in a container or pit in the sand and left for several months. The cycad starch either froths or becomes moldy, rendering the material safe to eat. It remains to be seen how effective these techniques may be in relation to the chronic (i.e., carcinogenic) effects of cycad as a food, but they appear to be completely effective in eliminating the acute effects.

Fire may also play a role in cycad productivity. Recent experiments on *Cycas sp.* in Cape York have shown that cycads are able to resist fire better than many competing plants and that, in the long run, recurrent burning would increase their productivity (Harris, 1977; Beaton, 1977). Moreover, periodic and regular burning may also stimulate and synchronize seed-production, as was shown by tests on *M. communis* on the Clyde and Moruya Rivers of New South Wales (Beaton,

1977). Such regular burning would not only have promoted greater productivity but would also have had the effect of concentrating the yields of usable kernel material at particular times of year, leading to the same kind of harvest conditions as described earlier for Bogong moths and Bunya pine-nuts. With this in mind, Beaton has suggested the useful concept of cycads as a class of "communion food," in addition to staples and starvation foods, which were used only when they could support large population gatherings, often in direct relation to ceremonialism of some kind (1977: 162).

Alternatively, I would like to suggest that the qualities of harvestable cycad indicate that, like Bunya pine-nuts and Bogong moths, this was a staple food. But for the Aborigines of the Australian uplands, it was a special kind of staple which (1) did not require the use of facilities or communal efforts of any kind to harvest it efficiently, but which nevertheless (2) permitted the aggregation of large numbers of people when it became available. The Australian uplands, all the way from the Victorian Alps in the south to the highlands of southern Queensland and Cape York in the north, present us with a distinctive and somewhat anomalous adaptive strategy that may, in fact, help us to understand certain essential elements of adaptive behavior in Australia and elsewhere.

"Special staples" and "Thomson's Paradox" in Aboriginal Australia

The recent knowledge gained about what I am calling "special staples" (following Beaton's seminal suggestions) in the Australian uplands can be applied back to the view presented earlier of Australian desert adaptations. There the hunting of large macropods and emus presents a somewhat attenuated version of this same kind of behavior. When available, natural surpluses of large game serve to support maximal social groups. But, like Bogong moth harvests, Bunya pine-nut collecting, and cycad harvesting, no facilities were required for the efficient procurement of large quantities of food. So there is no necessary reason for large groups to come together in order to carry out the harvest. In other words, these maximal groups are utterly different from the "critical mass" of personnel needed for natural harvests that require the employment of facilities. The Bogong moths, Bunya pine-nuts, cycads, and large game, in their respective areas, provided the Aborigines with a resource which, when available, allowed maximal groups of people to assemble in one place, but there is nothing intrinsic to the procurement of these resources that necessitated such large congregations of people.

The fact that some of these foods, especially cycad and perhaps Bogong moths as well, can be stored, seems to have had little or no effect upon this relationship. In each of these areas, Aborigines assembled in large groups in response to natural surpluses rather than stored accumulations of these staples. "Thomson's Paradox," referred to earlier in connection with his Arnhem Land observations, is that while people could prepare and store food for this purpose in many parts of Australia, they generally did not. Perhaps, as I argued for the Western Desert, the preparation of certain staples for storage was primarily a method intended for emergencies. Anyone who has studied Australian Aborigines will recognize this paradox. Aborigines, unlike hunter–gatherers in some other parts of the world (especially the Pacific coast of North America), did not aggrandize food or other key resources in anticipation of future shortages. Instead, they relied upon social networks, usually defined in a kinship idiom, to provide access to key resources when they were most needed in times of local scarcity. Thus no mechanism existed for individuals or individual families to aggrandize food supplies, while negative social pressures were present to discourage such behavior. Any attempt to build up food supplies by means of storage would run counter to the sharing ethic that was and still is, to varying degrees, a pervasive part of Aborigine social life everywhere in Australia. Alternatively it might be argued that aggrandizement of food surpluses creates the necessity for storage, which would limit mobility in an environment where mobility is essential. So one could suggest that storage runs counter to a great deal besides the sharing ethic. However, there was nothing to prevent Aborigines from preparing storage caches in secure areas like caves and trees, as indeed the Western Desert people did from time to time, mainly for the purpose of extending the range of especially long hunts. The technology of storage could have been employed without necessarily sacrificing mobility.

Having eliminated facilities and storage as factors to explain why desert and upland groups of Aborigines came together into maximal aggregates, what ideas can we use to explain why such aggregates occurred? The best answer appears to lie in the nature of the activities that occurred when so many Aborigines came together in one place. In all of the areas where we have examined the status of these special staples, there is evidence to show that these large aggregations of people provided the opportunity for ceremonies (especially initiations), trade, and social alliances (particularly betrothals). Rather than look to some "just so" kind of explanation like innate human gregariousness to account for these gatherings, perhaps we can see the activities that occurred during these gatherings as somehow adaptive at a higher level than that of the immediate need for obtaining food. Recent arguments by Peterson (1976) serve to reinforce and extend the idea presented earlier in connection with the desert Aborigines that large social aggregations were essential to arranging long-distance social relationships to create networks along which the sharing of food and access to resources could flow in times of need. The actual distances, directions, and extents of these networks might vary from group to group, but each group of Aborigines, whether in the desert or the uplands, can be visualized as having a sort of radius of social space around it created by its own particular range of sharing relationships.[4] The size of each of these radii, although modified perhaps by factors like terrain, linguistic affiliation, and others, can be viewed primarily as a function of the severity of stress imposed upon that group either by the physical environment or by social factors like intergroup hostility (though still, in all probability, in relation to competition for scarce resources). The more severe the stress, the larger the social radius. This hypothesis can be supported best by evidence from the Australian desert, where stress in the form of the direct impingement of the limiting factor of water is most readily apparent and gives rise to a variety of strategies that cumulatively result in a risk-minimizing adaptation that includes widely ramified social networks – that is, the largest such radii in Aboriginal Australia. Smaller radii in areas like the Australian uplands and coasts reflect greater periodicity and reliability of key resources as well as, in some cases, greater absolute abundance. But in most parts of Australia there is still an element of risk in the form of droughts or unexpected wild crop failures, even though these may occur only once in, say, every 100 years. Social networks and other social mechanisms for overcoming risk and scarcity played an essential role in the lives of the Aborigines of Australia, where such risk and scarcity can be expected to occur virtually everywhere at some time.

In arguing for such a hypothesis, exchange of information is at least as important as the direct or potential exchange of goods and access to key resources. Moreover, this information must be exchanged not only between groups (in space) but also from one generation to the next (in time). It is easy to understand how such transmission of vital information about the location of water sources, identification and location of food plants, movements and habits of game, and so forth, can occur in a region like the Australian desert, where the pressures for obtaining these resources are immediate and likely to occur frequently, at least every few years. The pedagogical nature of Aborigine myths and ceremonies in the sacred life with respect to desert geography is well known and widely reported, and this pedagogical element is evident in both the initiatory and "increase" rituals of all Australian desert people. But what about areas, like the Australian tropics, where emergencies occur only at wide intervals (like the 1973–4 eco-disaster among the Anbara) and may arise only once in several generations? In such cases, information passed on by one generation of knowledgeable people might well be forgotten or lapse through disuse before it is needed once

again. In other words, how can a society "remember" this information over the long interval until it is needed once again?

Goodale's (1970, 1971) studies of the kulama yam ceremony
among the Tiwi Aborigines of Melville and Bathurst Islands, off the
north coast of Arnhem Land, suggests one way of solving this problem. The kulama (probably a species of *Dioscorea*) is not eaten regularly by the Tiwi, although it is fairly abundant in their habitat. For
one thing, its flavor is consistently regarded as poor by the Tiwi, and
it also requires laborious leaching of toxic compounds to render it
edible. With these two strikes against it, why do these Aborigines
have an elaborate and prolonged ritual for it that involves, among
other things, procurement, preparation, and consumption of this
generally despised plant food? The ritual is performed infrequently
and has been observed only twice by anthropologists: in 1912 by
Spencer (1914) and in 1956 by Goodale. It has none of the usual
features of initiatory or increase ceremonies reported from other
Aboriginal societies and lacks the secret overtones that these usually
possess. Both sexes participate in all phases of this ritual, which
culminates in the consumption of this rather unappetizing food by
the participants. Goodale argues convincingly that, indeed, the kulama ceremony is no ordinary Aboriginal initiation or increase ritual,
but can be interpreted as a special ritual to ensure the transmission
of knowledge about how to gather and prepare this plant as an
emergency food source. The regular but infrequent performance of
this ritual and its apparently anomalous features in relation to other,
better known Australian rituals can be most economically explained
as a traditional mechanism of the Tiwi to ensure that the knowledge
of this plant's potential as a food resource is preserved over the long
intervals between emergencies.

So risk-minimizing can be inferred as an essential, structural element in Aborigine traditions even in situations where the risks are
infrequent and the opportunities to optimize resources are at their
greatest. The recognition of such underlying similarities among
Aborigines living in habitats as diverse as the desert, tropics, and
uplands inevitably calls to mind the intuitive but undoubtedly accurate statement by Lévi-Strauss:

> The day may come when all the available documentation
> on Australian tribes is transferred to punched cards and
> with the help of a computer their entire techno-economic,
> social and religious structures can be shown to be like a
> vast group of transformations. [1966: 89]

Although no one has yet attempted to computerize this information
about Australian Aborigines, the proposition that there are broad
structural similarities that reflect transformations based on common

adaptive responses is probably valid and can be tested by further examination of the available literature. "Thomson's Paradox" appears to represent widespread if not universal behavior among Australian Aborigines and may occur among many other human societies as well. Wherever it occurs, it is probably best explained as risk-minimizing behavior and will prove to be consistently and necessarily related to sharing networks scaled in extent according to the degree of risk over basic resources and to a sharing ethic, the compulsiveness of which is similarly scaled according to these same risks. These risks, in turn, are related to the operation of limiting factors in the physical and/or social environment as they affect human habitation in a given region. Traditional and introduced technologies can affect the magnitude of these relationships in various ways, but the relationships remain essential if the impact of these technologies is to be properly understood.

Some general propositions about Aboriginal subsistence
In the preceding two chapters we have looked at a descriptive model of Australian desert adaptive behavior along with at least a partial view of several other important and well-documented adaptations in other parts of Australia. After exploring the essential characteristics of these particular adaptations, we need to consider what possible general principles can be derived from them as a framework for proceeding with the approach I have called living archaeology. Earlier, I argued that the use of uniformitarian assumptions in perceiving general principles in human behavior is valid insofar as these assumptions consistently related to aspects of ecology and evolutionary biology that are already maintained on the basis of such principles. This view is implied by Watson and Watson (1969: 160) when they state:

> To claim that there are no uniform causes of human behavior and that there are no uniformities of human behavior (above a certain level) that can be described in terms of lawlike generalizations is to deny that man is a part of nature.

But if we accept this view, then how can we move effectively from a particular case, like that of the Australian Aborigines, to principles about human behavior in general? Perhaps the easiest thing to do is to view each particular society's adaptive model as a case study, with inferences to be drawn from each case and modified as new cases appear. As in the legal profession, each case is an empirical precedent, to be compared with later cases. General principles in law evolve as precedents are developed and then compared and perhaps modified, with principles or laws representing the then-current views of existing precedents. For example, divorce as it is defined legally today in the state of California is not based on immutable laws, engraved for all time on the bronze block of history. It is, instead, the product of rules that have been progressively modified and amended by successive precedents. Although rules of general principles exist, they are constantly being revised by the legal system's willingness to recognize current marriage practices. In theory, at least, each new case is a precedent capable of generating a new principle or of making a significant difference to the interpretation of an existing principle. Similarly, Schiffer (pers. comm.) has noted that in archaeology, a single case can generate a general principle for further testing. The descriptive models in these last two chapters should be viewed in this way. As Watson and Watson argue:

> It is important to recognize that any anthropological description defines a model and that any such model can be tested for "truth" (scientific relevance) by organizing its description in the form of one or more lawlike generalizations and then checking to see if it is useful for explaining or predicting in the area under consideration. [1969: 141]

In other words, we shall see what principles about human adaptation in general can be derived from the material covered in the last two chapters and use these as a framework for predictions of a more specifically archaeological nature. Some of these principles, or propositions, are as follows:

1. Limiting factors operate in the realm of human behavior and produce the same effects as they do upon species in nature. That is, they act to set threshold levels for the maximum population that can be supported under periods of maximal stress.

2. A "successful" adaptation is one that in the long run correctly assesses key resources as potential limiting factors, that is, in terms of periods of greatest scarcity rather than optimal availability, and responds appropriately.

3. Unlike nonhuman species, people rely upon traditions as the principal mechanism to overcome or mitigate constraints imposed by limiting factors. Social and symbolic traditions, like traditional technology and subsistence, must therefore bear a consistent (i.e., noncontradictory) relationship to the requirements imposed by limiting factors operating in their particular physical and/or social habitats.

4. Behavior that might appear to be maladaptive at one level of interpretation (like the disproportionate expendi-

ture of time in hunting large game by desert Aborigines)
may be viewed as adaptive at another level (as, for example, when large game serves as a special staple to permit maximal aggregates of population, with consequent
establishment of sharing networks).

5. The greater the element of risk imposed by a particular limiting factor, the more widely ramified and pervasive
will be the behavior within a society to create and maintain
social networks for sharing food and access to key resources. To the extent that risk is the paramount consideration, sharing will be the primary social response. This is
a relativistic proposition; that is, it must be considered in
relation to the particular ecology and human population
densities of the regions being examined. The geographic
expression in distance (i.e., kilometers) of expanded social
networks will vary accordingly.

6. Reliability in obtaining key resources to meet minimum requirements is more critical to a society's adaptive
success than the society's overall intake of resources. Or,
windfalls won't do.

7. Optimizing behavior (that is, strategies aimed at ex-
tracting maximal amounts of key resources), particularly
the increased use of facilities, will tend to occur whenever a society is not constrained by key limiting factors in
its environment and has access to a resource that can be
more efficiently harvested by means of facilities. (But
overdependence upon large quantities of a key resource
obtained by means of facilities may entail new risks in
the event that either the resource should at some time
fail or that the critical mass of personnel necessary to
build and operate the facility cannot assemble. In other
words, new limiting factors can arise.)

8. If the element of risk is too great, a society's population will tend to stabilize around the threshold imposed
by the key limiting factors in the habitat in relation to
the exploitive technology in use by the society. Mobility,
however, and the ability to exploit local concentrations of
resources will create temporary aggregations that exceed
this threshold average.

9. Even in cases where food staples abound, a greater
variety of foods will be obtained than can be accounted
for in terms of strictly quantitative dietary requirements.
"Having enough to eat" requires variety as well as bulk,
both to meet constant nutritional requirements and to
ensure a knowledge of alternative food sources in times

of scarcity. From day to day, flavor enhancement will often be the primary stated reason for obtaining such a wide variety of food, although other mechanisms to ensure variety of food intake will be present when the potential foods taste really bad or are difficult to procure.

10.   A change in technology and/or wild crop management can have the effect of expanding the variety of potential edibles without necessarily resulting in larger yields. Such innovations (including, quite possibly, steps toward early plant and animal domestication) may initially have been responses to minimize risk rather than representing an effort to increase yields. Of course, the relaxation of constraints imposed by any limiting factor in a given habitat will ultimately have the effect of increasing yields, but such increases – even to the level of a staple food – are a by-product of risk-minimizing behavior rather than a primary product of attempts to optimize resources.

11.   In certain habitats, the geographic range and yields of potential edibles can be increased by means of technological and managerial manipulations when stress occurs (or in anticipation of stress). These are the habitats first referred to by the Russian biogeographer N. I. Vavilov (1926) as "nuclear areas," in which ancestral varieties of today's domesticants existed in the wild. In those nuclear areas and adjacent regions where risks of scarcity were infrequent, and abundant alternative wild foods were available even in times of stress, no domestication occurred. Indeed, there was resistance to such innovations when they were introduced. Hence Arnhem Land and Cape York Aborigines did not practice plant domestication even after prolonged exposure to farming via Indonesia and New Guinea prior to European contact (J. P. White, 1971).

These are some of the general relationships that can be posited on the basis of the risk-minimizing model epitomized by the desert Aborigines of Australia and reflected by other Australian Aboriginal adaptations as well. These relationships show that even under the most optimal conditions, the behavior of all people, everywhere, is constrained by limiting factors of some kind, in the past as much as in the present. Under certain ecological conditions, not found in Australia but occurring in many other parts of the world, hunter–gatherers under stress with respect to basic food resources found ways to manage their wild crops that became what we call, in retrospect, domestication and agriculture, mainly in order to ensure a steady minimum intake for their dietary needs. In the Western Desert of Australia these stresses were so extreme that they restricted the range and manageability of wild crops and excluded introduced crops – making sustained agriculture impossible there, even today. In tropical Australia, especially Arnhem Land and Cape York, introduced domesticants could grow, but dietary stress was so infrequent as to make agriculture unnecessary and not worth the extra effort for groups of hunter–gatherers who were already living fairly well on wild foods. We have tended in the past to think of agriculture and domestication as somehow inevitable, so the Australian case is instructive. It shows why agriculture and domestication did *not* occur, even when the opportunity for domestication was present, as in the tropical north of Australia. Agriculture is not inevitable. The Australian case studies present a contrast to our ethnocentric ideas about early agriculture, based as they are upon our impressions of present-day agriculture in different parts of the world, that should encourage us to consider risk-minimizing behavior as a probable and immediate factor in the earliest human efforts to domesticate plants and animals.

The idea of limiting factors is as decisive for explaining human behavior as any other uniformitarianist principle in natural science. Do we seriously question the proposition that because people, along with everything else in nature, are subject to the effects of gravity today, they have been subject to these same effects in the same ways at all times and everywhere in the past? The "ecological connection" referred to in the last chapter permits us to establish linkages between human behavior and the uniformities of the natural world, which take us beyond the realm of analogies and into a different order of discourse at the level of general principles. But, as we shall see, these principles are not covering laws, that is, finely finished products to be dusted off and admired on appropriate occasions. They are transitory expressions of behavioral realities as we perceive them now in relation to specific cases, and they serve mainly as a framework for searching out and considering additional evidence that will bear on these questions. They are merely the first step, albeit an essential one, in doing living archaeology.

5

The anthropology of human residues

What is the "archaeological signature"[5] for any particular human society or mode of adaptation? Are there distinctive patterns of residue formation that characterize certain kinds of adaptive behavior among human beings? If, as I shall argue here, by observing the adaptive behavior of any living human society, we can derive predictions about that society's discards, we are doing living archaeology. This approach does not require that one then goes on to apply these ethnographic findings directly to an archaeological site or assemblage. Indeed, if one accepts the arguments of the preceding chapters, it should be clear that living archaeology can inform us directly only about residue behavior in contemporary societies and only indirectly about prehistoric human behavior. Yet these indirect arguments are more compelling than any direct reasoning based upon analogy. This chapter will start to explore the nature of this new kind of anthropology – the anthropology of human discard – and will examine the linkages between patterns of discard observed in living human socieities and their archaeological payoff as inferences about past human behavior in relation to the procurement, manufacture, use, and discard of stone artifacts by Australian desert Aborigines.

Alternatives to heaven

Where do the different material discards arising from human activities ultimately come to rest? This is really a new question for anthropologists and archaeologists, and empirical attempts to answer this question constitute the essence of living achaeology. This question is founded upon the assumption that material by-products of human activities as well as finished artifacts of all kinds do not go to heaven. Where, in fact, do they go? Until about ten years ago, this kind of question was almost unheard-of, either in archaeology or in anthropology. Archaeologists, if they thought about processes of discard at all, tended to see such discards occurring in a vague and rather undifferentiated manner, usually in the form of a midden or refuse heap. This was the archaeologists' "heaven." How many archaeologists in the American Southwest, for example, have excavated refuse heaps adjacent to dwelling structures with the expectation of finding a representative sample of Puebloan potsherds upon which to base their chronologies and cultural reconstructions? Did anyone ever ask: Where do potsherds really go in nucleated farming societies of this sort? At the simplest or most basic level, they might have asked: When and under what conditions do people go to the trouble of removing their rubbish and other discards instead of simply moving away when these residues accumulate to excess? Perhaps the answer to such a question lies in the degree of nucleation and permanence of settlement of a community, or perhaps it has more to do with the nature of resources being exploited. Despite the occasional early recognition by certain archaeologists like Schenck (1926: 170) that middens were not always undifferentiated loci of discard but might contain concentrations representing particular activities like past meals, the more usual assumption has been that refuse deposits are homogeneous samples of all past discards in a particular society or community.

Anthropologists rarely, if ever, considered human residues as a subject worthy of study or discussion at all. It was not until Heider's "cautionary tale" about the Dani and other Highland New Guinea societies ten years ago that the central importance of studying human discard behavior began to emerge clearly:

> I feel strongly that the archaeologist must recognize himself as a prehistoric ethnographer and must take more seriously the implications which ethnographic examples have for his own work . . . Studies of house-building and pottery-making are all very well, but for the archaeologist the emphasis should be on function and disposal rather than on manufacture: How are houses and pots used, and what happens to these afterwards?" [1967: 62]

The value of adopting this point of view was effectively demonstrated before long by Stanislawski (1969) when he studied the use, recycling, and ultimate discard of broken Hopi-Tewa Indian pottery. He found that Hopi potsherds are often used in a variety of ways that lead to their ultimate discard in many places other than the refuse heap. Some, for example, are pulverized and incorporated into new pots as tempering for the clay. Others may be used as actual implements, such as scrapers for smoothing the surface of new pots. Still others are inserted into the wall adobe of new buildings. And some may even serve an "archival" function by being stored in piles around the house and looked at from time to time by potters anxious to refresh their memories about designs used in the past. More recently, Longacre (1974) has argued for tagging pots in a Kalinga village in the Philippines, much as an ornithologist might tag birds, in order to monitor the movements of these pots through the Kalinga cultural system. Recent studies like these have done much to develop an awareness among archaeologists and ethnographers for the importance of empirically studying human behavior in relation to discard.

Discards are the human species' ultimate form of circumstantial evidence. Like circumstantial evidence in a court of law, discards cry out for an adequate explanation and must achieve a parsimonious fit with all other available evidence. At the most basic level of discourse, human residues cannot be explained away if they are physically present in an archaeologically supportable context. They are, in fact, the raw material for the anthropology of human residues. If one does not prematurely attach any ideational or behavioral meaning to these residues, but looks first at their physical occurence in relation to their geographic and biotic setting, then one can begin to discover just what the circumstances might have been that led to their coming to rest ultimately in the context in which they actually occur. Empirical observations of patterns of discard in living human societies enable us to model these circumstances and eventually to specify when and under what conditions certain characteristic patterns of discard will occur. In doing his, the steps that link these circumstances to their end-products, namely material residues, are not merely logical but are based on real cases that serve as precedents for general propositions about how particular patterns of residue formation are the "archaeological signatures" referred to earlier.

The linguistic metaphor

Having freely used a legal metaphor to describe the case-study process by which living archaeology generalizes from specific evidence, I would now like to apply a linguistic one to expand the argument about discard and use this to relate the residue-oriented approach of living archaeology to the broader interests of anthropology in general. Rowe (1959) and his colleagues have already demonstrated how one can infer "rules" of composition in prehistoric Peruvian pottery styles and other forms of visual art, such as the famous bas-reliefs of the Raimundi Stone at Chavin de Huantar (Rowe, 1962). These rules of composition, such as the complex pattern of visual "kenning" or alliterative reduplication evident in the headdress of the primary figure sculpted on the Raimundi Stone, are seen by Rowe and his associates as akin to the rules of grammar in a language. One can infer the "grammar" of a particular style by observing how various motifs are recombined in different contexts, just as a linguist infers the grammatical structure of a language from the elements of speech he observes in use in different situations. And one can also infer how these rules are transformed by observing how, through time, various elements of speech or style are recombined differently but along particular lines determined by preexisting patterns set by these rules.

For archaeologists like Rowe, the recognition of grammar-like rules of composition in complex, prehistoric art styles has provided a valuable tool for refining chronologies and also for inferring processes of prehistoric political and symbolic behavior. Menzel (1956), for example, has shown how the revival of a regional pottery style, within the Ica Valley in Peru, following the collapse of Inca authority due to sixteenth century Spanish intervention, serves as a model for explaining similar revivals during earlier periods in Peruvian prehistory. Although each revival contained materials that were different from what preceded it, there were continuities in the particular grammar of each regional style that showed how these rules of composition were transformed and carried on, even during periods of stylistic uniformity imposed by an imperial authority like that of the Inca. Thus one might explain the peculiarly cyclical pattern of Peruvian prehistory by observing transformations in the pottery and other art styles; with periods of wide regional uniformity representing phases of more or less imperial authority and periods of reassertion of local or regional styles as phases of weakened political control, when the authority necessary to impose an "imperial" style over a wide area waned.

Like language, residue formation is a universal human trait. Human societies, everywhere and at all times, practice discard. So just as Rowe and his colleagues have used a linguistic metaphor in studying prehistoric art styles, a living archaeologist can infer the "rules" that govern the patterning of human residue behavior in particular societies. In short, the anthropological study of human residues is comparable to other approaches in anthropology and linguistics that seek to infer structure from form and behavior. When a social anthropologist notes the existence of a rule among West Desert Aborigines of preferred second cross-cousin marriage, he is making an inference based upon interviews and observations of actual marriages. He soon discovers, too, that this rule is not absolute but may be modified by factors such as contact with other desert groups who practice mainly simple or first cross-cousin marriage, local demography, and accessibility of resources. Such shared rules or norms are often referred to as culture by anthropologists, but in living archaeology we cannot always rely upon interviews to give us reliable information about rules of residue behavior. Instead, we depend upon direct observations of behavior, with no prior assumptions about how that behavior may or may not be structured in the minds of the people we are observing.

Again, the linguistic metaphor serves us better than anthropological concepts of culture. One might wish to argue that a linguistic metaphor should be applied only to expressive behavior, as was indeed the case for the Peruvian data used by Rowe, Menzel, and others. At times such expressiveness is a feature of residue behavior, as, for example, when Western Desert Aborigines space their habitation campsites to express the quality of social relationships between extended family groups. In the Western Desert, increased distance between campsite clusters generally reflects increased hostility or distrust; decreased distance reflects more amiable relations. Distances tend to fluctuate constantly along a sliding scale of social relationships ranging from extreme hostility (fights and feuding, with extended family clusters camping up to two miles apart) to close harmony and interdependence (marriage alliances are the ultimate expression of such social harmony, with extended family clusters moving to within as close as 60 meters to each other). One quickly learns to "read" the spatial language expressing these Aboriginal social relationships between groups at any given time. In this case, the spatial arrangement of physical features such as campsites and hearths consciously express social relationships. One can reasonably infer the qualities of these relationships in a contemporary habitation campsite in the Western Desert even if there is no one present in camp at the time the spatial relationships between campsites are being measured.

But the linguistic concept of grammar does not rely entirely upon conscious expression, and the same is true when this concept is applied to residue behavior. Many, if not most, rules of grammar in language are used unconsciously. That is, one does not necessarily have to be conscious of the grammatical structure of one's own language in order to be able to speak it effectively. For the living archaeologist, as for the linguist, the grammatical "rules" for a particular society are operationally defined. Elsewhere, Stanislawski (1975) and I (1968) have even suggested that one can explore the possibility of "deep structures" in human residue formation that approximate the search by linguists and linguistically oriented anthropologists for universal patterns in human cognition. If such universal principles of residue behavior exist, it is unlikely that the people in any particular society will be consciously aware of them.

The relationship between conscious or unconscious emic categories in archaeological interpretation was succinctly expressed by Clarke (1968: 59–62) as the problem of the cognitive "black box." The idea of the black box is widely used today in the field of systems analysis as well as in common parlance, and it is useful to the living archaeologist as well. The idea seems to have had its origin in the early days of World War II, when the British developed a cavity-magnetron power tube that made radar both portable in aircraft and more accurate than units already in use. This important technical breakthrough occurred in mid-1940, when the Battle of Britain was in progress, so the decision was made to bring the device to the United States in order to duplicate the design for mass production (Skolnik, 1962: 12). At that time the development of an efficient aircraft-interception (AI) radar was both top-priority and top-secret. As these radar units were produced and entered service, aircrews were trained in their use but were purposely not trained in the operating principles or inner workings of the device. These items were, quite literally, housed in black boxes to be opened and serviced only by personnel with the necessary secret clearance.

With advances in aviation electronics in later years, these black boxes multiplied until the term "black box" came to refer to just about any device that can be used or operated effectively in complete ignorance of its inner workings. In a modern, technological society, everyday behavior involves black boxes to such an extent that we tend to take them for granted. How many people, when they turn the ignition key on their car, understand the inner workings of all the components of their car well enough to explain why it works – or in some cases, why it doesn't? We all use devices like this every day without understanding precisely how they work, just as the pilots and aircrews who used the early AI radar during World War II could locate enemy aircraft without a clear understanding of the inner workings of the device.

Clarke's idea that emic categories and cognitive codes exist as a black box for the archaeologist is well suited to living archaeology. Although some archaeologists have, at times, argued for the discovery of "mental templates" (Deetz, 1967: 43–49) or the "man behind the artifact" (Spaulding, 1953), the conviction in archaeology has grown that such efforts at reconstructing prehistoric categories of thought lie beyond any means of effective testing. Several recent studies in living archaeology (White, 1967; White and Thomas, 1972; White, Modjeska, and Hipuya, 1977) have revealed the difficulties involved in making reliable inferences about native systems of stone artifact classification in Highland New Guinea, and similar results were obtained in the Western Desert of Australia.

To explore this problem among Western Desert Aborigines, I first observed the widest possible range of stone artifacts in use among people – mainly desert dwellers or people recently arived from the desert at missions and reserves – learning as much as possible about how these different tools were used, the raw materials they were made from, hafting, the extent to which they were retouched, and other aspects of observable behavior related to these artifacts. Then I interviewed individuals, one at a time, while they collected stone for toolmaking and while they made and used these implements. I asked each individual for the Aboriginal term for each artifact along with an explanation of what it was that made one category different from another.

No doubt the Aborigines involved in this study were puzzled by all this interest in what, to them at least, was an unimportant bit of everyday behavior, which they regarded with the same casualness that we might, for example, treat tying our shoelaces. But they were cooperative and sorted the stone artifacts into remarkably uniform groupings, at least in terms of the single criterion that was most important to them – the angle of the working edge of the implement. Later, over a prolonged period of observation and in many different situations involving stone tool use, these categories consistently stood up, both in relation to behavior and to the terminology applied to these artifacts. Blocks of stone and flakes with working-edge angles of 40–89 degrees, with an average value of 67 degrees, were called *purpunpa* and were consistently used for wood-scraping and -chopping tasks in procuring and shaping mulga (*Acacia aneura*) and other hard woods. We can refer to this broad class of implements as "chopper-plane-scrapers." Stone flakes with acute working-edge angles of 15–59 degrees with an average value of 40 degrees, were called *tjimari* and were used as knives for cutting flesh, sinew, and fibrous materials. A few incidental exceptions to the behavior related to this simple, binary classification were observed, as, for example, on one occasion an Aborigine man wore out his last wood-scraping flake (termed "adzes" by Australian archaeologists) and replaced this flake by hafting an acute-edged *tjimari* in its place. The edge of this tool quickly wore down through use until it attained a more obtuse angle, but this was understood at the time to be a practical expedient in a situation where no suitable *purpunpa* were readily available.

Such minor exceptions aside, this was a simple and consistent system of classification that was consciously manipulated by the Aborigines involved and might seem to be the sort of emic categorization or mental template that an archaeologist could hope to reconstruct from his analysis of a prehistoric lithic tool assemblage. Such was not to be, however, for it soon became evident that these two categories, though consistently correlated with basic differences in use, cross-cut and were cross-cut by other attributes that would be taken seriously by archaeologists in arriving at *their* classifications. For example, no *tjimari* (flake knives) were ever observed to be hafted onto wooden handles (although some had small handles of spinifex resin attached to them for a better grip), while only the smaller *purpunpa* (i.e., adzes) were hafted when in use. The larger *purpunpa* (i.e., choppers, flake-scrapers, and spokeshaves) were, like the knives, unhafted. Hafting was correlated more closely with size and use than with any particular emic category. A wide variety of lithic raw materials was used for both

categories of tools by the Aborigines, even to the extent, as we shall
see later, of using stone that did not always possess the best edge-holding properties for the particular tasks in which they were employed.
Retouch was applied intentionally by means of direct percussion use-
ing a hammerstone whenever it seemed appropriate, regardless of
whether the artifact was classified as *purpunpa* or *tjimari*. In the case of
tjimari, retouch was applied mainly to shape the flake rather than to
sharpen it, and the working edge was left alone. Such flake knives
were used as long as the flake edge retained its natural sharpness and
discarded when the edge became dull from use. *Purpunpa*, on the
other hand, were usually retouched along the working edge, although
there were many cases observed when an unretouched flake or block
of stone with a naturally suitable working edge was used. These were
retouched later, after there had been some attrition of the working
edge, but sometimes they were not. Hafted adzes were accorded
unique treatment by being retouched sometimes with a wooden percussor or by pressure, with the teeth. At times the steep retouch along
the back or sides of a flake knife was indistinguishable from the steep
retouch of the working edge of a woodworking scraper. Repeated use
and resharpening of the smaller woodworking flakes (hafted adzes)
resulted in a distinctive combination of attributes such as step-flaking
and microwear along with characteristic changes to the shape of the
flake resulting in a discarded slug or flake remnant that was not seen
in connection with the larger, hand-held wood-scraping and -chop-
ping implements. Again, size, which was not a variable included in the
emic classification, was important. Any archaeologist could be expected to recognize and classify Western Desert Aborigine chipped
stone artifacts in terms of visible differences in size, retouch, and raw
material. But we also know, from having interviewed Aborigines as
they made and used these tools, that sorting according to these variables would not correlate at all closely with the emic categories or
mental templates that these people themselves use to classify their
chipped stone implements. No reliable or consistent relationship exists between the archaeologist's classification of such implements,
based as it is upon visible and measurable attributes of the artifacts
themselves, and the Aborigines' own way of classifying these items.

With this and other cautionary cases in mind, we are led to the
conclusion that it would be erroneous for archaeologists to assume
that any consistent relationship exists between their classification of
tools, architecture, or any other aspect of prehistoric material behavior and those of the native makes and users of these artifacts. Native
cognitive categories and processes in relation to materials thus represent an example of Clarke's black box. We can observe and model
inputs and outputs in a human society, whether past or present,
without specifying the content of the cognitive black box. It matters

little if emic categories are consciously expressed and manipulated by members of a particular society, since these categories, whether conscious or not, cannot be reliably inferred in the absence of living informants. Just like the linguist who infers the grammatical structure of the language he is studying from its use by native speakers in different situations, so the living archaeologist can infer principles that structure relations between behavior and materials in particular human societies. But such inferences do not imply the use of any kind of "mental stethoscope" to understand the conscious or unconscious operation of the minds of the people being studied, any more than the linguist's grammar implied this. As an archaeologist-turned-ethnographer, the living archaeologist needs to approach his study of human behavior as if the mind really is a black box, the inner workings of which he cannot expect to understand in any reliable way.

Toward a grammar of Aboriginal lithic technology

All of the flaked stone tools made and used by the Western Desert Aborigines of Australia can be classed as "maintenance tools"–that is, tools for making or maintaining other tools (Binford and Binford, 1969: 71). Although I have indicated that the Western Desert people regarded the manufacture and use of flaked stone tools as an activity of no great importance in itself, implying a casual and offhand attitude toward stone toolmaking, this view does not necessarily hold throughout the Australian desert. Recent studies by James O'Connell (1974, and pers. comm.) among the Alyawara, an Arandic-speaking group of Aborigines in Central Australia, have shown that these people regarded stone toolmaking as an important activity worthy of careful planning and technical skill. Although these Aborigines no longer make and use stone tools as part of their everyday behavior, they still possess the necessary skills and can produce a wide range of implements when asked to do so. The Alyawara understand the flaking properties of the different lithic raw materials occurring in their territory and can discuss these in some detail. They have been observed using heat-treatment to alter the texture and flaking characteristics of the stone they are about to use, and they can produce true blades by means of direct percussion applied to a specially prepared blade core. The Alyawara even have special songs that were sung to the stone prior to the removal of blades. These big blades were fashioned into several kinds of tools, including the *yilwuga*, which, along with its use as a scraper, was also used for scooping out edible starch from wild yams or "bush potatos" (*Ipomoea costata*).

O'Connell's studies among the Alyawara not only reveal the existence of a technically elaborated lithic technology in the Australian

desert that represents an extreme contrast with the much less elaborated stone technology of the Western Desert people, but they also
suggest some totally unanticipated uses for certain tools (i.e., *yilugwa*
as "spoons") that archaeologists might otherwise simply classify as
scrapers or endscrapers, without any specific attribution as to function. One could quibble with O'Connell over the reliability of his
informants' testimony about the use of these apparent endscrapers
as spoons, since a question still remains concerning the relative importance of this spoonlike function. Perhaps it served other uses as
well that O'Connell's informants have not fully described, in much
the same way we use a device called a screwdriver for many other
impromptu tasks besides turning screws (like opening lids on paint
cans, chiseling wood, etc.) (Schiffer, 1978: 236). But the main value
of this discovery lies in its unexpected nature. No archaeologist,
simply by inspecting these implements, would, in his wildest imagin-
ings, have inferred this spoonlike use as a possible function for this
type of tool. Here, then, is an illustration of how living archaeology
can help to free us from ethnocentric preconceptions about behavior
in relation to materials. The linguistic metaphor applies here, too,
since linguists must always be prepared for unexpected grammatical
transformations in the languages they study. These cannot be anticipated logically or on the basis of familiar patterns but must be discovered in the realm of real behavior observed at firsthand.

In the Western Desert it was possible to observe the quality and
amounts of different kinds of isotropic stone being collected by the
Aborigines and to monitor these lithic materials from their point of
collection to their final discard. Isotropic stone is rock that has the
property of fracturing more or less evenly in all directions from the
point at which a blow is struck, creating cone-shaped fractures that
detach opposite the point of impact at or near a 45 degree angle
away from the striking platform. These materials range from coarse
stone with many inclusions and/or internal planes of fracture to fine,
glassy materials such as obsidian. Their flaking and edge-holding
properties vary in relation to the tasks for which they are sought,
and one would, reasonably, expect them to be selected on that basis.
For example, a coarse basalt that is tough and hard to reduce by
percussion may, nevertheless, hold an edge better on a woodworking
tool than some finer materials, while, for cutting meat or skins a
glassier stone that will provide a sharp, albeit a rather fragile, edge
will be sought. Each region of the world offered a greater or nar-
ower choice of these materials to its ancient human inhabitants, but
Australia has been one of the few places where it has been possible
to observe the procurement of lithic materials for toolmaking among
people contemporary with ourselves.

Ideally, one can envision a situation in which lithic raw materials suitable for different tasks are more or less evenly distributed over the landscape. For example, stone that is well suited for adze-making occurs widely over the surface of the landscape occupied by the southern Alyawara, and it comes as no surprise, therefore, that one also finds that a substantial proportion of base-camp assemblages in this area can be expected to consist of stone derived from nonlocalized sources (O'Connell, pers. comm.). In such a "simple" situation as this, one would expect on purely utilitarian grounds that a wide variety of tool types would be produced from stone materials that are at least minimally suited to the mechanics of manufacture and use relative to each tool type. However, not all landscapes offer such an ideal distribution of lithic materials – indeed, there are few that do. Our utilitarian expectations may have to be modified in the light of actual geography, in which sources for suitable lithic raw materials are irregularly distributed, often in highly localized and infrequently occurring sources. The Western Desert of Australia is just such a place where utilitarian considerations of ease of manufacture and efficiency of use of stone artifacts must be balanced against contingencies involving ease of procurement in relation to actual sources of raw material.

The Western Desert Aborigines obtained their lithic raw materials from two distinct types of sources; quarries and nonlocalized sources. Quarries, while not always spectacular, possess a high degree of archaeological visibility. Chipping stations at large quarries usually consist of small circular or oval-shaped patches of ground swept clear of rocks and other surface debris, with occasional hammerstones lying nearby. These small cleared areas were prepared by men who sat down to remove flakes from cores with prepared striking platforms by means of direct percussion, as opposed to the more random technique of block-on-block flake removal, which takes place right at the stone nodule or outcrop being reduced. Although surface indications of chipping stations at quarries are rather faint, they tend to be long lasting and not highly susceptible to the effects of surface erosion. At quarries, Aborigines obtained flakes and small lumps or cores that were carried away and further trimmed for specific uses.

Nonlocalized sources of stone also occurred widely over the region and were extensively used by the Aborigines. The entire plateau upon which the Western Desert lies contains many ancient outcrops of resistant rock that are often surrounded by flats covered with pieces of rock eroded from these little monadnocks. After the original outcrop has eroded away, these flats of pebbles and rocky detritus – termed "gibbers" by white Australians – sometimes form a pavement of hard rocks over extensive areas. Rocks of manageable size and reasonable isotropism are distributed widely over the surface of many parts of the Western and Central Deserts of Australia. Stones from these nonlocalized sources were generally used as instant tools, for some immediate task at or near the place where the stone was collected. These included such tasks as removing a slab of wood from a mulga tree with the aid of a large chopper-plane, or the preliminary shaping and trimming of such a blank into a spearthrower with a hand-held chopper plane of more manageable size. Such chopper-planes were usually retouched unifacially to sharpen the working edge, although, at times, a naturally sharp stone was used without any application of intentional retouch. Aborigines, both male and female, sometimes picked up sharp stone flakes to use when roasting and butchering a kangaroo or other game. In nearly every observed case, the Aborigines disposed of stone tools that they collected and/or manufactured at nonlocalized sources of stone at the place where the tool was used. Regardless of whether or not they had been retouched by the Aborigines, these instant tools were rarely carried away to a habitation campsite or some other locality for further retouch and/or use.

Although precise calculations were impossible because of the fact that other activities like hunting and visits to sacred sites occurred at the same time, it was apparent that procurement of usable stone for toolmaking was the most time-consuming and laborious part of the entire stone toolmaking process. Quarried stone, in particular, was often collected by small parties of men who made a special effort to visit the quarry site, sometimes detouring from some other route for that purpose or else making an expedition from their habitation camp primarily to procure isotropic stone. These Aborigines removed selected flakes and cores that were small in comparison with the blocks, cores, and flakes lying about the quarry, mainly because these pieces could be carried conveniently back to camp. At no time during eighteen observed episodes of this kind did I ever see an individual or a party of men collect stone from a quarry source more than 32 kilometers (20 miles) from their habitation base camp.

Actual behavior at some quarries consisted of applying block-on-block percussion directly to large boulders, nodules, or outcrops whenever these showed above the ground surface and had natural angles on the surface that could act as striking platforms. In such cases, the wastage of raw material in relation to each usable flake or core was high, with 200–300 waste flakes per usable flake as a reasonable minimum estimate. Exact counts of waste flakes were difficult, since these would have required putting down a large ground sheet and collecting and counting all debris in a controlled manner. I found that such attempts at control interfered unduly with the activities I was observing, and in this aspect of the study, as in all others, I opted to keep my observations as nondirective as possible. Many of the flakes from block-on-block and core reduction went

White chert being collected from a quarry located near the
Warburton Ranges Mission and Puntutjarpa Rockshelter and
being tested for its flaking properties by means of direct percussion. At this quarry, unweathered stone is dug from just below the surface of the ground. White chert is readily available
in the Warburton-Puntutjarpa area and is ideal for making
tools to shape hardwood implements.

zinging off to a considerable distance from the point of impact, and
other, very small flakes were lost track of as they slipped between
and under flakes that were already present on the ground. In one
case I counted 660 waste flakes per usable flake after one block-on-
block episode, but even this must be viewed as a minimum estimate
on that occasion. Sometimes men visiting a quarry would dig one to
two feet below the surface of the ground to obtain lumps of unweathered stone. This was especially evident in the case of white
chert, a popular material for stone toolmaking but one that was
susceptible to weathering. Pieces of stone extracted in this way were
always reduced by means of direct percussion with a hammerstone
applied to a core with a prepared striking platform. The same man
who on one occasion was observed smashing in the most wasteful
manner possible on unprepared nodules or other surface blocks of
material, was observed on other occasions – usually those involving
great effort to extract pieces of usable material by digging – taking
care to prepare a striking platform and to reduce a piece of material

in a systematic and much less wasteful manner. Tjungurayi, for example, who regularly used a block-on-block method at certain localities, was careful to use a prepared core technique at other quarries like the one near Partjaṛ (where the quartzite is not unduly subject to weathering but occurs in the form of stream cobbles that must be pried loose with a digging stick from the clay and conglomerate soil matrix of a creekbed channel), with a resulting economy of raw material. Watching Tjungurayi at work, I never counted more than 62 waste flakes per usable flake in any single core reduction episode, although his average of fourteen waste flakes per usable flake by this method was much lower. Aborigine men carried small cores from the quarry to the habitation camp in their hands (never more than two or three, altogether in one trip) and the flakes were tucked into their long hair (to prevent the edges from being dulled by rubbing against each other).

At this point we need to think of Aboriginal lithic raw materials as flowing in two diverging streams toward their ultimate contexts of discard. On the one hand, we have the quarried material being carried back to camp for further shaping and use. On the other hand, we have raw material from nonlocalized sources being used more or less on the spot and left there after the particular task is completed. Quarried stone flows into the habitation base camp, close to a water source, while materials from nonlocalized sources end up in the context of various task-specific sites that are widely dispersed over the landscape, usually far from any reliable source of water. In terms of our Aboriginal grammar of behavior in relation to lithic residues, *rule number 1* is: Nonquarried stones serve as instant tools and are discarded at or near the locus where they are used. That locus occurs at or near the place where the material was collected. The corollary of this is *rule number 2:* Quarried stones are transported from the locus of collection to a habitation base camp where they can be further shaped and used.

Cores and waste flakes left behind at quarry localities are on the order of 100+ times greater by weight per episode than cores and flakes that are transported back to camp. Exact weights are not available because a kilogram scale and block-and-tackle strong enough to lift and weigh large cores on these quarries were not available. Many large cores were too heavy to lift without mechanical assistance, and those that could be lifted exceeded the limits of the scale I carried with me (13.6 kg. or 30 lb.). Cores and flakes transported from the quarry back to camp, on the other hand, were easy to lift and carry and could be weighed using the scale. The largest of these weighed 5.2 kilograms (11.4 lb.), but the average weight of 32 cores transported from these quarries was much less (0.63 kg. or 1.4 lb). These rather rough-and-ready weight measurements convinced me that

some kind of quantitative assessment of the amounts of lithic material
flowing through the Aborigine cultural system was essential if the full
implications of rules number 1 and 2 were to be understood. In
assembling this data later on, I was helped to sharpen my approach by
a question asked by a colleague,[6] namely: "How much isotropic stone
would an average adult male Aborigine be expected to use in the
course of a normal year?" And I might add the further question:
Where do these materials ultimately come to rest?

Pehaps the most distinctive stone artifact produced in the Western
Desert is the hafted adze. This class of artifact has been widely
reported and described in the Western and Central Deserts of Australia (Horne and Aiston, 1924; Mountford, 1941; Thomson, 1964;
Tindale, 1965; Gould, Koster, and Sontz, 1971). These discoidal and
unifacially retouched implements were used to scrape hard woods
(mainly mulga), and, as the working edge became dulled through
use, each implement was resharpened and used again. This process
of resharpening and reuse, sometimes involving rehafting of the
adze flake as well, was commonly repeated over twenty times for a
single adze before the tool was worn down to a remnant so narrow
that it could no longer be held in its haft. These remnant adzes,
termed "slugs" by Australian archaeologists, are probably the most
diagnostic class of stone artifacts found on post-Pleistocene age habitation sites in the Australian desert. Examples of stone adze flakes
and slugs excavated at Puntutjarpa Rockshelter in the Western Desert are illustrated in Fig. 5.

Hand-held flakescrapers were also used by Aborigines for woodworking tasks, although less often than hafted adzes. Sometimes a
man forgot to take his spearthrower (with the adze hafted onto its
handle) with him, and he found that he needed to resharpen a
wooden speartip or give the final shape to a spearshaft. Irregularly
shaped but fairly thick stone flakes were unifacially retouched by
direct percussion for use as scrapers; or, if a spearshaft required
trimming, a simple, unretouched flake was sometimes used as a
spokeshave. These tools were not saved or reused. They were produced, as needed, at habitation campsites or in task-specific localities, and they were made from either quarried or nonlocalized stone.
Together with the largest unifacial stone choppers used to detach
slabs of mulga wood and provide initial shaping or spearthrowers
and other hardwood implements, these flakescrapers, spokeshaves,
and adzes made up the general category of "chopper-plane-
scrapers." Since these are all maintenance, or, more specifically,
woodworking tools, the easiest way to calculate the amounts of stone
used in a year is to estimate the weight of lithic raw material expended on different woodworking tasks during the course of an
average year.

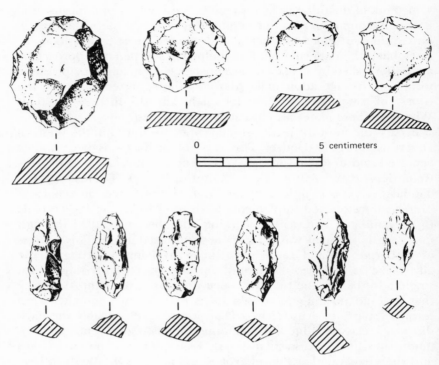

0   5 centimeters

Fig 5. Prehistoric stone adze flakes (top row) and adze slugs (bottom row) from the Puntutjarpa Rockshelter excavations. Slugs are the used-up remnants of adze flakes and are one of the most common and durable classes of material residues left by both past- and present-day Western Desert Aborigines.

An adult male Aborigine replaced his spearthrower (*miru,langkuru*), on an average, about once every two years, and he replaced his wooden club (*kupulu*) at the same rate. Throwing-sticks (*wayanu*) were replaced about once every year. Spearshaft wood dries out and becomes stiff and brittle quickly, so spearshafts (hunting spear: *kulata*) had to be replaced about every three weeks. Speartips (*tjirkali*) generally needed to be resharpened at least once every other day. Wooden digging bowls (*wira*) were replaced about once each year, but fine carrying bowls (*ngunma, piṭi*) tended to be kept and used for long periods – perhaps as much as ten years. Digging sticks (*waṇa*), despite hard use, lasted fairly well and needed replacing only about twice a year. Other, minor woodworking tasks like replacement of the sharp, bipointed wooden peg (*mukulpa*) used both as a spearthrower hook and as a barb on the foreshaft of the hunting spear, occurred at irregular intervals and accounted for such a small amount of stone tool attrition that they cannot usefully enter into these calculations.

On the basis of laboratory experiments and ethnographic observations, I estimate that one adze flake is good for an average of 3,058 useful strokes of hardwood (i.e., freshly cut mulga) scraping. This is an overall average figure that takes into account variations in lithic raw materials seen in use. This works out to an average of twenty resharpenings in the useful life of a single stone adze. An adze had to be retouched every time it was used for sharpening a mulga wood speartip, which works out to about 182 uses per year or 9.1 adzes per man per year for that particular task. A man also needed to replace an average of 17.3 spearshafts per year, and he was able to shape two spearshafts with a single adze flake, thus requiring an average of 8.7 adze flakes each year for this task. One adze flake was sufficient for shaping two clubs, and, similarly, one adze flake sufficed for shaping two throwing-sticks. One adze flake was generally adequate to perform the final shaping on one spearthrower. My data on wooden digging- and carrying-bowls is less reliable, because I observed a few cases and can offer only a rough estimate. Adzes were used in the final finishing of these implements and probably required about the same amount of effort as a spearthrower – that is, one adze flake per bowl. Adzes were rarely, if ever, used in shaping digging-sticks. My figures do not distinguish occasional substitutions of hand-held flakescrapers and/or spokeshaves for adzes when these tasks were performed.

In addition to these utilitarian tasks, we must also consider wood-scraping activities related to the manufacture of sacred boards and other ritual paraphernalia. These are hard to estimate, since ceremonies took place at irregular intervals and at variable rates. On some ritual occasions, woodworking activities were considerable. As a general estimate I would add another three adze flakes to the annual inventory, bringing the total now to 23.05 (Table 8). This is a reasonable estimate of the average number of adze flakes and other retouched tools of quarried stone required by an Aborigine living under traditional circumstances in a normal year.

About the same number of large "chopper-planes" were required by a man for woodworking, on the average, as retouched tools of quarried stone. These implements were used for cutting stalks, roots, or branches for making spearshafts, for making the initial "V"-shaped cut in the trunk of a mulga tree when preparing to detach a slab of wood for making into a spearthrower or sacred board, and in the preliminary shaping of every kind of wooden artifact, including digging-sticks. The crucial difference between "chopper-planes" as instant tools and retouched adzes and flake-scrapers manufactured of quarried stone is that "chopper-planes" were discarded immediately after use; hence, 1 use = 1 tool. My minimum estimate for use of "chopper-planes," including prelimi-

Table 8. *Average number of adze flakes used per man per year*

Utilitarian and domestic tasks	Average number of flakes
Resharpening speartips	9.1
Replacing spearshafts	8.7
Replacing spearthrowers	0.5
Replacing clubs	0.25
Replacing throwing-sticks	0.5
Replacing wooden bowls	1.0
Total	20.05
Other tasks	
Replacing sacred paraphernalia	3.0
Total	23.05

Table 9. *Average number of "chopper-planes" used per man per year*

Utilitarian and domestic tasks	Average number of "chopper-planes"
Replacing spearshafts	17.3
Replacing spearthrowers	0.5
Replacing clubs	0.5
Replacing throwing-sticks	1.0
Replacing digging-sticks	2.0
Total	21.3
Other tasks	
Replacing sacred paraphernalia	2.0
Total	23.3

nary shaping of sacred boards and ritual objects, is 23.3 per man per year (Table 9).

Mention should be made here of parallel research on the quantitative aspects of stone toolmaking and tool use among Western Desert Aborigines by Hayden (1977). Hayden's estimates, based on studies of the rates at which retouched stone tools were used and replaced by a nuclear family of Pintupi Aborigines (Western Desert people from the vicinity of Lake Macdonald but residing at the settlement of Papunya, Northern Territory, when the study was made), presents us with higher figures. Hayden's informants stated that they replaced retouched stone tools at the overall rate of 117 per year, or 2.5 to 10 per week per person. According to Hayden's data, his

Pintupi informants performed tasks more frequently and used more tools per task than was the case for the Western Desert people I observed. Nevertheless, Hayden's figures are of the same general order of magnitude as mine and could be viewed providing the parameters within which to consider the flow of lithic materials within many Australian desert hunter–gatherer societies. How can we account for these differences? No conclusive answer is possible at this time, although there are several factors that should be considered. For one thing, both Hayden's and my figures are estimates; in Hayden's case based on informant testimony, in my case based on direct but intermittent observations. For another, there was at least some use of metal tools by the desert-dwelling Aborigines I observed, although this was minimal, and there was even more dependence upon metal and glass by the Aborigines residing within 100 kilometers (60 miles) of the Warburton Ranges Mission, where European influences were stronger. I do not know how much such influences affected Hayden's informants, but I can see this as a factor that could have led to reduced totals in my study. And, of course, these differences could be due to genuine regional variations in stone toolmaking behavior among Western Desert Aborigines as a result of differences in such variables as local availability of raw materials, differences in traditional tool-use, and others. Obviously more work will be needed to sort these factors out and assess their relative degrees of importance in order to account for these differences.

The case of flake knives is more problematical. Since these were used mainly for cutting meat and sinew, and since successful hunts in the Western Desert were rather uncommon and occurred at irregular intervals, it is hard to offer an accurate estimate of the rate at which such artifacts were used up. In most cases, flake knives were made of stone from nonlocalized sources. Sometimes naturally sharp-edged flakes found lying on the ground were picked up and used as flake knives, thus constituting an important variety of instant tool. There were also cases observed, however, where sharp waste flakes left over from adze production on quarried stone were picked up by someone in the habitation camp and used for a cutting task. So, as instant tools, some flake knives could be made from quarried as well as from nonlocalized stone. At reserves and missions in recent years, pieces of broken bottle glass have increasingly come to replace stone for impromptu cutting implements, and I have included episodes involving bottle glass "knives" with my flake knife observations under the heading of nonlocalized sources of stone. My best general estimate is that approximately twenty of these flake knives are used by one person each year, but I am well aware of the weaknesses in this estimate. Women use these at least as much as men, and women sometimes perform the final finishing of wooden bowls, using hand-held flakescrapers. So I admit to being somewhat arbitrary in referring to the use of stone tools as a primarily male activity.

Now we can combine the figures for frequency of tool use with those for individual tool types. I weighed only nine ethnographic adze flakes before they were retouched, hafted, and put to use, and I obtained a mean weight of 41.4 grams for these. I regard this as an inadequate sample, however, and suspect that the true mean should be lower. "Chopper-planes" (the heavyweights of the class termed *purpunpa* by the Aborigines) were more variable in weight, which is not surprising considering their ad hoc nature, ranging from 4.7 kilograms to 97.0 grams, with a mean weight of 809.2 grams. Ethnographic flake knives had a mean weight of 40 grams. The total weights for these different artifact classes are summarized in Table 10. Thus, about 18.9 times more stone from nonlocalized sources passed through the hands of an average Aborigine stone toolmaker during a normal year than stone derived from quarries. It also means that about 99.95 percent of the total lithic material was used by the Aborigines in task-specific localities that are relatively ephemeral and widely dispersed over the landscape, while only about 0.05 percent saw use in the context of a habitation base-camp. This latter figure may have varied, of course, depending mainly upon how many flake knives were used at task-specific localities as opposed to habitation base-camps. But even if all 800 grams of flake knife material were used in the habitation area, it would still not affect the basic magnitude of the relationship.

Thus we can derive *rule number 3:* Despite the fact that quarried stone represents only a minute fraction of the isotropic stone used in the total cultural system, much more quarried stone than stone from nonlocalized sources is discarded within the context of habitation campsites. The case of the Western Desert Aborigines reveals that the stone tools occurring at habitation base camps represent only the tip of the iceberg when it comes to accounting for the total amounts of isotropic stone used within the society. Yet *rule number 4* presents us with a statement that could serve as a genuine cross-cultural principle: Lithic raw materials that are labor-expensive to procure and/or to work with will tend to be used in artifacts that have relatively long use-lives.[7] Finally, we can state *rule number 5:* The widest variety of artifact types within the total lithic assemblage are used and discarded in the context of habitation base-camps. This latter rule may be regarded as a corollary of a wider definition of habitation base-camps as localities, like Tikatika, that represent the widest observable range of activities performed by the widest range of the population, including people of both sexes and all ages.

Table 10. *Total amounts of lithic raw materials needed per man per year*

Artifact classes	Total amounts
Nonquarried:	
"chopper-planes"	17.237 kg.
flake knives	800 gr.
Quarried:	
adze flakes and	
equivalent flakescrapers	954 gr.

In dealing with rules of grammar in the formation of material residues, we are sometimes, like the metaphorical linguist I have invoked from time to time, confronted with variations that constitute "rules within rules"–those derivative but nevertheless special rules that operate to alter and amend the basic rules under certain, specified conditions. For example, when nonlocalized sources of usable isotropic stone occur naturally near a water source, we encounter a peculiar situation in which nonlocalized lithic raw materials were extensively used and discarded in the context of a habitation base-camp. The artifacts produced from these raw materials were by no means limited to instant tools but included significant numbers of retouched implements like adzes and flakescrapers that presumably had long use-lives. This was clearly the case at Puntutjarpa Rock-shelter, where during the recent Aboriginal occupation of the site (i.e., within the last 200 years) quartz, which is abundantly available on "gibber" flats less than half a mile from the habitation campsite, was the single most popular lithic raw material for toolmaking there, accounting for slightly over 50 percent of the stone used. This popularity of quartz at Puntutjarpa was a constant feature of human behavior at this site for at least the last 10,000 years. Although it was not equally preferred for making every tool type, every type of stone artifact made and used at Puntutjarpa at any time in its history of human habitation included at least some made of quartz. While quartz, with its pronounced internal planes of cleavage, is a difficult raw material to flake, its abundance close at hand made it more attractive for stone toolmaking than it otherwise might have been. Thus the chance factor in desert geography brings about situations where nonlocalized sources of lithic raw material occur within a short distance, generally less than one mile, of a habitation campsite. A similar proviso applies whenever a quarry occurs at or very close to a water source (which, inevitably in the Western Desert, means a habitation campsite, though not necessarily a large one). In such cases, unusually high percentages of the lithic raw material from that quarry can be expected to appear in the stone artifact inventories from that site. Most quarries in the Western Desert occur in areas distant from natural water sources, so this latter situation is rare. But a few cases are known, such as the large habitation base-camp at Partjar, in the Clutterbuck Hills, where in 1966–7 I observed large amounts of locally available yellow quartzite in use for making a variety of stone tools including flake knives, flakescrapers, and adzes. Perhaps we can generalize from such examples to propose *rule number 6:* Whenever random factors of geography place sources of usable stone, whether in the form of quarries or nonlocalized in nature, at or in close proximity to a water source where a habitation base-camp will occur, ease of procurement will outweigh other factors and unusually high percentages of artifacts of these locally available stones will be made, used, and discarded at such campsites. This "modifier" does not invalidate rules 3 and 4, but it helps us to appreciate the interaction of variables like efficiency of a particular kind of stone for making and using certain kinds of tools in relation to others like ease of procurement.

Such interactions are not limited to variables of a strictly utilitarian nature like those stated above. The Western Desert Aborigines have a term, *yiraputja,* which they applied to any durable and portable substance that they regarded as having been left behind by a mythological Dreamtime being in its travels across the landscape. To some extent, this is a residual category that includes unusual stones and materials introduced into the physical environment in an unusual manner. For example, tektites (heat ablated, glassy stones of presumed extraterrestrial origin that are found widely on the surface of many parts of the Western Desert), prehistoric stone tools different from those currently in use (like backed blades), and pieces of bakelite plastic, old eyeglass lenses, and other oddments of European origin were among the items termed *yiraputja* whenever they were found. More often, however, this category included stone like quartz crystals, peculiarly shaped agates, pieces of mica, and so forth, that occur naturally in the Western Desert but are uncommon and distinctive in appearance. Occasionally these materials were fashioned into tools, but more often they were saved and incorporated into the bundle of special goods (*mapanpa*) used by sorcerers for curing and other purposes. There have even been a few cases observed of an Aborigine picking up a prehistoric tool, such as a backed blade, and reusing it as a hafted adze after some retouching. *Yiraputja* always had something about them that was distinctive in color, shape, or texture, but they were not at all uniform in appearance. Strictly speaking, these were a form of usable stone that is nonlocalized in occurrence, but in their use they conformed more to rule number 4.

Although there is, admittedly, something subjective about my use here of "distinctive appearance," one can posit another modifier (*rule number 7*): When stones of distinctive appearance are found in nonlocalized sources they are retained and used for tasks or activities that involve relatively long use-life. Thus the operation of rule number 4 is not entirely dependent upon investments of labor in relation to quarrying or manufacture but may include additional considerations that are harder to define objectively but are, nonetheless, real. In the case of stones belonging to the category *yiraputja*, it is the retention of the item that constitutes the labor-expensive behavior referred to in rule number 4, even though such behavior is not especially laborious or energy-expensive. Stones of "distinctive appearance," while constituting a tiny proportion of the total lithic assemblage, can be expected to show up readily in any archaeological analysis of the lithic residues of any habitation campsite.

One could continue to generate rules and grammatical "modifiers" of those rules in relation to the lithic residues of the Western Desert Aborigines, but these examples should suffice before the exercise becomes pedantic. The principal value of applying a linguistic metaphor in this way to lithic discards is the manner in which it enables us to perceive linkages between behavior and residues in a living human society. These linkages are like the "behavioral chains" and "C-transforms" referred to by Schiffer (1976: 14–15) although without any of the mechanistic overtones that such flow-model procedures sometimes imply. The idea of grammar works well when applied to the structuring of human behavior generally, and this is as true in relation to materials as it is to language, social structure, ritual, or any other observable human activity.

Perhaps the ultimate extension of a grammar of material residues appears whenever someone designs a formula based upon such relationships as the general basis upon which to make archaeological inferences. Such an effort is already underway by Barbara Luedtke (1976), who has proposed the following formula to help explain the patterning of lithic residues in a series of Late Woodland Period (700–1300 A.D.) archaeological sites in Michigan. This formula expresses the amount of chert needed in relation to known uses:

$$C = \sum_{i-1}^{n} \frac{T_A}{T_T} (S + M + R)$$

Here, C equals the amount of chert (or other lithic raw material) needed per person per year (or any other unit of time); T_A equals the amount of each task accomplished with a given tool per year (measured in hours of work, number of strokes, etc.); T_T equals the life span of the tool (measured in the same units as T_A); S equals the average weight of the tool at the time it is discarded; M equals the amount of unused manufacturing debris associated with the tool; and R equals the amount of unused resharpening debris associated with the tool (Luedtke, 1976: 12). Or, stated more simply:

> The amount of chert needed per year is equal to the sum of the number of tools needed, times the average weight of these tools plus their associated chipping debris. [Luedtke, 1976: 12–13]

Admittedly, my Australian data is poor in relation to M and R, since I did not weigh the actual amounts of debris produced in the course of manufacturing and resharpening each tool. These amounts were small, however, and could be estimated from known amounts of lithic raw material that were transported back to the habitation camp for further work and weighed before actual core-reduction and tool manufacture took place.

As Luedtke herself is quick to point out (1976: 14), this formula does not take into account problems like recycling of tools into other forms and for other uses, nor does it cover the possibility of functional substitution of materials like shell or bone for items made of stone, making direct extrapolation between cultures that are technologically dissimilar quite risky. She goes on to note:

> However, in a situation where no other data are available, one is perhaps justified in using values derived from one culture to help construct the lithic demand equation for another. Replicative experiments are another source of data, and are especially useful for estimating tool life expectancies. Using such sources of data, order-of-magnitude estimates can be achieved, indicating amounts of chert needed under given circumstances. [Luedtke, 1976: 14]

In particular, she examines data from the Western Desert Aborigines and Duna-speaking societies of Highland New Guinea studied by J. P. White and Charles Modjeska, which furnished "ball park" estimates for her studies of the Late Woodland Period in Michigan (Luedtke, 1976: 19–22). Up to this point, however, her approach is not a test so much as it is an extrapolation, albeit a reasonable one. The question is: Can the application of such formulas ever be more than an exercise in extrapolation, which is really a controlled form of analogy? Citing Western Desert Aborigine data as well as observations by Warner among the Murngin, a group of Arnhem Land Aborigines, Luedtke notes, "Other, less utilitarian properties may influence lithic preferences" (1976: 23) – in particular, enhanced social value of chert due to color, texture or other aspects of rock structure, and distance from the source as factors that could influence people's procurement behavior. It is in this direction that we must now begin to search for an approach that will explain the total pattern of lithic residues in contemporary and prehistoric societies more adequately than the argument by analogy.

The search for an "archaeological signature"
Despite our clearer picture of the order of behavior underlying lithic residues in Western Desert Aborigine society, we are still short of identifying the "archaeological signature" referred to at the beginning of this chapter. The fundamental problem in the case of the Western Desert Aborigines, as with many other human societies, is that the chipped stone artifacts were almost exclusively maintenance tools or by-products of the manufacture of such tools. By their very nature, tools that are used to make and maintain other tools can tell us little or nothing directly about subsistence and other activities related to procurement of basic resources.

So far this study has shown how, given the grammatical relationships between behavior and the final context in which different materials are discarded, our perception of the total range of Aboriginal behavior addressed to lithic technology depends as much upon what is not present at a particular site as upon what is. For instance, the predicted absence or low frequency of occurrence of large "chopperplanes" from the residues in a habitation base-camp could be as important to our understanding of the behavior at that site as is the presence of adzes, flakescrapers, and other implements with relatively long use-lives. Similarly, the amount of usable lithic material present in such a habitation site represents only a tiny fraction of the stone actually used by the Aborigines. So the presence of retouched implements together with the relatively small amounts of stone they comprise in one kind of site (habitation base-camps) implies the presence of other tools that account for the bulk of the lithic raw material in other localities (task-specific sites). These observations bear out the general proposition recently voiced by Jelinek (1976: 31):

> The traditional view of artifact materials as representative of a fully functional cross section of the range of activities carried out during a site occupation must . . . be modified to consider this material as largely trash in the view of the people who were responsible for its deposition (that is, this artifactual material is, to a degree, a negative impression of the functional system and its necessary tools).

So far, living archaeology has provided us with a view of the "negative impression" of Aborigine economic and adaptive behavior in the Western Desert. The next step will be to show how, despite these apparently unpromising characteristics, further examination of the lithic technology of ethnographic Western Desert Aborigines can furnish the "signature" for the particular kind of risk-minimizing mode of hunter–gatherer adaptation described earlier.

6

The materialist approach in living archaeology

In order to achieve a "signature" of lithic residues that will usefully identify the nonseasonal and risk-minimizing, hunter–gatherer mode of adaptation characteristic of the Western Desert of Australia, I shall adopt a materialist approach that has, as its foundation, two related principles. One is the Principle of Totality, already alluded to in Chapter 2, whereby the living archaeologist is concerned not only with the statistically dominant patterns or "behavior in the aggregate" observable in human residues but also with idiosyncratic or statistically minor patterns that otherwise might be regarded as unimportant exceptions to the more dominant patterning. And the other is the Argument by Anomaly. Before we can go on with the analysis of Western Desert Aborigine lithic technology, this latter argument needs to be explained.

Argument by anomaly

In archaeology, or, for that matter, in any aspect of social science, how do we know what we know? When are we really satisfied that some statement about human behavior is valid, as opposed to other statements that appear open to differences in interpretation or other weaknesses? I have already debunked the idea of analogy as unconvincing, and in doing so I presupposed the epistomological imperative of finding a more convincing approach than the use of analogy. In this chapter I wish to substitute argument by anomaly for argument by analogy. An analysis of the way Australian desert Aborigines selected and used different lithic raw materials will demonstrate how effective argument by anomaly is, as compared with argument by analogy, in furnishing a convincing "archaeological signature" of the traditional Western Desert way of life.

The use of anomaly for discovering unknowns is well established in the physical and natural sciences. Perhaps the best known example, though not necessarily the best one, is the discovery of the outer planets, Neptune and Pluto. In 1841 an undergraduate at Cambridge University, John Couch Adams, calculated that an unknown planet was causing the planet Uranus to deviate from its presumed orbit. In astronomy, a deviation of this kind, in which the gravitational attraction of one mass impinges upon the predicted orbital path of another, is termed perturbation. Adams's announcement of his calculations in 1845, which pointed to the existence of a planet beyond Uranus, was ignored. At almost the same time a French atronomer, Urbain Leverrier, published calculations that were virtually identical, but these, too, were ignored. However, a Berlin astronomer, Johann Gottfried Galle, was persuaded to test Leverrier's calculations with his telescope, and on his first attempt on September 23, 1846, he found the planet Neptune less than one degree from its predicted position.

The discovery of Pluto followed the same pattern but represents a more ambiguous example of the use of astronomical anomalies in orbital paths for the discovery of hitherto unknown bodies in space. Early in the 1900s W. H. Pickering and Percival Lowell predicted the existence of yet another planet from perturbations to Uranus and Neptune. In 1919 an attempt was made to provide visual confirmation with a photographic search from the Mt. Wilson Observatory, but this effort failed because of a defect in the critical photograph, and, on another picture, a bright star obscured the image that might have revealed the planet. Another attempt in 1930 by C. W. Tombaugh, however, succeeded in finding Pluto only five degrees from its calculated position. Although the discovery of Pluto looks like a convincing follow-up on the earlier use of orbital anomalies to discover Neptune, it now appears that Pluto's mass is too small to account for the perturbations that originally led to its discovery (Hunten, 1975: 131–2). So in this latter case Pickering and Lowell appear to have been right, but for the wrong reasons, and the search continues for whatever it may be that is causing Uranus and Neptune to deviate from their predicted orbital paths.

Despite the ironies attending the discovery of Pluto, we can see how the use of anomalies has proved to be a valuable tool for inferring the presence and location of planetary and other bodies. We can apply this same logic in living archaeology. By looking at the totality of human behavior relating to residues, we can discover anomalies that are just as circumstantial as the orbits of the outer planets in relation to their mass. These anomalies cannot be dismissed as "mere idiosyncrasies" or "particularist exceptions." They demand an explanation, and the explanation of these deviations or idiosyncrasies may prove more interesting than explanations for dominant patterns or "behavior in the aggregate." After all, the general orbital path of Uranus, while explainable in terms of physical laws of mass and movement, has proved to be of less interest to astronomers than the discoveries that were possible once the deviations from this general path were known. The laws of physics provided the framework needed to assess the significance of this anomaly, but in astronomy, as in the physical and natural sciences generally, these laws are not ends in themselves but are tools for making new discoveries. Each new discovery tests the law. Earlier, I suggested that instead of trying to discover laws of human behavior, the living archaeologist is concerned with using relationships that have already achieved the status of law in other fields as frameworks for making discoveries about human behavior that can be tested against the evidence of the past. Propositions generated by living archaeology are not laws unto themselves but are mainly extensions of laws or lawlike formulations that already exist in such guises as Liebig's Law of the Minimum, the Law of Supply and Demand, or the Principle of Least Effort. What matters most is not the law but the testing of propositions derived from laws, since it is the testing process that leads us to discover those things that are most worth knowing about past human behavior.

Argument by anomaly also gets us past one of the principal objections so often voiced against the use of laws in anthropology and archaeology. This is the "So what?" problem. Since most laws, in the end, come out sounding like self-evident statements, one is always tempted to belittle them by asking: So what? Is this not merely demonstrating the obvious? The argument is not a valid objection to the use of laws, but it does reflect a reaction to the other attitude that one sometimes encounters in social science, namely, the "Eureka! I've discovered a law!" syndrome. Examples of this abound in the archaeological literature, although the two best known are Wittfogel's "hydraulic hypothesis" for explaining the rise of autocratically administered civilizations through increased dependence upon large-scale irrigation (Wittfogel, 1960) and Leslie White's argument that the evolution of human society in general is the product of increased efficiency in harnessing energy (White, 1959). The value of these lawlike formulations lies not so much in their intrinsic validity as in the use to which they have been put since they were first propounded. Taken at face value, these lawlike formulations about the evolution of human civilization were compelling in their logical simplicity and comprehensiveness. It was not so much the errors or exceptions to these "laws" that led many scholars to reject them but, rather, their very strengths, namely, the simplicity and comprehensiveness that made them appear reductionist at worst and uninteresting at best. They seemed to be simple answers to very complex questions. But they also led scholars to test them in various ways, and from these tests have emerged valuable studies that have unquestionably made archaeology more interesting. Laws or lawlike formulations themselves are not the goal so much as they are an intermediate step in a continuous process of probing for new awareness in social science. It remains to be seen whether Wittfogel's or White's generalizations will ever achieve the status of law in the same sense as one finds laws used in the natural and physical sciences. In a way, it hardly matters, since the primary value of these formulations lies in their applicability as frameworks for further testing and discovery, especially when anomalies appear to predictions derived from them. There is nothing trivial or obvious about the need to explain anomalies that can be recognized only in relation to such general frameworks.

Righteous rocks and the Western Desert Aborigines

It is a well known ethnographic fact that Australian Aborigines in general, and the desert people in particular, sometimes made exceptional efforts to obtain isotropic stone for purposes or reasons that had more to do with their sacred life than with more mundane considerations such as flaking or edge-holding properties. Take, for instance, the case of the Kimberley point. These objects are among the finest examples of the stoneworker's craft anywhere in Aboriginal Australia. They have been thoroughly described in the literature, both in terms of their manufacture and use by ethnographic Aborigines of the Kimberley District of northwestern Australia (Love, 1936: 72–7; Elkin, 1949) and also in relation to subsequent experiments to replicate the unique method of pressure flaking with a hardwood flaker reported for their manufacture (Crabtree, 1970). These bifacially-retouched projectile points are among the few flaked stone implements in Aboriginal Australia that we know, from ethnographic accounts, were used as "extractive" tools in the sense advocated by Binford and Binford (1969) to refer to tools used primarily to extract primary resources directly from the physical and biotic environment. In the Kimberley region, historic Aborigines like the Worora used these implements as the tips of their throwing-spears for hunting kangaroos (Love, 1936: 75). For hundreds of years Aborigines in northwestern Australia have made these implements out of European-derived glass, mainly from bottles washed ashore and from telegraph insulators, as well as from locally available isotropic stone. The pressure-flaking technique used to manufacture these implements spread to adjacent areas (Micha, 1970: 289), but the points themselves were traded even farther afield into the Central and Western Deserts, where they were reported from the desert south and southwest of the Fitzroy River near Halls Creek (Petri, 1954: 52–3), to localities along the Trans-Continental Railway in the southern part of the Western Desert.

Of special importance is a reference by Spencer and Gillen to the presence of Kimberley points among the Kaitish, Unmatjera, and Ilpirra–all Central Desert groups residing immediately to the north and northwest of Alice Springs, Northern Territory, about 880 kilometers southeast of the Kimberley District:

> Spears of this nature and their detached heads are used for magical purposes. [One typical Kimberley point] was found in the possession of a man of the Ilpirra tribe, to whom it had come from the far north. It was supposed that the head had been endowed with evil magic by its original owner, and that a wound inflicted by it, however slight, would have fatal results. It is a matter of fact that a native will simply lie down and die, if he believes that the spear which has wounded him was charmed. The only possible cure for a wound of this kind is the exercise of strong counter magic. [Spencer and Gillen, 1904: 675–6]

An account of individual behavior like this must be treated with caution, for it could be atypical of behavior within the society generally. One of the recurring problems of Australian ethnology, especially in the study of material culture, has been the tendency to generalize about behavior from a single, possibly aberrant, example. It is often hard to know from reading descriptive ethnographies whether one is dealing with an idiosyncrasy or a normative pattern. In this case, however, we are also given a circumstantial account of this Ilpirra man's use for this implement, which is consistent with the ethnographic practice of sorcery as known widely throughout the Australian desert. While this Ilpirra man's possession of a Kimberley point was probably unusual and highly idiosyncratic for that society, his use of it was typical of the system of belief and behavior for that region that has been termed sorcery by anthropologists who have studied it. So by the time Kimberley points reached this part of the Central Desert they were endowed by their recipients with properties comparable to other items in the sorcerer's kit. Although not necessarily secret, they were treated as sacred to a degree.

Aranda Aborigines in the Central Desert were in possession of some Kimberley points (Spencer and Gillen, 1927: 537–8), and Tindale (1965: 154–6) reported finding two Kimberley points among Ngatatjara-speaking people at the Warburton Ranges Mission in 1935. Another report from this same expedition and locality contains a photograph of a Kimberley point being used to circumcise a male novice along with the note that the operator bit the edge of the point to chip off some flakes and sharpen the implement as the operation progressed (Hackett, 1934: 16). This latter occurrence is important, because these implements were used there exclusively as circumcision knives and not at all as spearpoints. Thus, some 1,100 kilometers (680 miles) from their place of origin, these artifacts were being used and curated (to apply a concept used by Binford, 1973:

242) in a manner completely different from that observed in the Kimberley District. The Worora and other Kimberley Aborigines used these items as extractive, utilitarian implements, namely, as speartips. When the speartip shattered during use, as frequently happened, replacement was rapid, making Kimberley points one of the most common classes of stone artifact discards in that region. At Warburton, in the Western Desert, we are seeing the far end of a cline in which these implements were used exclusively for secret functions within the context of the sacred life. There, women and children were not permitted to see these objects, which were kept hidden when not in use and were regarded as *yiraputja* (items of a "special substance" referred to in Chapter 5). The farther these implements traveled from their place of origin, the more exalted their status became. What were purely profane objects in the Durkheimian sense became increasingly sacred when transported farther away into a situation where they were scarce and where the social context was different. The geographic distribution of Kimberley points supports rule number 4 presented earlier, that lithic materials that are labor-expensive to procure and/or to work with will tend to be used in artifacts that have relatively long use-lives.

But this rule does not explain why people took the extra trouble to obtain these exotic implements. No simple, utilitarian argument can explain this. Isotropic stones capable of producing sharp edges suitable for circumcision and other bodily operations connected with the sacred life were abundantly available in the Western and Central Deserts and were often made into flake knives for just this purpose, as I saw happen on six occasions in 1966–7 at Warburton, Laverton, and Cundeelee in the Western Desert. The Western Desert Aborigines did not need Kimberley points to carry out these particular operations – that is, there was nothing intrinsic to the task that required this kind of tool. Here then is the anomaly. The lawlike statement of relationships in rule number 4 may be valid, but it does not adequately explain the totality of behavior that went on in this part of Australia. It helps us to generalize from this anomaly, but it is not the last word when it comes to explaining why anomalies of this kind occur.

For a more adequate explanation we must examine this kind of anomaly in greater detail. During the course of archaeological excavations at Puntutjarpa Rockshelter near Warburton in 1969–70, a systematic survey was conducted to locate all sources of usable isotropic stone occurring within a 40-kilometer (25-mile) radius of the site. This effort was assisted by Aborigines at the Warburton Ranges Mission, many of whom were still visiting these localities to obtain stone for their toolmaking activities. We were also aided by the Western Mining Corporation, Ltd., then in the process of surveying for copper ore in the region. The Western Mining Corporation's coverage of this area was complete, with teams on motorbikes and other vehicles inspecting literally every square foot of ground. These teams informed us of any outcrops or other natural occurrences of potentially usable stone, thus expanding the completeness of the raw material survey beyond the limited means available to ourselves.

Seven classes of usable isotropic stone were found to occur within the 40-kilometer radius of Puntutjarpa Rockshelter, in the following contexts:

> 1. *Warburton porphyry.*   A hard, dark bluish-gray stone with pronounced granular inclusions but with little tendency toward internal planes of cleavage. This material came mainly from a large quarry immediately south of Mt. Talbot in the Warburton Range, 10 kilometers northeast of Puntutjarpa. Redeposited pieces of this material were also found in creekbeds passing through the flats between the Warburton and Brown Ranges (including Hughes Creek, which approaches to within 500 meters of Puntutjarpa).
>
> 2. *Quartz.*   Hard white or semitranslucent stone with pronounced internal planes of cleavage. Quartz was abundantly available from nonlocalized sources throughout the area around Puntutjarpa, mainly on "gibber" flats and quartz outcrops nearby. Surface scatters of this material occurred to within 500 meters of Puntutjarpa, on the flats on both sides of Hughes Creek.
>
> 3. *Quartzite*   A variable category of stones with fine granular texture and few, if any, internal planes of cleavage. Color varied from pale yellow to dark red and reddish-brown. Most specimens collected were hard, with a semisilicious surface shine, but some specimens tended toward a dull surface and were "sugary" in texture. Like quartz, this material was widely available in nonlocalized surface and creekbed sources.
>
> 4. *Red chert.*   A hard, fine-grained dark red chert with some tendencies to fracture along internal planes of cleavage. There was only a single source for this material within the 40-kilometer radius of Puntutjarpa, at a small quarry near The Sisters, a conspicuous landmark about 16 kilometers southeast of Puntutjarpa.
>
> 5. *Opaline.*   White stone with shiny surfaces but soft internal texture, tending at times to crumble into a white powdery consistency. All opaline in the Puntutjarpa area

was redeposited and occurred within creekbeds, including Hughes Creek.

6. *White chert.*   Hard white to semitranslucent stone with no internal planes of cleavage, varying in texture from dull to smooth. Rough cortex was often present, and some pieces showed a partial pinkish to dark reddish-brown coloring. Five quarries for this material were found near Puntutjarpa, with the most distant being three localities about 32 kilometers from the site and the closest being 23 kilometers away.

7. *Agate.*   Hard, brown to semitranslucent stone, sometimes with pronounced internal banding and smooth texture with few internal planes of cleavage. Few large pieces of this stone were seen, but small lumps of agate occurred widely on gibber plains in the vicinity of Puntutjarpa.

The red chert and Warburton porphyry quarries were no longer used by the local Aborigines at the time of this study, but sources for white chert were still visited and used. The 40-kilometer radius was a somewhat arbitrary distance chosen because it approximates the greatest distance Aborigines in the Western Desert today have been observed to carry lithic raw materials on foot from quarries to their habitation base-camps. It is arbitrary because it does not make allowances for variations in terrain or for the exigencies of actual movement, as, for example, when a collecting party detours to hunt lizards or track a kangaroo. Note, too, that copious supplies of various raw materials (Warburton porphyry, quartz, quartzite, and agate) were available from nonlocalized surface sources to within 0.8 kilometer of Puntutjarpa.

During the entire 10,000-year history of human occupation at Puntutjarpa, we find a reliance upon all seven classes of locally available raw materials for making stone tools of every kind. But we also find a low level but pervasive use of exotic cherts and chrysoprase. In this instance, the term "exotic" refers to any isotropic stone that cannot be found occurring naturally within the 40-kilometer radius around Puntutjarpa. Fig. 6 presents stone tool types by stratum in Trench 2 (the principal excavated trench) at Puntutjarpa, and Fig. 7 shows the numbers and percentages of different lithic raw materials occurring by stratum there as well. No effort was made in this table to group these raw materials in relation to the different classes of stone tools there, but one can see that all kinds of raw materials, including exotics, are represented throughout the sequence and were used by the ancient inhabitants at all times during the occupation of the site. Quartz was the most heavily favored material at most times, with white chert running a formidable second. Not to be

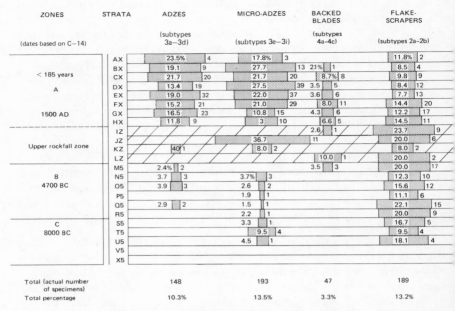

Fig. 6. Stone tool types by stratum; Trench 2, Puntutjarpa.

ignored, however, are the exotics that account for an overall average of 2.6 percent of the lithic raw material used in tools throughout the history of the site without interruption. Even at this gross level of analysis, it is apparent that something was "pulling" isotropic stones of exotic origin into the deposits at Puntutjarpa.

With this overall pattern in mind, let us look more closely at the relationship between lithic raw materials and a particular type of artifact at Puntutjarpa: the flaked stone adze. This is merely one of six major stone artifact types distinguished at the site, but it has perhaps the most distinctive morphological characteristics and is best known in terms of its ethnographic uses in relation to those characteristics. In this discussion I am including all adzes, including the smallest ones (termed "micro-adzes" elsewhere). A total of 341 flaked stone adzes and adze slugs were recovered from Trench 2 at Puntutjarpa from strata ranging over the entire 10,000-year sequence there. Visual inspection of qualitative attributes together with analysis of metrical attributes shows that there was a continuous tradition of adze manufacture and use that has changed little (except for size – adzes have tended to become larger through time) throughout the last 10,000 years in this area right up to the ethnographic present (Gould, 1977: 94–100). As Table 11 shows, the lithic raw material overwhelmingly favored by the ancient inhabitants at Puntutjarpa at all times for making this type of tool was white chert,

LARGE CORES (subtypes 1a–1c)		MICRO-CORES (subtypes 1d–1e)		HAND-AXES (prov. type 5)		RETOUCHED FRAGMENTS PLUS UTILIZED FLAKES (prov. type 9)		TOTAL (actual number of specimens)
11.8%	2					35.3%	6	17
2.1	1	8.5%	4			31.9	15	47
4.3	4					29.3	27	92
9.2	13	4.9	7			33.1	47	142
8.9	15	7.1	12			31.5	53	168
6.5	9	5.8	8			29.0	40	138
18.0	25	12.3	17			25.9	36	139
19.7	15	10.5	8			23.7	18	76
18.4	7	21.1	8			34.2	13	38
16.7	5	13.3	4			13.3	4	30
16.0	4	20.0	5			44.0	11	25
		40.0	4			30.0	3	10
16.4	14	25.9	22			31.8	27	85
16.0	13	34.7	28			29.6	24	81
28.6	22	22.0	17			27.3	21	77
37.0	20	22.2	12			27.8	15	54
16.2	11	23.5	16	1.5%	1	32.4	22	68
28.9	13	22.2	10			26.7	12	45
23.3	7	16.7	5			40.0	12	30
19.1	8	11.9	5			50.0	21	42
27.3	6	13.6	3			36.4	8	22
		40.0	2			60.0	3	5
								0
214		**201**		**1**		**438**		**1431**
15.0%		**14.0%**				**30.6%**		

with an overall average of 60.7 percent. White chert was heavily favored for adze-making by the ethnographic Aborigines residing around the Warburton Ranges Mission. Yet exotic stone, as defined above, was used in adze-making too, throughout the Puntutjarpa sequence, with an overall average of 26.7 percent. To understand these results we must comprehend the total pattern presented by the data and not just the statistically dominant trend represented by white chert.

As regards efficiency of procurement, we already know that white chert was far easier to obtain than the exotic materials, but what about mechanical efficiency? How did the exotic stones at Puntutjarpa compare with locally available materials in their relative efficiency at performing certain tasks (specifically, scraping hard woods)? All of the signs of edge damage, shape and size of slugs, and step flaking on the archaeological adzes matched the characteristics that were diagnostic of this kind of use on the ethnographic specimens observed in this study. A simple wood-scraping experiment was designed and carried out to replicate the ethnographic use by holding all variables constant except lithic raw material, which was varied in each repetition of the experiment. These experiments are described in detail elsewhere (Bronstein, 1977), so a brief summary here will suffice. A variety of isotropic stones was collected from the Warburton Ranges area and other localities in the Western Desert to provide a sample for the

ZONES	STRATA	WARBURTON PORPHYRY		QUARTZ (including quartz crystal)		QUARTZITE	
(dates based on C-14)							
< 185 years	AX	4.4%	34	51.4%	396	8.8%	6
	BX	5.7	93	52.8	865	6.9	11
A	CX	7.1	187	52.0	1363	7.9	20
	DX	6.5	246	54.5	2073	6.7	25
	EX	5.9	269	53.7	434	7.2	32
	FX	6.8	253	50.9	1899	8.4	3
1500 AD	GX	9.1	438	48.7	2333	10.9	E
	HX	10.8	400	47.8	1751	12.5	4
Upper rockfall zone	IZ	14.7	457	41.2	1285	16.8	
	JZ	13.6	181	45.7	610	16.3	
	KZ	19.8	318	45.1	725	14.6	
	LZ	15.7	100	50.2	319	13.1	
B	M5	14.3	1168	46.7	3803	19.9	
	N5	11.1	1093	54.0	5321	16.7	
4700 BC	O5	10.1	885	55.1	4835	15.4	
	P5	11.3	696	52.8	3241	15.9	
	Q5	14.3	665	46.8	2181	18.5	
	R5	15.7	596	40.4	1530	20.9	
C	S5	15.7	299	39.4	751	19.2	
8000 BC	T5	14.5	205	35.8	505	15.7	
	U5	12.3	56	28.7	131	12.1	
	V5	10.5	8	34.2	26	9.2	7
	X5			22.2	4	5.6	1
Total (actual number of specimens)		8,647		38,381		11,228	
Total percentage		11.2%		49.5%		14.5%	

Fig. 7. Relative percentages of lithic material by stratum; Trench 2, Puntutjarpa.

experiment. Exotic materials in this case were multicolored cherts from the Lake Throssel region, about 320 kilometers (200 miles) southwest of Warburton, and chrysoprase from the Wingellina Hills, about 240 kilometers (150 miles) east of Warburton. From these materials, replicas of a total of 25 adzes were produced by means of direct percussion with a small hammerstone. These adzes were hafted, in turn, to a Western Desert Aborigine wooden club that had formerly been used ethnographically in this same way. These adzes were hafted with spinifex resin adhesive, also produced by present-day Western Desert Aborigines.

Each adze operation required the operator to draw the hafted adze toward himself in the manner observed among contemporary Aborigines, with the angle of the bulbar face of the adze held as constant as possible against the fresh mulga wood being worked at an angle of 30–45 degrees throughout the experiment. These strokes continued, with force applied as evenly as possible, until the working edge had dulled to the extent that it no longer removed wood shavings, whereupon the adze was resharpened in its haft by means of direct percussion with a wooden percussor, and the work continued. Table 12 shows the number of useful strokes of wood-working wear obtained from each class of isotropic stone in the course of this experiment. Each phase of the experiment ended

RED CHERT		OPALINE		WHITE CHERT		AGATE		EXOTIC (including Wingellina chrysoprase)		TOTAL (actual number of specimens)
.5%	4	.9%	7	24.2%	86	3.1%	24	6.6%	51	770
.5	8	.7	11	22.3	365	4.3	71	6.8	111	1637
.5	14	.8	21	21.2	557	4.4	115	6.0	157	2622
.3	11	.9	33	20.5	782	4.6	176	6.0	220	3806
.4	17	.8	36	23.2	1050	3.6	163	5.3	229	4535
.3	10	1.2	45	23.7	882	4.3	162	4.4	163	3727
.3	16	1.1	51	20.1	962	5.2	250	4.6	219	4792
.1	5	.9	32	21.5	791	3.2	117	3.5	129	3687
.0	1	.5	16	21.4	667	3.5	109	1.8	57	3116
		.4	5	19.2	256	2.6	35	2.2	30	1335
.2	3	.2	4	16.6	267	2.2	35	1.2	20	1606
.2	1	1.6	10	16.4	104	1.4	9	1.6	10	636
.0	3	.3	25	16.5	1343	1.2	101	1.0	81	8146
.1	6	.4	38	15.7	1542	1.0	103	1.0	97	9845
.1	7	.3	22	16.3	1429	1.5	134	1.2	103	8768
.0	3	.2	13	16.9	1038	1.7	107	1.1	68	6140
.0	1	.2	11	16.8	784	1.5	72	1.7	81	4657
.2	6	.2	6	19.1	725	1.4	53	2.2	82	3790
.3	5	.1	2	21.2	404	1.8	35	2.4	46	1908
.2	3	.5	7	26.4	372	2.1	30	4.7	67	1411
		.4	2	40.4	184	2.9	13	3.3	15	456
				46.1	35					76
				72.2	13					18
124		397		14,738		1,914		2,055		77,484
.2%		.5%		19.0%		2.5%		2.6%		

(bracket grouping rows 10–12: 6693)

when the adze flake was reduced to a slug that became so narrow it could no longer be held in its haft when subjected to the mechanical forces imposed by this wood-working activity. These experiments, while informing us about the use-life of these implements vis-à-vis different lithic raw materials, also furnished exact replicas of adze slugs found archaeologically and ethnographically in the Western Desert.

The results of this series of experiments provide a baseline for evaluating the relative mechanical efficiency of these different types of stone in performing the kinds of wood-scraping tasks observed ethnographically in the Western Desert. Table 12 shows that white chert is by far the best material for scraping hard mulga wood. The preferences shown by Western Desert Aborigines, both past and present, for making adzes out of white chert can be understood readily in terms of both the mechanical efficiency and ready availability of this type of stone. Although exotic cherts rate second in mechanical efficiency to white chert, their edge-holding abilities are so much poorer than white chert, and their efficiency in relation to procurement is so low, that the fact that 26.7 percent of the adzes at Puntutjarpa were made from this kind of stone must be regarded as a significant anomaly. At the bottom of the scale we find opaline, representing a class of raw material with a mechanical efficiency of

Table 11. *Numbers and percentages of lithic raw materials used in making adzes and micro-adzes, Puntutjarpa Rockshelter*

Stratum	Warburton porphyry	Quartz	Quartzite	Red chert	Opaline	White chert	Agate	Exotic	(Dates based on C-14 zone)
AX	—	—	—	—	—	2 / 28.6%	—	5 / 71.4%	—
BX	—	1 / 4.5%	—	—	—	16 / 72.7%	1 / 4.5%	4 / 18.2%	← 185 YEARS
CX	—	—	—	—	1 / 2.4%	20 / 48.8%	4 / 9.8%	16 / 39.0%	—
DX	—	1 / 1.7%	2 / 3.3%	—	3 / 5.0%	37 / 61.7%	1 / 1.7%	16 / 26.6%	*A*
EX	—	—	2 / 2.9%	—	2 / 2.9%	42 / 60.9%	4 / 5.8%	19 / 27.5%	—
FX	1 / 1.9%	1 / 1.9%	2 / 1.9%	—	1 / 1.9%	36 / 67.9%	—	13 / 24.5%	—
GX	1 / 2.6%	5 / 13.2%	2 / 5.3%	—	1 / 2.6%	19 / 50.0%	3 / 7.9%	7 / 18.4%	← 1500 A.D.
HX	—	—	—	—	—	16 / 76.2%	1 / 4.8%	4 / 19.0%	—
IZ	—	—	—	—	—	—	—	1 / 100.0%	—
JZ	—	—	—	—	—	1 / 100.0%	—	—	*Upper rockfall zone*
KZ	—	—	—	—	—	2 / 66.7%	—	1 / 33.3%	—
LZ	—	—	—	—	—	—	—	—	—

M5	—	—	—	—	—	1 / 50.0%	—	1 / 50.0%	
N5	—	—	1 / 16.7%	—	—	4 / 66.7%	—	1 / 16.7%	
O5	—	—	1 / 20.0%	—	—	4 / 80.0%	—	—	← 4700 B.P.
P5	—	—	—	—	—	1 / 100.0%	—	—	B
Q5	—	1 / 33.3%	—	—	—	1 / 33.3%	—	1 / 33.3%	
R5	—	—	1 / 100.0%	—	—	—	—	—	
S5	—	—	—	—	—	1 / 50.0%	—	1 / 50.0%	
T5	—	—	—	—	—	3 / 75.0%	—	1 / 25.0%	← 8000 B.P.
U5	—	—	—	—	—	1 / 100.0%	—	—	C
V5	—	—	—	—	—	—	—	—	
X5	—	—	—	—	—	—	—	—	
Totals	2 / 0.6%	9 / 2.6%	10 / 2.9%	—	8 / 2.3%	207 / 60.7%	14 / 4.1%	91 / 26.7%	341 / 100%

Table 12. *Comparison by lithic raw material of useful strokes in working hardwood (Acacia aneura) with experimentally produced adzes*[a]

Lithic raw material	N	0–500 strokes	500–1000 strokes	1000–1500 strokes	1500–3000 strokes	3000–5000 strokes	5000–8000 strokes	8000–10,000 strokes	10,000–15,000+ strokes	Average of strokes
White chert	7			1			4	1	1	7,555
Exotic cherts	9		2	2	2	1		1	1	4,073
Warburton porphyry	3		1	1		1				1,602
Quartz	1		1	1						2,072
Quartzite	3		1	1			1			2,659
Opaline	1	1								78
Chrysoprase (exotic)	1					1				3,369
Total population	25	1	4	6	2	3	5	2	2	Overall Average 3,058

[a]After Bronstein (1977: Table 48). Note that, because of scarcity, no red chert or agate was available for these experiments.

152

only 1.03 percent of that of white chert. The wonder is that Aborigines used opaline at all for wood-scraping tasks, yet we find a total of eight adzes from Puntutjarpa that were made of this stone. It is possible that the opaline used in toolmaking at Puntutjarpa is not of local origin (though local material, of course, would be easiest to procure) but may have been collected from distant sources. Such an argument cannot be based on any presumptive desire by the Aborigines to obtain such material for its edge-holding properties vis-à-vis woodworking, since these are demonstrably poor. While the experiments point clearly to a mechanical explanation of preferences by the Aborigines for white chert in making adzes, they are increasingly ambiguous in explaining the relative preferences as one moves down the scale of technical efficiency for each class of isotropic stone. These results show that the continuous, low-level use of exotic cherts for adzemaking at Puntutjarpa cannot be explained by simple utilitarian arguments of efficiency of use or ease of procurement.

As shown elsewhere, adzes have relatively long use-lives in comparison with other items in the ethnographic Western Desert Aborigine stone toolkit. Although one might be tempted to argue that the disproportionate number of flaked stone adzes at Puntutjarpa derived from exotic sources might in some way be related to this fact, the results of Bronstein's experiments demonstrate that the exotic stone materials present at the site had less suitable edge-holding properties for this particular class of implements than did the locally available white chert. There is an anomalous relationship in this case, which is: if white chert was obviously the most efficient lithic raw material for adzemaking, both in terms of efficiency of procurement and use, why was exotic stone used at all for this purpose?

Yet this anomaly is precisely what one would predict for people living as nonseasonal, risk-minimizing hunter–gatherers like the present-day Western Desert Aborigines. It is, in fact, a signature of this particular mode of adaptation. It did no good to ask Aborigines about their preferences with regard to specific kinds of stone for certain tasks, despite the fact that they revealed such preferences in their behavior. Perhaps this was due to the casualness of their attitudes toward stone toolmaking and the everyday use of stone tools. In the Warburton area, the preference for white chert for adze making was virtually absolute, with the only exception being specific pieces of chert brought in or traded from distant, named localities. At Laverton, on the southwestern fringe of the Western Desert, a similar tendency was noted in 1966. There, Aborigines regularly made special visits to a large quarry containing dark bluish-gray chert, located on Mt. Weld Station, about 24 kilometers (15 miles) from the Laverton Aboriginal Reserve. Other experiments have shown the Mt. Weld material to have edge-holding properties comparable to the white chert found near Warburton when used to shape mulga wood, and at Laverton this type of stone was used entirely for adze making and for manufacture of circumcision knives. At Laverton, as at Warburton, tasks like the removal of the slab of mulga wood from the tree trunk for making a spearthrower were performed with stones that were immediately available on the ground where the woodworking activities took place – at least when no steel axes were available for this purpose.

One must realize that at Warburton and Laverton in 1966–70 the Aborigines were making increased use of steel axes and chisels for woodworking tasks. I found it interesting that stone tools were still made and used as much as they were on these Reserves, considering the ready availability and longevity of metal tools. Not surprisingly, it was the more traditionally oriented Aborigines, both old and young, who tended to persist in making and using stone tools.

When interviewed about the exotic or unusual cherts from which some of their adzes and knives were made, the Aborigines at Warburton and Laverton (and the nomadic desert dwellers discussed earlier) stated that these items came from specific localities that were a considerable distance away. In every case, the Aborigine possessing such imported stone artifacts was able to name and describe the exact place where the raw material was collected and give its totemic affiliation (that is, he was able to name the ancestral mythical character connected to that place), even though the man being interviewed may not himself have gone to that place to collect this stone. Sometimes I tested this knowledge by bringing isotropic stones back with me from the vicinity of various sacred sites that I had visited in the company of their cult-lodge "owners." Upon my return to Warburton, I would show these stones to the initiated men in the community, who in all cases correctly named the locality from which the stone had been collected and identified the mythical ancestor associated with it. These stones were then passed on to members of the appropriate cult-lodge, who were always glad to have them. The exotic cherts in their possession had been collected at or near various sacred sites, where they occurred near geographical landmarks of totemic significance. Adzes of such material were not regarded as sacred objects themselves, and they were carried openly in camp where women and children could see them. When asked, the Aborigines always discussed these with pride, not in the craftsmanship of the tools (which was sometimes poor) but in the raw material. The patrilineal totemic affiliation of the man being interviewed was always the same as that of the site from which the particular piece of isotropic stone had come. Worn adze slugs made of such exotic materials were simply discarded in the habitation camp area. No attempt was made to curate these items beyond their normal use-life.

In other words, these tools of imported stone were relics that were esteemed by the owner and his associates because of their close physical proximity to some important mythical and sacred event. They had become "righteous rocks." It was almost like watching a pilgrim from the Holy Land showing off a piece of the True Cross or some other souvenir of sacred importance. The stone had been collected at or near the sacred site and carried away by a member of the patrilineal cult-lodge affiliated with that site, in many cases then to be passed on to other members of the same cult-lodge as a token of their mutual affiliation by virtue of common patrilineal descent from the same mythical ancestor. Thus it was that these objects came to rest in habitation base-camps, often hundreds of miles from their place of origin.

How much of this behavior, many episodes of which were observed in the context of Aboriginal Reserves where contact with Europeans has been intense, should be regarded as reflecting traditional values or behavior? When visiting previously uncontacted or little contacted Aborigines in the Mt. Madley area of the Western Desert in 1970, I observed behavior exactly like this, so we can be assured that it was a normal feature of traditional desert life. But I suspect that on Reserves and in other contact situations this behavior has increased and reflects a growing desire by these displaced Aborigines to reassert and maintain their ties to distant sacred sites that are too far away now for them to visit regularly. This interpretation fits well with general tendencies for increased ceremonialism often observed on Aboriginal Reserves in and around the Western Desert. Access to motor vehicles now enables Aborigines to carry these relics farther than was probably the case in the past. For example, I have seen adzes of Wingellina chrysoprase at Laverton, over 800 kilometers (500 miles) southwest of the Wingellina Hills (where several important quarries associated with sacred sites are known to exist [Crawford and Tonkinson, 1969]).

Widespread distribution of such materials today may be due in part to post-contact factors, although there is evidence for far-ranging, Kula-like trading networks over much of the Western and Central Deserts in early- and pre-contact times (McCarthy, 1939: 425–9). At Laverton in 1966 I observed trade of this kind in progress. Sacred objects like incised boards and stones, decorated and incised pearlshells, emu-feather bundles, and other items were exchanged between male members of different totemic cult-lodges in a formal, ritualized manner. At least some of the incised stones were *churinga* of Central Desert origin, while the pearlshell objects came ultimately from the Kimberley District coastline, approximately 1,250 kilometers (780 miles) away as the crow flies. Unlike the exchange and transport of isotropic stones and artifacts made from them, this trade took place between patrilineages (i.e., totemic cult-lodges) rather than between members of the same patrilineage. While there is evidence for a traditionally active and widespread transport and trade of lithic and other materials, there is also evidence to suggest that present-day traffic in these items under modern, "reservation" conditions may be even more intense and widespread than in the past.

I am not suggesting that such sacred associations and trade, either of the intra- or inter-lineage variety, arising from these associations necessarily existed in the prehistoric past to account for the presence of exotic lithic materials for adzemaking at Puntutjarpa Rockshelter. To do that would be to commit the error of affirming the consequent, which I pointed out earlier. Just because the Western Desert Aborigines did it that way in the recent past does not mean they did it that way in the remote past. The argument by anomaly allows us to explain this situation more convincingly and economically than the argument by analogy. In the presence of exotic stones for adzemaking at Puntutjarpa, we have a "perturbation" that departs from any expectations or predictions based upon strictly utilitarian principles of mechanical efficiency or economy of effort. By explaining the circumstances of this anomaly, we can infer relationships between the ecological requirements for human adaptation in the Western Desert and the particular way in which people who have adapted in this manner will discard their lithic materials – inferences that are more compelling than any explanation based upon the use of direct analogy. Unless one wishes to indulge in fantasies such as imagining thousands of stone tools and flakes with tiny feet migrating on their own across the countryside like so many beetles, or in a kind of Deus ex machina view with beings from outer space sprinkling these items over the landscape like so many cosmic litterbugs, one must accept the premise that the presence of exotic lithic materials, as defined earlier, is circumstantial evidence of social networks along which such materials flowed. The question then is one of explaining the role of such networks in relation to the essential problems of adapting to the conditions of life in the Western Desert.

Anthropologists working in the Central and Western Deserts of Australia have already noted the importance of widely ramified kin networks that facilitate the sharing of food and access to basic resources (Spencer and Gillen, 1899; Berndt, 1959; Meggitt, 1962; Strehlow, 1965). Fascination with the complexities of how these networks operated, especially in relation to kin-terminology, sections and subsections, and cult-lodge affiliations, should not obscure the overriding concern particular groups of Aborigines had with using these networks as a means of overcoming risks of drought and other problems of scarcity in their respective habitats. In a region where water and other related basic resources are not regularly available on an annual seasonal basis, and where amounts of these resources may be limited even in the best of years, the ability of families to travel long distances to other areas that are better off than their own and to take up temporary residence with the people living in these places as a means of overcoming the economic uncertainties that act as limiting factors, was the key to long-term adaptive success in the human settlement of the Western Desert.

The presence of exotic lithic raw materials in the toolkits of present-day Aborigines in the Western Desert is prima facie evidence for such long-distance social networks and the resource sharing upon which they were based. One can generalize from this case by proposing that widely ramified, long-distance social networks will arise in human societies that live directly off the land wherever and whenever basic resources are subject to extreme fluctuations on an irregular and unpredictable basis. The more severe and unpredictable these fluctuations are, the more widely these social networks will extend from any given point within the region. If one provisionally accepts such a proposition, the exotic lithic raw materials at Puntutjarpa are most economically explained as evidence that such a system of widespread social networks geared to the requirements of overcoming or minimizing risks in a nonseasonal, high-risk region like the Western Desert was operating at Puntutjarpa continuously for at least the last 10,000 years. This argument is consistent with present faunal, floristic, and geomorphological evidence from Puntutjarpa that indicates little, if any, change in climate or resources during the post-Pleistocene period at or around the site. The same basic ecological conditions prevailed then as now, and the limiting factors imposed by these conditions were overcome by the Aborigines by means of an adaptive strategy – long-distance social networks – that can still be observed operating in the Western Desert. Isotropic stones of exotic origin thus serve as an "archaeological signature" of a nonseasonal, risk-minimizing mode of hunter–gatherer adaptation in the Western Desert of Australia and, it is likely, anywhere else that similar limiting factors have affected human settlement.

The inferences based upon this argument by anomaly cannot tell us exactly how these social networks were organized or operated in the prehistoric past. Were the exotic stones at Puntutjarpa passed on through inter- or intra-lineage exchanges? Did lineages exist at all there in prehistoric times? The answers to these questions lie beyond our available evidence. But by looking first at the material relations of different types of stone and stone tool classes, the functions of which are reasonably well understood, as they occur together in their final context of discard at the ancient habitation campsite of Puntutjarpa Rockshelter, we can recognize that something has continuously and consistently led to the presence of imported stones for making implements for working hardwood. A utilitarian examination of the procurement and edge-holding efficiency of these tools demonstrated that these imported stones were anomalous, since lithic materials with superior edge-holding qualities for this task were available much closer to the site. The dominant pattern (or "behavior in the aggregate") of using white chert for adzemaking, which is easily understood in relation to utilitarian arguments, is less interesting than the statistically minor pattern relating to the use of exotic lithic materials for making this class of implements at Puntut-jarpa. Whatever the "something" was that was drawing exotic stones to Puntutjarpa in varying frequencies for adzemaking at all times in the history of the site, it cannot have been a strictly practical consideration. By initially applying a utilitarian argument to the material relations of the lithic discards, we can reliably infer the operation of nonmaterial and nonutilitarian factors. These exotic rocks are "righteous" because the circumstances of their presence demonstrably depend more upon ideational and symbolic aspects of human behavior than they do upon practical ones.

At this point, one might feel compelled to ask: What about places like California, where many people lived aboriginally off the land in optimal physical environments and yet traded lithic materials in different directions and sometimes over long distances? The key point to keep in mind in such cases is that one must look first at utilitarian explanations for these long-distance imports before attempting to apply the sort of risk-minimizing argument I have proposed here. If there is a general principle of human adaptive behavior at work in the relationships I have described for the Western Desert Aborigines, both past and present, it can be tested effectively by applying utilitarian arguments having to do with efficiency of procurement, manufacture, and use before going on to consider higher-level explanations. My prediction would be that in optimal habitats, where stress imposed by some limiting factor is less directly felt than in a place like the Western Desert, long-distance trade and/or transport of "exotic" stones was due primarily to practical, utility-oriented considerations having to do with tool use rather than considerations based upon the need to extend social networks in order to gain access to basic resources in distant areas. I would urge that scholars working in areas like California consider applying such a test to their materials whenever they find evidence for long-distance transport and/or trade.

Tests of this kind could be applied to different societies in various parts of the world, and not just to hunter–gatherer groups. Micronesian atolls, for example, offer promising opportunities for research along these lines, since these are places that are periodically

subject to environmental stress in the form of tidal waves and typhoons, with the latter being especially severe because of the danger
that they will contaminate the lens of freshwater underlying each
island (Alkire, 1972: 4). One could suggest that the extraordinary
skills developed by many Micronesian atoll dwellers in boatbuilding,
seamanship, and long-distance navigation are an essential component of an adaptive response to periodic stress that typhoons impose
upon basic resources – especially water. Moreover, accounts of Micronesian seamanship emphasize the frequency and gusto with
which long-distance voyages are undertaken, even when no compelling economic or social reason is given for the voyage (Gladwin,
1970: 38). So here, too, we may have an anomaly of sorts in which
long-distance voyaging, with all the opportunities this activity presents for trade and even the movement of families off distressed
islands to better-favored areas such as the high islands in many parts
of Micronesia, may be most easily explained in relation to adaptive
requirements imposed by a limiting factor. Of course, the actual
sharing of food and access to resources in a case like this would be
structured quite differently from what one finds among Australian
Desert Aborigines, with a heavier emphasis on redistribution of
goods, since rank and lineage chiefs are an important part of Micronesian social structure in many areas (Alkire, 1972: 24–9). But from
an ethnoarchaeological point of view, one would expect to see physical residues of some kind that would serve to indicate the persistence
of long-distance social networks as mechanisms to overcome environmental stress. No doubt the anthropological universe abounds
with potential cases of this kind, where limiting factors in the natural
environment can be identified and studied in relation to specific
behavioral responses that can be expected to produce distinctive
physical residues.

Materialist approaches to human behavior
By looking first at the utilitarian relationships of material residues in
their final resting place, we can avoid the pitfall of prematurely
imputing high-level symbolic or ideational explanations, thereby
making it possible to infer accurately when and under what conditions these ideational variables were operating to account for the
totality of the material residues. But this materialist approach to
human behavior should not be confused with a materialist philosophy. The fact that exotic stones at Puntutjarpa can, ultimately, be
regarded as an expression of human adaptive responses to the requirements of life in the Western Desert in no way undermines the
importance of ideational factors in explaining patterns of discard
and residue formation there. As this case study shows, living archaeology is a peculiar kind of anthropology – one with an unabashed

materialist bias. As anthropologists we are interested in questions of symbolism and meaning, but as archaeologists we are inclined to examine such questions from a materialist point of view. Instead of assuming beforehand, as some Marxist philosophers of materialism might have us do, that symbolic and social variables are somehow to be viewed as epiphenomena in explaining behavior when compared with variables of a material nature, living archaeology uses the materialist approach to confront the totality of variables that may account for the observed patterns of residues. Symbolic systems can play an essential role in human adaptation, and, as the case of "righteous rocks" among Western Desert Aborigines and at Puntutjarpa shows, they can be approached from the same materialist point of view by the archaeologist doing living archaeology as such items of behavioral hardware as technology and subsistence.

7

The importance of being different

Anomalies, as described in the preceding chapter, are not things unto themselves, but must be seen in relation to contrasting regularities. Such regularities may be general laws or lawlike statements of relationship, or they may relate to local or regional patterns. However general or localized they may be, these regularities are essential as a point of reference if one is to recognize and explain anomalies when they occur. Even if the regularity being compared is only provisional, it can still serve as a basis for discovering anomalies. Indeed, all statements of regularity are provisional to a degree, since they are always being tested and thus are expected to be subject to modification in the light of new evidence. So, like anomalies, laws and lawlike statements are relative and must be understood in relation to the process of testing to which they are constantly subjected in science. When that testing stops, these laws cease to be scientific propositions and become dogma.

The foregoing is merely a restatement of the earlier notion that laws, like anomalies, are not self-contained and permanent truths. It is the dissonance between law and anomaly in science that makes new discoveries a possibility, and this is as true in archaeology as it is in any branch of the physical and natural sciences. To demonstrate this idea, I shall make a trial effort in this chapter to extend the argument by anomaly to the Central Desert of Australia, using regularities in the Western Desert as a point of reference. I consider this a trial effort because it deals with material gathered in archaeological surveys and excavations in the Central Desert during 1973–4 that is still being analyzed in a variety of ways. The work on this project is far from complete, and the results of this work will, doubtless, affect our earlier ideas about prehistoric human adaptation in the Western Desert. Yet, incomplete as our findings are at this stage, we can begin to explain variability in Australian desert prehistory only if we follow Collingwood's (1946: 273) classic dictum and start right away by asking questions. How do we know what questions to ask when confronting an archaeological terra incognita like the Central Desert? The answer is that these questions must arise in regard to relationships perceived earlier, in this case in the Western Desert. In other words, new questions can be asked only in relation to questions that were asked earlier. They must be asked in the right order, and that order is derived from the recognition and subsequent reexamination of regularities in the light of anomalies to them. From the viewpoint of the Western Desert discussed earlier, the Central Desert is different in several important ways. While the Central and Western Deserts are more alike than different, at least when seen in global perspective, it is the differences rather than the similarities between them that tell us the most about prehistoric human adaptation in this part of the world.

Extending the anomaly[8]

The Western Desert of Australia was defined in largely negative terms in Chapter 3 as a region of extreme scarcity and unreliability of water and related key resources. It was cited as the ultimate case of stress due to high risk in arid Australia, and a risk-minimizing model was presented to explain how people have adapted traditionally to such conditions. But arid Australia is not an undifferentiated desert mass. Although there are few sharply defined subregions or ecological zones within the Australian desert as a whole, there are shifts in key variables that can be examined to see what effects they might have had on human settlement.

Perhaps we ought to visualize a radiating series of hypothetical transects, each extending outward from the Western Desert until a significant ecological shift is observed. A line drawn northeastward from the Warburton Range as a kind of arbitrary central point within the Western Desert leads into the Tanami Desert, an area of low rainfall but increased annual seasonality. This seasonality increases as one proceeds farther north and approaches the tropical monsoon system of Arnhem Land and the Australian tropics generally. Although unmistakably a desert, conditions in this region are more predictable than those in the Western Desert. The Walbiri Aborigines, whose traditional range extends over much of the Tanami, can be viewed in relation to this increased reliability of water and related resources.

A line extending eastward from the Western Desert leads to the west edge of the Simpson Desert, the driest part of Australia (with an annual average rainfall of less than five inches) but one which contains permanent artesian springs of drinkable water and river channels that sometimes carry large volumes of water from other areas. Unlike the Western Desert, this is a region of coordinated drainage, and this drainage pattern more than makes up for local deficiencies in rainfall. A significant amount of almost any heavy rainfall over a vast catchment area of Central Australia, including Alice Springs and the Macdonnell Range as well as a large area to the south, will flow eventually into one or more of a series of braided stream channels (most notably, the Finke, Neales, Alberga, Todd, and Macumba Rivers and their many tributaries and branches) that lead into this area. Incongruous as it seems, flooding is a major problem today in this driest of Australian deserts, and the Commonwealth Government of Australia is currently relocating the Central Australian Railway line from Marree to Alice Springs to a route farther west where such flooding as occurred in 1973 (the same exceptional rains that caused the molluscan eco-disaster among the Anbara in Arnhem Land) will not be as serious. There is something altogether bizarre about experiencing massive floods in and around these channels under a sunny, cloudless – and rainless – sky. The nature of this drainage pattern, with its long-distance transport of water collected from a huge catchment area, could be expected to have had decisive effects on aboriginal human settlement along the west edge of the Simpson Desert.

Another transect could be extended in a northwesterly direction through the Great Sandy Desert all the way to the coast, at Eighty-Mile Beach. The ecological conditions here have a touch of the bizarre, too, although in a manner altogether different from the Simpson. The Great Sandy Desert is the northwestern extension of the Western Desert, and it extends, quite literally, to the water's edge. It is one of those exceptional coastline areas in Australia that do not experience relatively high rainfall. Today one can drive along the main highway from Port Hedland to Broome and observe classic Western Desert topography and flora, mainly parallel sandhills and spinifex along with patches of mulga, termite hills, and other familiar features, sloping gently downhill in a northwesterly direction to the Indian Ocean, which is sometimes visible from the road. Here, then, is the Western Desert, much the same as we know it elsewhere, but with an additional coastal-marine component that could have made an essential difference to the way of life of the aboriginal inhabitants. The idea of a Western Desert mode of adaptation that included fishing and shellfish collecting presents intriguing possibilities for further research.

Each of the preceding suggestions is intended to show some of the latent possibilities that appear when one begins to consider different parts of arid Australia in relation to a baseline habitat and its characteristic mode of adaptation – in this case the Western Desert and the risk-minimizing adaptation practiced there by aboriginal human populations. By extending hypothetical transects outward from the central part of the Western Desert until a shift in a significant ecological variable occurs, we are laying the groundwork for recognizing anomalies in relation to variations in human behavior. Do significant correlations exist between floristic boundaries, for example, and variations in human behavior along these transects? If such correlations occur, can we then posit behavioral linkages between such a biotic shift and the observed variability in human residues? Arid Australia can be regarded as a kind of large-scale, natural laboratory for examining human adaptive behavior with respect to variations in key ecological factors. In 1973 we began to apply the approach by anomaly by extending a transect to an area of the Central Desert of Australia that lies in the James Range, Northern Territory.

A different desert

Somewhere in the vicinity of the Finke River and its tributary channels we encounter a kind of geomorphic Rubicon that gives definition to some of the important differences between the Western and Central Deserts. By the time one has traveled northeastward from Warburton to the Finke, one has already crossed at least two floristic boundaries that might have affected aboriginal adaptive behavior. Edible quandong (*Santalum acuminatum*), which was an important staple food both in good years and in times of drought in large areas of the Western Desert, has disappeared; although, somewhere in this area one also begins to encounter edible "bush potatoes" (*Ipomoea costata*) and "yams" (*Vigna lanceolata*), which assumed the role of dietary staples among many Central Desert people.

There is, however, a geographic contrast of potentially greater importance that sets the Central Desert off from the Western Desert, and this has to do with water supplies (always a fundamental concern in any desert area). Despite the predominance of sandhill country, the terrain to the northeast, after one crosses the Finke, is more varied than is generally true for the Western Desert. Here, as in the Western Desert, rainfall is low and basically nonseasonal. But, unlike the Western Desert, surface rainfall catchments are more common and closer together, mainly because of the rocky ranges that occur intermittently in more or less east–west lines throughout the area. Hilly topography like the James Range, the Ooraminna Range, the Waterhouse Range, the Train Hills, the Rodinga Range, and the Macdonnell Range characterize this region at least as much as do sandhills and stony "gibber" plains. These ranges are scored by deep cavities and gaps, like a mouthful of enormous old, decayed teeth, that contain well-shaded pools of rainwater and even some freshwater springs. There are a few places like this in the Western Desert, most notably in areas such as the Rawlinson and Petermann Ranges, but these tend to be few and far between, especially in the west.

The James Range region in particular, lying parallel and in close proximity to the Finke River drainage, can be viewed as an area that was transitional both in terms of desert geography and Aboriginal behavior. Looking westward from this "boundary" area and taking the point of view of an anthropologist long acquainted with the Aranda and other Central Desert Aborigine groups, T. G. H. Strehlow describes the Western Desert:

> This vast stretch of country is not really a desert, except for the extreme poverty and unreliability of its surface waters. In the absence of reliable rainfall records it can merely be estimated that the general amount of rain received is only two-thirds or half that of the Aranda-speaking area. Hence the Western Desert lacks – except in its eastern border lands – those large river systems, flowing springs, and permanent waterholes that once permitted the Aranda to develop their intricate social and cultural institutions. [Strehlow, 1965: 122]

In comparing these two regions and the human societies inhabiting them, Strehlow noted how some social institutions found among the Aranda were noticeably less well developed in the Western Desert. In particular, the Western Desert people appeared to have weaker subsection systems (a debatable argument), fewer myths and sacred songs, and sacred traditions that were generally shorter and poorer than those of the Aranda. Perhaps most interesting was Strehlow's idea that Aranda respect for totem animals – which meant that an Aranda man did not kill or eat his own totem animal – fostered de facto game reserves within the environs of sacred sites (Strehlow, 1965: 143–4). Nothing like this is described for the Western Desert, where the Aborigines could not afford the luxury of such behavior and, as far as we can tell, ate whatever they could catch or collect. Recent studies (Strehlow, 1965: 123; Tindale, 1974: 229) also tend to place a boundary between the Pitjantjatjara and Arandic linguistic blocs in the western end of the James Range, more or less in line with and to the west of the James Range. Of course, any attempt to identify cultural or linguistic boundaries between groups in this region must be tempered by a recognition of the high degree of nomadism and the widespread visiting that were characteristic of both groups as they were observed in the early historic period.

Strehlow was commenting on the Western Desert Aborigines from the Aranda point of view. Looking the other way across the Finke, from a Western Desert perspective, one can see the Central Desert as a region of expanded opportunities due to the availability of certain key resources, especially water. Much earlier, C. Strehlow (1920: 3–4) noted that the Aranda and "Loritja" (a Pitjantjatjara-speaking group whose range probably extended east of the Finke) of the area near the Hermannsburg Mission ate a wide variety of edible seeds and bulbs that they processed using two different types of stone-grinding implements; Mahlstein ("milling stone") and Reibstein ("grinding stone"). This is of interest because the historic Western Desert Aborigines did all of their seed and plant preparation on a single type of grinding slab appliance (*tjiwa*), suggesting a slightly greater variety of stone-grinding implements in this Central Desert area than one finds further to the west. Spencer and Gillen omitted any detailed discussion of Central Desert stone-grinding implements in their work, but they illustrated and described a wider variety of flaked stone tools than one finds among historic and ethnographic Western Desert Aborigines. To these also can be added the manufacture and use of ground-edge stone axes in the Central Desert, something rarely seen in the Western Desert and acquired there only through trade. These and other ethnographic descriptions, when compared with existing information about the Western Desert people, point to the Central Desert as an area of slightly greater technological specialization.

Both Central and Western Desert Aborigines practiced the art of rock and cave painting in historic times, and a general comparison of these art styles suggests a gross difference that may be important. Western Desert cave and rock paintings consist entirely of small designs, often in large numbers in any one place. Central Desert Aborigines, on the other hand, often created single large designs that cover all or most of the area being decorated. The famous vertical-striped patterns documented by Spencer and Gillen (1899: 170–9) at Emily Gap, a few kilometers east of Alice Springs, and the serpentine painting at the Walbiri sacred cave of Ngama, 29 kilometers (18 miles) southwest of Yuendumu, Northern Territory (Meggitt, 1962: 68, 226), are perhaps the two best documented examples, but other massive designs at sacred localities in the Central Desert area are known from our 1973 surveys in the Ooraminna Range and the Train Hills. Smaller-sized painted designs occur at Central Desert sites, too, sometimes with the larger motifs but more often without these present, in panels that closely resemble their Western Desert counterparts. In the Central Desert one also finds small caves decorated with negative handprints in red ochre, something that is totally absent in the Western Desert. Aside from some possible minor exceptions, all of the painted motifs familiar to an observer of Western Desert Aborigines can be found in many Central Desert sites, often in contexts and combinations similar to those in the Western Desert. But the Central Desert area shows greater stylistic complexity than the west in historic times, with the additional presence of large-scale and negative handprint motifs. Without getting into the finer points of stylistic comparison, it is apparent that ethnographic Central Desert rock and cave paintings are more varied than those of the Western Desert. Both Western and Central Desert sites contain many examples of rock engraving, too, although the practice

Bold designs of a characteristic Central Desert rock painting in
a small cave to the east of the James Range. These designs
show signs of have been "freshened" or touched up at intervals,
in contrast to the superposition of motifs found extensively in
the Western Desert and, to a lesser degree, in the Central Desert as well.

of rock engraving was prehistoric and did not occur ethnographically except in the attentuated form of rock poundings described by
Mountford (1976: 74–81). The farther west one goes into the Western Desert, however, the simpler the rock engravings become, with
fewer motifs and less numerous designs in any one place of occurrence. Although relatively complex motifs occur at localities like the
Cleland Hills (Edwards, 1968) in the eastern part of the Western
Desert, by the time one reaches the Warburton Ranges engraved
designs consist of nothing more than engraved circles, concentric
circles, and occasional emu or macropod tracks.

So when looked at from a Western Desert perspective, the ethnographic literature suggests a kind of added complexity for social and
ceremonial activities, stone toolkits, and artistic styles in the Central
Desert. While these aspects of human behavior in these two subregions of the Australian desert were clearly cognate and possessed
essential similarities, the variations are also apparent and require
explanation. Contemporary and historic ethnographies imply an
"additive" relationship in which the Central Desert people possessed

James Range East Rockshelter during the 1974 excavations.
The photograph was taken from the opposite side of the gap in
the James Range in which this site complex lies.

most of the attributes found farther west along with additional ones
that were unique to the Center. These ethnographies also indicated
that the James Range and neighboring regions would be a worth-
while area for examining this relationship archaeologically, since it
was the geomorphic "borderland" where these contrasts became
most evident. Finally, the James Range itself was found to contain
rock formations with stratified caves and rockshelters similar in basic
size and character to those excavated and tested in the Warburton
Range area (especially Puntutjarpa). Here, it seemed, was a good
place to start exploring the ecological and cultural anomalies of the
Central Desert in relation to the Western Desert model of aboriginal
risk-minimizing behavior.

The James Range East site complex
The James Range East site is a cluster of small rockshelters situated
on both sides of a small but steep-sided gap in the James Range on
the property of Deep Well station, Northern Territory, about 775
kilometers (480 miles) northeast of the Warburton Range. There is a
small and rather ephemeral waterhole a short distance from the
principal rockshelters, but the best water source is a series of shaded
pools in the bottom of a rock gully about one-fifth of a kilometer
east of the site. These pools are easily reached from the rockshelters
and could have served as the principal water source for the Aboriginal inhabitants. As at Puntutjarpa Rockshelter, the sediments in the
James Range East deposits appear to be entirely aeolian in origin,
but they show greater differentiation in color and/or texture than

was true at Puntutjarpa. Again, like Puntutjarpa, the excavated deposits in the principal rockshelter contained two sequential rockfall layers, although at James Range East the larger and more extensive rockfall was the earlier of the two – the reverse of the Puntutjarpa rockfall layers.

The principal excavations occurred in Trench 1 within the North Cave (Figs. 9 and 10), with Trench 2 extending across the front of the North Cave to the Main Cave, and Trench 3 continuing out onto the sandy, open-air flat in front of the Main Cave (Fig. 8). A detailed progress report on the James Range East excavations is currently in press, so I shall limit my discussion here to points that are germane to exploring and explaining archaeological variability in the Australian Desert. As shown diagrammatically in Fig. 11, these excavations have revealed a two-part stratigraphic sequence containing evidence of Aboriginal habitation extending from the historic to protohistoric present back at least 5,000 years. The later phase of human occupation has been termed *James Range II,* and is marked by a series of layers of dark sediments containing hearths, stone artifacts, and abundant faunal remains. The earlier phase of human occupation, termed *James Range I,* occurs in underlying layers of yellowish-brown and red sandy sediments. There sediments contained stone artifacts but lacked any datable hearth material. On stratigraphic grounds, however, James Range I clearly predates James Range II. A sequence of eight radiocarbon dates was obtained from various hearths and charcoal concentrations ranging from 2690±260 B.C. to 1755±80 A.D. There were no reversals in the radiocarbon series, and the dates in this series were consistent with the depositional history of the site as far as we have yet been able to reconstruct it. But no radiocarbon dates were available from levels below a depth of 28 inches in deposits associated with James Ranges I cultural residues. This ladder of radiocarbon dates makes it possible for us to make specific comparisons between human residues at the Puntutjarpa and James Range East Rockshelters over the last 5,000 years.

A total of 1,286 flaked stone tools, cores, and fragments showing signs of intentional retouch were found in the excavated levels of Trench 1 at James Range East, along with 79 ground and pecked stone tools (mainly fragments) and 19,668 unmodified stone flakes. This comes to 915 flaked stone tools, cores, and flakes per cubic meter. While hardly what one would regard as a poor site for artifact residues, Trench 1 at James Range East is quantitatively overshadowed by Trench 2 at Puntutjarpa. There a total of 1,431 flaked stone tools, cores, and fragments were found, along with 37 ground stone implements and 76,018 unmodified stone flakes. This averages 3,459 flaked stone implements, cores, and flakes per cubic mater – that is, 3.8 times the flaked stone artifact density at Trench 1, James Range East, with the difference consisting mainly of un-

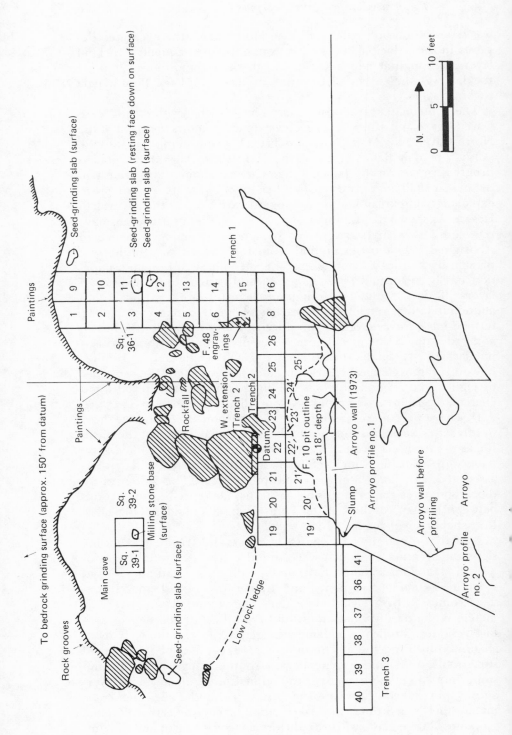

Main cave

To bedrock grinding surface (approx. 150' from datum)

Rock grooves

Paintings

Paintings

Seed-grinding slab (surface)

Milling stone base (surface)

Sq. 39-2

Sq. 39-1

Low rock ledge

Seed-grinding slab (surface)

Seed-grinding slab (resting face down on surface)

Seed-grinding slab (surface)

Sq. 36-1

Sq. 36-2

Rockfall

W. extension Trench 2

Trench 2

F. 48 engravings

Datum

F. 10 pit outline at 18" depth

Trench 1

Slump

Arroyo wall (1973)

Arroyo profile no.1

Arroyo wall before profiling

Arroyo profile no. 2

Arroyo

Trench 3

N

0   5   10 feet

1 9
2 10
3 11
4 12
5 13
6 14
7 15
8 16

26 25 24 23 22 21 20 19
25' 24' 23' 22' 21' 20' 19'

40 39 38 37 36 41

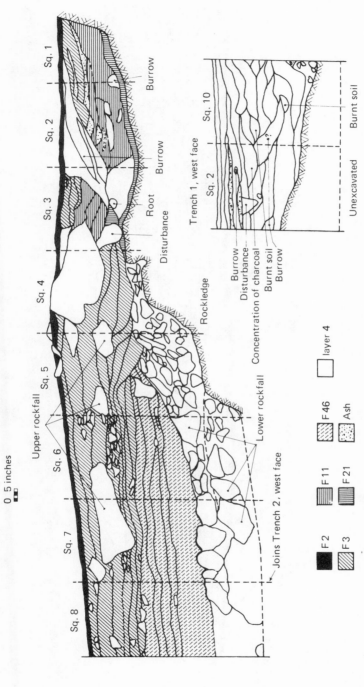

0 5 inches

Burrow

Burrow

Root

Disturbance

Upper rockfall

Sq. 1   Sq. 2   Sq. 3   Sq. 4   Sq. 5   Sq. 6   Sq. 7   Sq. 8

Rockledge

Concentration of charcoal

Lower rockfall

Joins Trench 2, west face

Trench 1, west face

Sq. 10   Sq. 2

Burnt soil

Unexcavated

Burrow
Disturbance
Concentration of charcoal
Burnt soil
Burrow

F 2   F 46
F 3   F 21   layer 4
F 11   Ash

Fig. 9. James Range East; Trench 1, South Face.

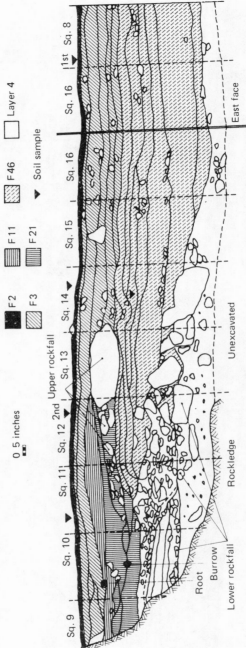

Fig. 10. James Range East; Trench 1, North Face.

modified flakes. Yet there were over twice as many ground and pecked stone implements at James Range East than Puntutjarpa. The overall ratio of one identifiable flaked stone implement to fifteen unretouched flakes at Trench 1, James Range East, is low compared with the overall average ratio at Trench 2, Puntutjarpa, of 1:53. When roughly contemporaneous strata at Puntutjarpa and James Range East are compared, the differences in these ratios are even more dramatic. Around 180 A.D. the ratio at Puntutjarpa was 1:34, while at James Range East it was 1:16. Around 1500 A.D. the ratio at Puntutjarpa was 1:33, while at James Range East it was 1:12. And around 2000 B.C. it was 1:21 at Puntutjarpa, while at James Range East it was 1:23. So it seems that, while core reduction and stone toolmaking activities took place at James Range East throughout the history of human occupation there, these activities were less important there than was true at the same time periods at Puntutjarpa. Perhaps these differences can help us to understand why only two hammerstones were recovered from Trench 1 at James Range East (and, indeed, from the entire James Range East excavation), whereas nine hammerstones were found in Trench 2 at Puntutjarpa.

To what extent are the simple differences between amounts of tools and waste flakes at these two sites reflected in the attributes and relative frequencies of the types of stone tools that were present? Figures 11 and 6 summarize the percentage frequency distribution and absolute numbers of various classes of flaked stone tools by stratum in Trench 1 at James Range East and in Trench 2 at Puntutjarpa, respectively. By inspection, the artifact classes represented at these two sites under the same typological heading ("adzes," "micro-adzes," "backed blades," etc.) are similar, although detailed and specific comparisons of qualitative and metrical attributes within each category are in progress that should inform us about the actual degrees of similarity between these two sites. So, in a sense, these categories are provisional. We already know, for example, that a much higher percentage of "Tula" adzes and adze slugs and their micro-adze counterparts are present in the James Range East assemblage than is the case at Puntutjarpa, where the ratio between Tula and non-Tula type adzes and slugs was almost 1:1 throughout the sequence.(Tula adzes are unifacially retouched scrapers fashioned on semidiscoidal flakes with the working edge opposite the striking platform of the flake; non-Tula adzes are the same as Tulas except that the working edge or edges occur along the lateral edges of the flake. Examples of Non-Tula adzes and Tula adze slugs are illustrated in Fig. 5, and metrical attributes of Tula and non-Tula adzes and slugs are presented in Gould, 1977: 82–3). We also know that the shapes of backed blades found at James Range East vary to a much greater degree than was true for backed blades at Puntutjarpa. At James Range East, for

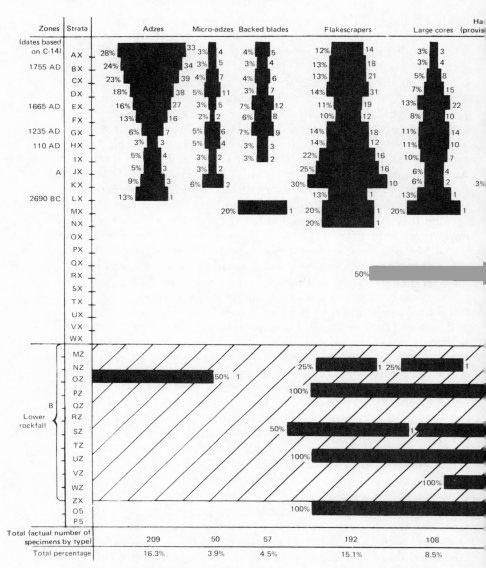

Fig. 11. Flaked stone tool types by stratum; Trench 1, James Range East Rockshelter.

example, we encounter backed blades of angular shape (triangular, trapezoidal, etc.) that are utterly absent from the Puntutjarpa assemblage. So already it is apparent that some specific differences exist within as well as between these stone tool categories, and these differences will be explored as research continues with this material.

However, at the level of analysis represented in Figs. 6 and 11, we can see that the similarities in stone tools at these two sites outweigh

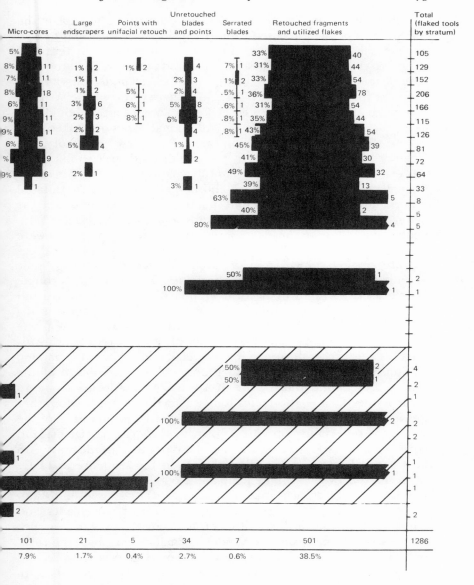

the differences. In other words, the lithic traditions represented at Puntutjarpa and James Range East are cognate and have been throughout the duration of human habitation at both sites. But, since we have declared ourselves to be in search of anomalies, it is primarily the differences rather than the similarities that concern us here. Variability exists between the lithic inventories at James Range East and Puntutjarpa, albeit on a small scale, and explaining this variability should prove more interesting than trying to explain the similarities. For the purpose of this discussion, it is sufficient to deal only on the simplest level of differentiation, that is, in terms of categories that even a casual observer would agree are different.

All of the major stone tool types, both of flaked and ground stone, that were found at Puntutjarpa and elsewhere so far in the Western Desert are also well represented at James Range East, although not always in the same proportions. Additional types of flaked and ground stone tools appear in the James Range East inventory that have not been found at all or to any significant degree so far in the Western Desert generally or at Puntutjarpa in particular. These additional tool types include large endscrapers, points with unifacial retouch, unretouched blades and points, serrated blades, lenticular seedgrinders, single basin grinding slabs, and ground edge axe fragments. In addition to these types, several individual specimens were found in Trench 2 at James Range East that represent other types that are already known from the archaeological and ethnographic literature on Central Australian Aborigines. These include a couple of Leilira blades (used by historic Aranda Aborigines as knives and heads for fighting picks) and muller bases and a single fragment of a double-basin grinding slab as well as an unusual adze slug of a type known to occur in the Lake Eyre region of northeastern South Australia. At this gross and preliminary level of comparison, the general relationship between the post-Pleistocene lithic assemblage of the Central Desert and that of the Western Desert appears to be an additive one. That is, the James Range East site complex (and other sites in the James Range region surveyed in 1973) contains all of the stone tool types and subtypes known in the Western Desert and more besides. As Fig. 11 shows, the tool types that are distinctive to the Central Desert appear relatively late in the sequence at James Range East, between around 4,000 and 2,000 years ago. These items present some differences that are technological, as opposed to simply formal, in such things as the appearance of true blades and points made on blades as well as ground edge axes. Large struck flakes of sandstone (from the Sonder Formation, in which the rock-shelters of the James Range East site complex occur) were also found in association with many of the groundstone fragments, supporting the idea that slabs of local sandstone were being quarried and reduced at the site as part of the process there of manufacturing seed-grinding implements. Yet despite all of this technological and typological enlargement of the total lithic inventory, the percentage total of all these additions never exceeded the peak of 11.7 percent (Stratum BX) around 1800 A.D. and averaged 5.4 percent overall. Thus all typological and technological variability in the lithic inventory at James Range East in comparison with Western Desert stone tools occurred within the last 4,000 years and involved less than 12 percent of the total toolkit at all times during that period.

Seen in a wider Australian perspective, there are two levels of additive change reflected in the Puntutjarpa and James Range East lithic assemblages. At one level we can consider these additions as part of a number of changes taking place all over Australia (except for Tasmania). Both at Puntutjarpa and James Range East we can observe the appearance of adzes, micro-adzes, and backed blades during the post-Pleistocene. Elsewhere (Gould, 1969; 1973) I have argued that the addition of these kinds of implements to a desert assemblage consisting of a rather generalized array of large items subsumed under the heading, "Australian core tool and scraper tradition," (Bowler, Jones, Allen, and Thorne, 1970: 52) is the regional desert version of an Australian-wide tendency to add small tools to the already existing large tool assemblage. This "Australian small tool tradition" embraces a wide range of tool types that may differ from one part of Australia to another. Pirri points, Kimberley points, Tula (and non-Tula or "Burren") adzes and slugs, backed blades, and blades without backed retouch (such as butted blades like those found widely in South Australia and pointed blades such as are found in many late sites in southwestern Australia) are among the varied implements that can be regarded as "small tools." While it is likely that most or all of these small tool types were hafted when used (Mulvaney, 1966: 87–8; 1975: 229), J. P. White and D. Thomas (White and Thomas, 1972: 278–9, Plate 7:1) have also noted that certain ethnographic New Guinea people have been observed making use of tiny, untrimmed stone flakes for cutting and scraping tasks, suggesting that small size alone is not necessarily indicative of hafting.

The idea of stone toolmaking "traditions" here is not all-encompassing in terms of culture or technology as a whole. A tradition can exist alongside other traditions, and variations or subtraditions can exist within a tradition. The tradition concept provides a framework for considering localized variations in time and space. In the case of the Australian small tool tradition, different tool types were added (and in a few cases, subtracted) at different times in different areas. The adzemaking subtradition seems, on present evidence, to have been the first to appear, with two stratigraphically confirmed occurrences of Pleistocene age in widely separated parts of Australia. Several small adze slugs of non-Tula type were found in contexts dating around 13,500 years ago at Seton Cave on Kangaroo Island, South Australia (R. Lampert,[9] pers. comm.), and a partially worn micro-adze, also of non-Tula type, was found in contexts of approximately the same date at Devil's Lair Rockshelter near Cape Leeuwin, in the southwestern corner of Western Australia (Dortch, 1973: 106–7).

178   *The importance of being different*

These finds are consistent with the appearance of micro-adzes and adzes in the earliest occupied levels at Puntutjarpa at some time probably between 10,000 and 12,000 years ago. The subtradition of adzemaking was already well established by the time Puntutjarpa Rockshelter was first occupied by man. This adzemaking subtradition continued unbroken throughout the post-Pleistocene of arid Australia, with little change aside from a general tendency for adzes to increase in size until the ethnographic present. The presence of adze and micro-adze slugs is compelling evidence for hafting, since it is mechanically impossible to replicate the characteristic attributes of shape, step flaking, and edge damage of these slugs by hand holding them during use as hardwood scrapers. Such replication is possible only with the mechanical assistance of hafting.

In the Western and Central Deserts, backed blades appear as a later component of the small tool tradition. At Puntutjarpa it is hard to fix a firm date for the initial appearance of backed blades, but, on stratigraphic grounds, it is unlikely to have occurred before about 4,000 years ago. At James Range East they seem to have appeared sometime around 3,200 years ago, although one example was found in stratigraphic contexts dating to over 5,000 years ago. A single occurrence like this, however, is more easily explained as having been shifted out of position by some kind of disturbance within the site deposit, perhaps due to scuffing and trampling by the ancient inhabitants or movement caused by a burrowing lizard. However, backed blades at both Puntutjarpa and James Range East went out of use by the historic period, and there is not a single documented case of ethnographic desert Aborigines – or, for that matter, of historic Aborigines anywhere in Australia – manufacturing backed blades. This particular small tool subtradition appeared relatively late and then disappeared shortly before the arrival of Europeans in Australia. The sudden and late disappearance of backed-blade making in protohistoric times is surely one of the most intriguing and puzzling questions in Australian archaeology.

The adzemaking and backed blade subtraditions are both represented at each of these sites, and their histories there seem to conform in general to their occurrence as part of the small tool tradition as known more widely in Australia. At this level of analysis, they are most easily understood as regional expressions of the general phenomenon I have termed the Australian small tool tradition. But the presence of additional small tool types at James Range East suggests that additional variations on this general theme were taking place in the Central Desert in late post-Pleistocene times. The presence of various small blades, both retouched and unretouched, along with unifacial points, may be connected in some way to widespread subtraditions of small point manufacture to the north and northwest (mainly bifacial points, including the famous Kimberley points as well as other varieties) and to the south and southeast (mainly unifacial points, generally referred to as pirris). A few true pirri points, with unifacial pressure retouch, were observed on surface sites during our 1973 Central Desert survey as far north as the Northern Territory–South Australian border, and one (probably an "import") was found on a surface habitation site about 800 meters (880 yd.) southeast of the James Range East rockshelters. None, however, were found in the excavations. The unifacially retouched points excavated at James Range East all showed steep and rather ragged percussion retouch with one possible exception. This was a point on which some unifacial pressure flaking may have been tried along one lateral edge of the piece. It is hard to see the blade and point-making subtraditions at James Range East as anything but the most tentative kind of technologies, although, unlike backed blades, they did continue into the historic period, with some types being made and used by Aranda and other Central Desert Aborigine groups. One must keep in mind that the problem of explanation here has more to do with internal rather than external factors. It is all very well to note pointmaking technologies in adjacent regions and suggest possible historical connections. But an adequate explanation for such technological specializations must still be based upon the internal characteristics of the cultural system that adopted them, however they were introduced.

Seed-grinding implements reflect the same additive relationship as flaked stone artifacts. While faceted cobble seed grinders and flat grinding slabs at James Range East are indistinguishable from their Western Desert counterparts, lenticular seed grinders and single-basin grinding slabs were not seen in the Western Desert at all. Moreover, double-basin grinding slabs were plentiful on the surface around the James Range East rockshelters, and a fragment of one was excavated in Trench 2 there. Cobbles with pecked depressions (mullers) were also seen on surface sites throughout the Central Desert area, including the James Range, during the 1973 survey, although none were actually found at James Range East, either on the surface or in the excavations. On a percentage basis, the variability in the seed-grinding inventory accounts for an average of 1.8 percent of the total variability in the stone toolkit at James Range East and reaches a maximum of 5.0 percent around 1800 A.D. (Stratum BX). While stone toolmaking may have been less important as an activity at James Range East than it was at Puntutjarpa, the same cannot be said for seed processing, at least insofar as this activity is reflected by the presence of stone seed grinders and seed-grinder fragments. A total of thirty-seven seed-grinding implements were recovered from Trench 2 at Puntutjarpa, compared with seventy-

three at Trench 1, James Range East. It should be mentioned that
anytime two or more fragments were found that fitted together or
appeared to be pieces of the same implement, they were all counted
together as a single implement before these figures were totaled.
Seed-grinding implements are the only unambiguously extractive
class of stone appliances in the Western and Central Deserts, so it
seems fair to conclude that seed processing was a more important
domestic activity at James Range East than it was at Puntutjarpa, at
least during the last 5,000 years.

No complete ground edge stone axes were found at James Range
East, and it is entirely possible that the five axe fragments found
there are all pieces of a single axe. These fragments are all of a dark,
fine-grained stone (probably diorite) that is certainly not available
locally in the James Range area. Petrological analyses should eventually inform us about the source of this raw material, since Aboriginal
quarries for such stone are known from various, distant parts of
South Australia and Northern Territory. A careful reconnaissance
of the area around the James Range East site complex was made,
though without the absolute completeness of coverage that was possible at Puntutjarpa, and only two sources of isotropic stone were
found within a 40-kilometer (25 mile) radius of the site. These were
both quarries containing gray quartzite. So except for the Sonder
Formation sandstone, used in making many seed-grinding implements, and this quartzite, we can tentatively posit that all other lithic
raw materials in use at James Range East were exotic—that is, were
derived from sources outside this radius. Of special interest is the
presence of a few seed-grinding implements made of granite. The
nearest natural sources of granite are along the Northern Territory–
South Australian border, about 170 kilometers (105 miles) to the
south of the site and in another area beyond the Harts Range, about
180 kilometers to the north. Although a wide variety of cherts was
used for making flaked stone tools at the James Range East site
complex, a diligent search failed to turn up any local sources of this
material. As analysis of the James Range East material proceeds, the
relationship between local and exotic stones and various categories
of stone tools will be examined in detail with the aim of further
testing the propositions presented in Chapter 6. It is already worth
noting, however, that at Puntutjarpa only locally available stones
were used to manufacture seed-grinding implements, so the James
Range East occurrence of granite for this purpose provides yet
another point of contrast and correlates with the increased variety
and number of seed-grinding implements there.

The additive relationships that are apparent even from this rather
superficial examination of the lithic inventories at Puntutjarpa and
James Range East are also reflected in the rock art present at these

sites. Neither James Range East nor Puntutjarpa is the most spectacular rock art site in its respective region, yet each contains good
examples of the regional styles and techniques and can be regarded
as an important rock art locality. At Puntutjarpa both the Main Cave
(containing Trench 2) and the West Cave, seven meters away, contained paintings, and there were additional paintings present at
some nearby rockshelters slightly farther to the west in the same
escarpment. These paintings were being added to by local Ngatatjara Aborigines from the Warburton Mission during the 1967 test
excavations at the site, and between 1967 and our return to the site
in 1969, several new designs had been placed on the ledge above the
entrance to the West Cave. In every case observed in the Western
Desert generally and at Puntutjarpa in particular, the new designs
were simply painted over the old ones, often overlapping or partly
obscuring the earlier motifs. No effort was ever made to freshen or
"touch up" a design that was already present, and the overall effect
was one of successive superpositions that created a kind of palimpsest of motifs covering the rock surfaces. The designs were varied
and included circles, concentric circles, a sort of "wagon wheel"
motif, serpentine motifs (some of them clearly snakes, others just
wiggly lines), emu tracks, and seminaturalistic representations of goanna lizards and centipedes. Most were monochromatic, but a few
were rendered in two colors. The only pigments used overall were
red and yellow ochres, charcoal, and white (from calcined bone or
white ash). Emu fat was used as a fixative for these pigments on
those occasions when I could observe Aborigines actually applying
new designs to the cave walls.

There were no rock engravings at Puntutjarpa, although these are
known from several localitties in granite formations north of the
Warburton Range, about 30–35 kilometers from the site. The Ngatatjara Aborigines of the Warburton area regarded these engravings
as designs that had been painted on the bodies of novices in episodes
of the Dreamtime myths that depict initiations. That is, the bodies of
these novices were said to have been transformed into stone (i.e., the
domelike formations of granite at these sacred sites) along with the
painted designs, which were likewise transformed into the engraved
patterns on the rocks. Both the rocks at these Dreaming sites and the
engraved designs were regarded as sacred, since they were thought
to embody the substance of the Dreamtime ancestors – in this case,
the Wati Kutjara (Two Men), an important Western Desert myth
cycle whose track passes close to Warburton. The mythical associations at Puntutjarpa were much less sacred, although they were well
known to the local Ngatatjara inhabitants (including women and
children) and had to do with the Dreamtime travels of Ngintaka, the
perentie lizard. At this point in the story line, the Dreamtime peren-

tie lizard was being chased by mythical human beings. The pursuit, according to the myth, went from west to east, following the line of the present Brown Range escarpment in which the rockshelter is located. This escarpment is part of a larger formation of quartzite rock that continues much farther to the east, through the Townshend Range, Ranford Hill, and finishing in the Hocking Range, and the Ngintaka myth is consistently associated with it. At Puntutjarpa, the perentie lizard dug a shallow burrow to escape his pursuers, but he left the tip of his tail sticking out. His pursuers grabbed his tail (this often happens on real lizard hunts, too) to try to pull him out, but instead, he pulled them in after him, whereupon they and the burrow all were transformed into rock – that is, the present Brown Range formation. About 50 meters west of the Main Cave at Puntutjarpa, there is a large crack in the face of the escarpment through which one can see daylight from the bottom, and this is said to be the burrow into which Ngintaka went and later pulled in his pursuers. This crack is the actual Dreaming site. It takes its name from this episode, since *puntu* is an archaic word for man, and *-tjarpa* is a suffix meaning into or inside, hence Puntutjarpa means "men (or people) inside (the ground)."

The point of this digressive excursion into Western Desert mythology is simply to point out that while the rock engravings at nearby sacred sites were regarded as sacred in and of themselves, since they were part of the transformed features of the mythical beings, like the rocks and other sacred features of these sites, rock and cave paintings were not. Paintings of this kind often represented the same motifs as one finds in the rock engravings (mainly circles and concentric circles), but the painted designs were said to be *watilu* ("man-made") as opposed to *tjukurpa* ("Dreaming"), which applied to features of the actual sacred site itself. In terms of a grammar of rock art residues, the ethnographic Western Desert Aborigines no longer produced rock engravings but regarded these as part of a special sacred category produced by their Dreamtime ancestors, while rock and cave paintings, such as those observed at Puntutjarpa, were mere representations of sacred motifs like body paintings and tracks of totemic beings that men with knowledge of such matters could produce as they wished. Cave and rock painting was a flourishing art form in the Western Desert in 1966–70 and probably still is. These painted designs were applied to the surface of sacred sites or to nearby rocks but were not part of any initiatory or increase ritual, and they were not accorded any of the ritual deference shown to actual sacred materials. Of course, only fully initiated men (either members of the cult-lodge affiliated with the site in question or men who had been introduced to the site by members of that cult-lodge) could actually apply designs to the sacred rocks, since only they could safely come into physical contact with the Dreaming site itself. The "palimpsest effect" described earlier arose from repeated revisiting and addition of new designs upon the rock surfaces at and near the place as tokens of mutual affiliation and respect for the sacredness of the site in the rather loose manner described earlier in connection with isotropic stones found at or near sacred sites.

Animal track designs – mainly macropod and emu tracks, but sometimes also tracks of mallee hen and other, smaller birds – were present at Puntutjarpa. Usually one finds such designs in rock defiles and near natural hunting blinds where men have concealed themselves to await the approach of game, in cases like that seen at Tjalputjalpu, near Tikatika. These designs were not regarded as sacred in any way but were applied in the context of the hunt. Although this is a difficult notion to test objectively, several informants claimed that this was a means of hastening the arrival of game; in other words, a loose form of hunting magic. The Main Cave at Puntutjarpa, in addition to being located near a minor sacred site, was also a hunting trap of some importance, since the escarpment was used in connection with hunting kangaroos along the gentle south slopes of the Brown Range. Hunts were described in which game was driven, either by chase or by use of fire, over the edge of the cliffs on the north side of the range and then given the coup de grâce by other men positioned in the Main Cave and other rockshelters along the base of the escarpment.

The most elaborate paintings at James Range East were in the Main Cave, and similar, though less elaborate paintings, were present in the North and South Caves as well. These paintings consisted entirely of motifs already familiar in the Western Desert, arranged in the same palimpsest kind of superposition. Concentric circles, linear designs, animal tracks, and other monochromatic and bichrome designs (with the same four colors in use overall) were present on the cave walls and nearby rock surfaces. These designs can be regarded as cognate with and indistinguishable from the general range of Western Desert paintings, including those at Puntutjarpa. The East Cave, however, was unique in containing only negative handprints in red ochre, which is a motif not found so far anywhere in the Western Desert. None of the localities in the James Range East complex contained the large, unified motifs seen covering whole rock surfaces at sites like Emily Gap and Jessie Gap (about 70 kilometers to the north), Ooraminna (about 25 kilometers to the north), or Wallabi Gap, near the Train Hills (about 40 kilometers to the southeast). However, such large painted designs continue to be produced by some Central Desert Aborigines like the Walbiri and were being painted well into historic times by other groups like the Aranda (Spencer and Gillen, 1899: 171). Meggitt (1962: 68, 226) described the large serpentine painting and subsidiary motifs at Ngama Cave, near Yuendumu, as representing the snake, dingo, and wallaby totems and noted that these designs were retouched annually as part of increase (i.e., "maintenance" rituals for these species). A recent film (Sandall, 1967) shows the cult-lodge at Ngama renewing these designs in the context of ritual activities.

Thus these large-scale paintings of the Central Desert – one cannot help but think of them as compositions in mural art as opposed to the graffiti-like designs described earlier – were painted and retouched as part of some corporate ritual act. Unlike the Western Desert paintings and their Central Desert counterparts, these designs were continually freshened up rather than being partially obscured by new designs. Even though such large-scale paintings with signs of periodic retouch were not present at the James Range East site complex, they were an important ethnographic feature of many of the major sacred sites of this Central Desert region. As a form of human residue, the cave and rock paintings of the Central Desert include several important additive elements, in contrast to the Western Desert, that imply a cognate but somewhat different grammar of expressive art.

Engravings were discovered on a large rock slab on the surface inside the Northeast Cave at James Range East, and further engravings were found on the upper faces of two boulders in the upper rockfall layer excavated in Trench 1 in the North Cave. Unless one is willing to make the rather improbable assumption that both of these boulders fell with their engraved surfaces facing upwards when the rockfall occurred, it seems likely that these pecked engravings were made sometime after the rocks fell and came to rest in their present positions. The ancient Aboriginal artists chose rock surfaces that were smooth and showed the designs to best advantage. All of the pecked designs at the James Range East site complex were of emu tracks, but other nearby sites like Ikulpa (in the James Range, about 8 kilometers to the east) and Ewaninga (about 40 kilometers to the north) contain a wide variety of engraved motifs along with emu tracks. Emu track designs do occur in Western Desert rock-engraving sites, although it is hard to tell if they were pecked in the same fashion, and many of the motifs observed at Ikulpa and Ewaninga are also shared with the Western Desert. From a superficial examination, it looks as if the similarities in rock engravings between these two subregions outweigh the differences, although none of the sites seen so far in the far Western Desert can match those of the Center for sheer variety and numbers of designs. Further comparative studies of these rock art styles are planned. Within the present chronological framework for the James Range East site, the two engraved boulders rest stratigraphically within the same time period estimated for a rock-free habitation area at the back of the North Cave – that is, sometime after the upper rockfall event but before the upper surface of these rocks were covered by sediments, thus placing them in age sometime between 2000 years ago and 1700 A.D. Of course, the artistic tradition of rock engraving may be much more ancient than these dates would indicate, but they do at least demonstrate how rock engraving persisted in the Central Desert until very late post-Pleistocene times.

All of these additive relationships presented by the James Range East site complex and its immediate archaeological environs will be compared with the Puntutjarpa materials in detail, as research continues, especially as regards lithic residues, site features such as hearths and possible living areas, and rock art remains. But even at the preliminary and rather superficial level of comparison attempted here, certain obvious, overall relationships emerge. From these, one gets an inkling of the consistently richer inventory of human residues appearing in Central Desert Aboriginal sites. Everything seen before in the Western Desert can be found in the Central Desert, both in general and in specific cases where it is possible to compare contemporaneous dated periods. This additive relationship of the prehistoric Central Desert to Western Desert technology and rock art continued into the historic period, where it is documented ethnographically among Aborigine groups like the Aranda, Loritja, and Walbiri and Pitjantjatjara-speaking Aborigines of the Western Desert, respectively. Seen from a Western Desert perspective, post-Pleistocene Central Desert prehistory, even at this early stage of archaeological exploration, seems to be different in certain characteristic ways. Having established that consistent kinds of variability exist, the next step is to start to attempt an explanation for this for this variability.

8

Explaining the differences

As with other aspects of the analysis at James Range East, paleoecological studies are in progress and can be reported on in a preliminary way only. Even so, we are starting to see indications as to which
relationships are likely to be decisive in explaining the variability
between post-Pleistocene human societies in the Western and Central Deserts of Australia. By discovering and explaining these differences, we will ultimately establish criteria for explaining differences
of this sort more generally in prehistoric and contemporary human
societies. So even at this preliminary stage, it may be useful to examine the lines of analysis that show the most promise in supplying
convincing explanations for variability in human residues.

Paleoecological correlations and explanations
Identifiable fossil pollen was discovered in the excavated fill at both
sites and is presently being analyzed in relation to the general desert
flora of each subregion.[10] The analysis of pollen from Puntutjarpa is
nearly complete, and work on the James Range East pollens is underway. Numerous flotation samples containing charred plant and seed
remains were collected at each of these excavations, although the
analysis of these materials is in abeyance at the moment awaiting a
trained person to make the identifications. Geomorphological studies
on the sediments at James Range East and the nearby region[11] are
nearing completion. In general, the sediments at James Range East,
like those at Puntutjarpa, are aeolian in origin. But the internal stratification and differentiation of sediments within the North Cave deposits at James Range East are more pronounced than was true at the
Main Cave, Puntutjarpa, and explanations for these differences are
being sought. The presence of two large rockfall layers within the
excavated deposits at each site is also intriguing. Were these strictly
localized events? Or were they part of a more general pattern keyed
to some kind of widespread climatic or tectonic events in the Australian desert? The presence of numerous intact hearths (twelve at Puntutjarpa, twenty-two at James Range East) at all levels except the basal

ones at Trench 1, James Range East, argues for the essentially undis-turbed nature of the deposits, although in rockshelters like these a certain amount of mixing between levels must be expected. In each excavated rockshelter there were rock-free areas at the rear of the cave that were used as habitation campsites. At Puntutjarpa there is evidence to show that the rock-free areas associated with the lower rockfall were made by the human inhabitants when the cave was reoccupied following the rockfall event, but in the other cases these rock-free areas appear to have been natural – that is, places on the then-existing cave floor where no rocks fell. Under conditions of rockshelter occupation, where scuffing and other physical distur-bances by the ancient inhabitants usually obscures the features of individual campsites or activity areas, hearths and rock-free areas provided a welcome measure of archaeological definition for at least some of the ancient living surfaces in these caves.

Perhaps the most promising line of research right now is faunal analysis.[12] The faunal remains from Puntutjarpa Rockshelter were characteristic of a desert habitat comparable to today's, extending over the entire range of human occupation there (Archer, 1977), although one must keep in mind that many of the species repre-sented, such as red kangaroo, have the ability to adapt to a wide range of arid and semiarid habitats and are not restricted to extreme desert conditions. At both Puntutjarpa and James Range East there is a preponderance, both by weight and numbers of pieces of identi-fiable bones, of remains of large macropods, that is, red kangaroo (*Megaleia rufa*) and the euro or hill kangaroo (*Macropus robustus*). As both Frith and Calaby (1969: 39) and Newsome (1971: 34) have noted, red kangaroos inhabit the arid lands of Australia that occur roughly within the 15-inch isohyet, with the same being true for the euro, enclosing a total range of approximately 5.2 million square kilometers (2 million sq. miles). There is overwhelming evidence at both Puntutjarpa and James Range East for hunting and consump-tion of these species by man during post-Pleistocene times. Yet, despite this overall similarity, there are gross differences in the size-range of pieces of bone present and in the relative extent of break-age for these species at these two sites. The bones at Puntutjarpa were broken into exceedingly small bits, rarely exceeding two centi-meters in diameter or length. Macropod teeth there were usually split open, as were the epipheses of longbones. By contrast, the macropod remains at James Range East occurred in consistently larger pieces, although still much broken up when compared with the faunal remains from sites in many other parts of the world. At James Range East, for example, we found whole macropod teeth and epipheses. In some cases we even found portions of kangaroo jawbones with a few teeth still attached. A quantitative study is now underway by Archer to compare the size ranges of identifiable macropod and other bones at these two sites, but the general differences are already apparent by inspection.

While rockfall damage and dogs may account for some of the breakage, they do not fully explain everything about this breakage. Rockfalls occurred only intermittently at each site, yet the breakage patterns within each site remained more or less constant, even in the soil layers that intervene between the rockfalls. Dogs presumably were present at both the Western and Central Desert Aborigine camps, so dogs cannot be used to explain differences in the extent of breakage between these sites unless one can first posit some reason for dogs not having been present at James Range East. At Puntutjarpa the pattern of extreme breakage extends to the earliest levels of human habitation (10,000+ years), although dogs are considered by archaeologists, on present evidence, to be relative latecomers to the Australian scene – probably within the last 8,000 years (Mulvaney, 1975: 138; Macintosh, 1974: 91–2). If one were to attribute the extreme pattern of bone breakage throughout the Puntutjarpa sequence to dogs, one would then have to argue that the basal levels at Puntutjarpa reflect the earliest direct evidence for the presence of dogs in Australia. I am making no such claim. Archer (1977: 164) has also suggested that bones may be broken in the act of catching an animal. The explorer George Grey noted that among the Aborigines in northwestern Australia:

> A native hunting for food has his eyes in constant motion, and nothing escapes them; he sees a kangaroo rat sitting in a bush, and he walks toward it, as if about to pass it carelessly, but suddenly when on one side of it, he stamps on the bush with all his force, and crushes the little animal to death . . . [Grey, 1841: 290]

This argument might apply to larger animals as well, especially when they were hunted, as at Puntutjarpa in historic times, by driving them over cliffs. But, while bones were undoubtedly broken in such hunting, it seems improbable that such events accounted for the extreme breakage observed in the faunal residues at the Puntutjarpa excavations. How then are we to begin to explain this anomaly?

Of kangaroos and men in the Australian desert
A recent series of elegant quantitative studies in the Central Desert of Australia (Newsome, 1965a; 1965b; 1965c; 1971) provides a model of adaptive responses by populations of large macropods to the rigors of desert life. Using a light aircraft, Newsome systematically surveyed a 4,000-square-mile area of the Central Desert immediately to the north of the Macdonnell Range (about 70 kilometers north of

The red kangaroo (*Megaleia rufa*), generally the most robust macropod in Australia and found widely in arid and semiarid areas, is much sought-after by Aborigines.

the James Range East site complex) during the drought year of 1962. Unfortunately, no comparable studies of density, movement, and fluctuations of large macropod populations are available from the Western Desert, but it should still be possible to propose some general contrasts that will help to explain archaeological differences in patterns of bone breakage at Puntutjarpa and James Range East.

Newsome found that the highest densities of kangaroo population tended to occur during drought periods when red kangaroos concentrated on grassy plains where short green herbage (mainly *Eragrostis sp.*) was available and where some kind of mulga scrub woodland was available nearby for cover and shade. The highest density observed in his study was on the Mt. Hay plains in October 1961, where there were 8.9 kangaroos per square mile. These same kangaroos virtually vanished into the mulga scrub woodlands after the onset of rains, where they became more dispersed. On an overall average, their highest density on open, grassy plains was 5.3 per square mile, during drought, while their lowest was 1.1 per square mile, during good seasons. Conversely, the average overall density of red kangaroos in acacia scrub woodlands during drought was only 0.3 per square mile, while in good seasons it increased to 2.2 (Newsome, 1971: 36). Looked at another way, 64.7 percent of kangaroos observed in the study were sheltering in the acacia scrub woodlands within one-third of a mile of open plains and water courses during drought, and only 17.4 percent were farther away than one mile from these sources of food. After rains, on the other hand, only 29.5 percent could be found within one-third of a mile of these woodlands adjacent to grassy plains and water courses, while 51.8 percent were farther than one mile away. So areas of mulga scrub woodland adjacent to grassy plains and water courses, where herbage persists, can be viewed as "drought refuges" for the red kangaroo (Newsome, 1965b: 289).

The implication of this study is that, during drought, food was more important to kangaroos than water (Newsome, 1965b: 298). This is easier to understand when we find that the red kangaroo's favorite drought food, the green shoots of *Eragrostis sp.*, contain between 16 and 25 percent water by weight during dry weather. When this food source is scarce, kangaroos may need to drink (Newsome, 1965b: 298). As Newsome (1965c: 754) notes: "During drought, kangaroos seek the dwindling supply of green herbage . . . and choose it to eat in the face of an abundance of other types of vegetation." Yet, even when this food is available in areas of treeless spinifex plain, red kangaroos tend not to inhabit these places or do so in very small numbers (on the order of 0.2 to 0.3 per square mile) because of their need for shade and shelter reasonably close to where they feed. There is also evidence to show that kangaroos move into localized areas covered by storm rains. Newsome (1971: 36) noted that there were larger concentrations of kangaroos in areas of drought after a storm had passed through, and he also observed strong concentrations here and there that were most easily explained by kangaroos chasing patchy occurrences of rain.

In general, what Newsome describes is an opportunistic pattern of concentration and dispersal in response to changes in weather based on two mechanisms: movement and reproduction. Red kangaroos exhibit what Newsome (1971: 36) calls "native restlessness," moving often and over wide areas, with no home ranges. He comments:

> The data indicate . . . that the red kangaroo can be quite nomadic though localized in their daily movements for food, water, and shelter. Their longer movements seem to be associated with finding food in drought or, at least with deserting an area bereft of green herbage. [Newsome, 1971: 36]

Kangaroos also possess remarkable and rather complex reproductive mechanisms that are adaptive under desert conditions. This is the physiological phenomenon known as "embryonic diapause" (Dawson, 1977: 80), in which a viable embryo is carried by the female kangaroo in an arrested state. This phenomenon takes different forms among different macropods, and:

> Among red kangaroos its signficance would appear to be associated with a rapid rebuilding of the kangaroo population after a reduction in numbers due to a drought in the arid Australia interior. [Dawson, 1977: 80]

The joey (i.e., the immature kangaroo carried in the pouch) and young-at-foot (a joey large enough to live outside the pouch but still depending on its mother's milk for nourishment) may suffer progressively and die from the effects of malnutrition due to poor herbage during drought, but the blastocyst has a good chance of survival and will resume development when conditions improve. Thus a female red kangaroo can have three offspring "in the pipeline" at once, and as Dawson points out:

> One can . . . see the adaptive advantage in an arrangement whereby the female will, except under the severest conditions, harbor a developing offspring. [Dawson, 1977: 81]

In general, female red kangaroos keep producing offspring when their other young die from starvation or malnutrition arising from drought. These two mechanisms, movement and a unique system of reproduction, more than account for fluctuations in local populations and the related ability of red kangaroos to sustain themselves during droughts. The red kangaroo, and his close relative, the euro, are alive and well in arid Australia.

In earlier discussions I noted that large macropods were an irregular and relatively poor source of meat for the Western Desert Aborigines except on infrequent and unpredictable occasions when localized falls of rain in areas of predominantly mulga scrub prompted large increases in the density of game. How does this proposition relate to the model of macropod opportunism presented by Newsome and others? We have no reliable figures yet for kangaroo population densities in the Western Desert, although subjectively they appear to be lower than they are in the Central Desert. The observed tendency of red kangaroos in the Western Desert to become concentrated in certain areas of mulga scrub cover may be due to the habit observed by Newsome of macropods to concentrate in areas of storm rains, or they may arise from essential differences in the geography of the Western Desert (especially the Warburton area) as compared with the Center. In the Western Desert, much larger areas are dominated by sandhills and sandplains covered with spinifex and few, if any, trees. This is the kind of country that red kangaroos like the least, even after rains, and places like the flats between the Warburton and Brown Ranges, near Puntutjarpa, can be viewed as a kind of vegetational oasis, consisting of a corridor of mulga scrub woodland and small flats of grasses (including *Eragrostis sp.*) bounded to the north and south by vast areas of spinifex-coverd and relatively treeless terrain. This area and the others like it in the Western Desert probably conform more closely to what Newsome (1971: 34–5) classified as "mixed open plains and woodlands" that, in the Central Desert, have relatively low densities of 0.3 to 2.2 macropods per square mile, than to his other categories of "open plains" or "woodlands." In a relative sense, then, kangaroos tend to be concentrated in the Warburton and other similar "oasis" areas even when there are widespread rains, and predation of macropods by man in the Western Desert was concentrated in those areas.

Newsome's model implies different responses by red kangaroos to different kinds of rainfall, with dispersal occurring when rains are widespread and concentration when there are storm rains in specific, limited areas. According to the Newsome model, concentrations of game will also occur during droughts in "drought refuges" where edible green shoots of *Eragrostis sp.* are available in close proximity to mulga scrub woodland. In all three situations in the Western Desert – namely, drought, generalized rains, or spotty storm rains – large macropods would tend to concentrate in vegetational oases or corridors like that one that runs east–west through the Warburton-Brown Ranges.

Puntutjarpa Rockshelter occupied a key strategic location on the south side of that corridor, for it was slightly elevated above the surrounding terrain, faced to the north across this corridor of mixed grassy plains and mulga scrub woodlands, was well shaded, and had water supplies nearby. Any movement of game through this area could be observed from this vantage point. While it was a relatively attractive kangaroo-hunting-ground in comparison with the surrounding areas of spinifex covered sandhills, sandplain, and ṛiṛa, the densities of game there would hardly compare with those of the more extensive open plains and woodland habitats of the Center.

Moreover, the essential nature of opportunism in the Western Desert by man and kangaroos is different. Water is a less immediate limiting factor for red kangaroos than it is for man, since kangaroos need to drink only when deprived of green *Eragrostis* shoots, while the Aborigines need to drink all the time. Movements by man in this region were always tied to available sources of drinking water, and the corridor or vegetational oasis running through the Warburton and Brown Ranges was not an oasis for man, since it contained relatively few and rather poor water catchments. In many parts of the Western Desert, the kangaroo could go into places where aboriginal man could not always follow.

So not only did the Western Desert Aborigines probably have less large game available to them than their Central Desert counterparts, but they also had fewer and more widely spaced water catchments whose occurrences in time and space did not always correspond to periods and localities of maximum macropod density. The constant and immediate need for water was a more serious constraint to the Aborigines' pursuit of kangaroos in the Western Desert than it would have been in the Center, where water catchments are both more common and more dependable.

How did these general conditions translate into behavior? In December 1966, I observed a maximal grouping of 107 Aborigines who camped together for 2½ weeks at Waṇampi Well ("Snake Well"), a bore located 32 kilometers (20 miles) east of the Warburton Mission, in the center of this mixed open plains and acacia scrub woodland corridor. This windmill bore had only recently been installed, and the Aborigine men I spoke with there were unanimous in expressing their pleasure at being able to hunt relatively large numbers of kangaroos in an area that had previously been difficult and risky for them to enter. This new water source provided a base for venturing after macropods, which they did with gusto until they depleted the local supply of game (which had recently been enhanced by the improved herbage arising from a succession of localized rains).

Even more to the point was the behavior I observed in relation to butchering macropods. As I mentioned earlier, the Western Desert people made exceptional efforts to conserve every available bit of edible protein in small game by pounding the meat, bones, and skin together into a pulpy mass whenever appropriate and eating the entire mashed up animal. For larger animals, especially macropods, the preferred technique was to break open all of the bones, including even the phalanges, skull, jawbone, and teeth, using a spinifex spine to tease out every last bit of meat or marrow from the interstices of shattered bone. Sometimes the spinifex spine was used as a toothpick afterwards. If old people with poor teeth or weak jaw muscles happened to be in camp, the kangaroo tail was pounded, after roasting, into the same kind of pulpy mass that we saw earlier with lizards and feral cat vertebrae.This made it easier for the elderly to eat, and, like these other methods, it conserved available protein to the utmost.

Thus in the Western Desert, relative scarcity of game was translated into extreme behavior by people in breaking up or pounding roasted carcasses in order to obtain every last scrap of edible mate-

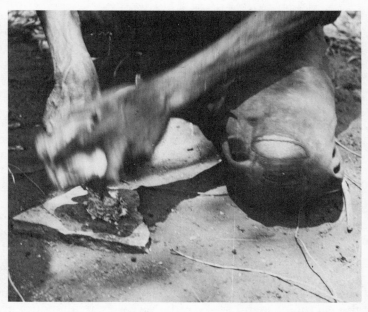

The vertebrae of a feral cat being pounded, after roasting, on an impromptu rock anvil by a Western Desert Aborigine. This is an example of behavior directed toward conserving edible protein in an area where hunting is difficult.

rial. The result in the case of kangaroos was a scatter of tiny pieces of shattered bone that were too small to be held in the hand any longer while attempting to extract meat. No empirical accounts exist in the literature to tell us about patterns of butchering and consumption of game among the Central Desert Aborigines. But, given the relatively higher densities of game and easier access to game made possible by having more good water sources over parts of the landscape well suited for macropods, one would expect that the Central Desert Aborigines of the post-Pleistocene period did not have to go to anything like the extremes of carcass reduction that we saw in the Western Desert. Under such conditions, Michael Archer and I predict that large game, especially kangaroos, would not be broken into as small pieces as they were in the Western Desert. In other words, the relative size of pieces of butchered bone is the "archeological signature" for relative degrees of stress imposed by the limiting factor of available water. Differences in butchered bone sizes in the James Range East deposits in relation to faunal materials found at Puntutjarpa can be explained more simply by variations in desert geography as they affect the availability of large macropods and water than by any alternative hypothesis based upon destruction of bone due to injury during the hunt, by dogs, by natural factors like rockfall-related disturbances within these sites, or cultural preferences. For the living archaeologist, this causal linkage between ecological factors and material residues is proof of the importance of being different in the Central Desert.

Differences that make a difference

It would be dangerously facile for me to make the simple claim that the relative richness apparent in such aspects of prehistoric behavior as stone toolmaking and rock art in the Central Desert as compared with the Western Desert were the product of a relatively richer environment. It would be even riskier to argue that this additive relationship extended to the social and ceremonial differences observed by T. G. H. Strehlow for the historic Central Desert Aborigines in contrast to their "culturally deprived" Western Desert counterparts. Just because water and game were more readily available in the Center does not mean that human behavior necessarily became more elaborated in any particular way. Such an argument, like the one discussed earlier in relation to the beginnings of agriculture, places such explanations in the realm of innate human tendencies – that is, they are made to seem inevitable. Such absolute historical inevitability is a "just so" story writ large, and it explains nothing.

From the preceding discussions we can see that there is a correlation between the better water and game resources of the Center than those of the Western Desert and the additive qualities of the archaeological residues in the Center. We saw, too, that the "archaeological signature" of ecological stress in relation to human behavior was not an absolute, unitary phenomenon that could be used as a key for explaining all known hunter–gatherer and other archaeological complexes where faunal residues occur. Rather, it is a relativistic relationship based upon the discovery and explanation of anomalies. The small bone fragments that appear as residues at Puntutjarpa and among contemporary Western Desert Aborigines are not necessarily diagnostic of ecological stress of the sort described above for all times and in all places. Small pieces of bone like those in a Middle Paleolithic site in the Middle East or a Paleo-Indian site in North America might mean something entirely different. The significance of these small pieces of bone emerges only by contrast with another case where the ecological differences are understood and controlled for.

Can the additive relationships in the lithic inventory and rock art of James Range East and the adjacent region be explained as anomalies in relation to the Western Desert model? The residues at James Range East and Puntutjarpa reflect roughly the same range of human activities: butchering and consumption of game, manufacture and use of stone tools, sleeping and resting, processing and con-

sumption of edible seeds, and rock painting. There are differences
in degree, such as the greater emphasis on stone toolmaking evident
at Puntutjarpa than at James Range East, and there are even some
differences in kind, such as the presence of residues that reflect the
manufacture of seed-grinding implements and the practice of making rock engravings, both present only at James Range East. But the
total array of residues in both sites indicates that these localities were
both occupied by maximal segments of the population (i.e., both
sexes and all age groups) who carried out the widest range of different activities likely to occur at any one place. Puntutjarpa and James
Range East were both habitation base-camps as opposed to task-
specific sites of some kind. Perhaps these localities were both visited
at times during their occupation and used as task-specific sites, but
we have no reliable way of distinguishing such task-related episodes
stratigraphically from the wide range of habitational activities.

This difficulty can best be understood if we make a rough-and-
ready distinction here between general activities, such as lithic technology, and the sequence of tasks or episodes that make up these
activities, such as stone tool procurement, manufacture, use, and
discard. In any rockshelter excavation it should be possible to infer
the range of general activities from a careful review of the lithic and
other residues, and one should also be able to posit the different
tasks vis-a-vis each general activity represented there, either on a
presence–absence or percentage basis. Rockshelters, however, pose
special stratigraphic problems by virtue of their confined space and
frequently soft deposits and the fact that these deposits were disturbed or mixed to varying degrees by scuffing, digging, sweeping,
and other behavior during successive reoccupations (Bordes, 1972:
42–3; Jelinek, 1971: 16). For these reasons rockshelter habitation
sites are generally better for purposes of working out chronological
and typological sequences than they are for identifying the loci of
particular tasks. Certainly these strictures apply to the excavations at
both James Range East and Puntutjarpa, although by the same token
we would not expect the vertical distribution of artifacts and other
residues to be entirely random. The natural and arbitrary excavation
units used at these two sites were designed to provide a framework
for observing varying frequencies of tool types, debitage, lithic raw
materials, faunal remains, and other residues without implying that
each excavation unit represents a unit of exact contemporaneity.

The problem in relation to the horizontal patterning of task areas
within these sites is more acute, partly because they are rockshelters
and therefore were subject to disturbances by factors of the kind
mentioned above, but also because of a factor that one can see operating among contemporary Western Desert Aborigines. I shall call
this factor the Principle of Interference, and it can be decisive in our

appreciation of the way in which any habitation base camp, whether in a rockshelter or an open-air location, may turn out to be a poor place to look for evidence of workshops, food processing areas, or other task-related loci. The Principle of Interference can be stated as follows:

> The wider the range of different general activities per-
> formed at a particular site, the greater the likelihood is
> that the by-products of each task performed in relation to
> each of these activities have become detached from the
> original locus where each task was carried out.

All contemporary Western Desert Aborigine habitation base-camps represent an inclusive array of different general activities performed by people of both sexes and every age group. These activities included technological pursuits (mainly finishing stone and wood implements), processing and consumption of food, sleeping and resting, and a multitudinous variety of social interaction and verbal activity. Task-specific sites, on the other hand, were related to a particular, limited task-group consisting usually of one sex and/or age group. Aborigine task-specific sites in the Western Desert included hunting blinds (consisting of brush screens, tree platforms, or small rock walls situated close to a waterhole), woodworking extraction sites (usually consisting of one or more acacia trees from which slabs of wood have been removed for further shaping into spearthrowers, throwing-sticks, and other implements), earth ovens (for roasting large game), men's traveling camps (consisting of a row of sleeping hearths and a brush windbreak arranged in a linear fashion), quarries (containing isotropic stone for toolmaking), and various ceremonial or ritual sites.

Sometimes a task-specific site appeared as a locus within a habitation base-camp, as, for example, when a kangaroo was killed nearby and was roasted in an earth oven and butchered within the confines of the habitation site, or when a suitable mulga tree occurring near the camp was used to procure a slab of wood. Observations revealed that even relatively well defined activity areas within habitation camp-sites rapidly became obscured as a result of interference occasioned by other tasks. Waste flakes and other stone-chipping debris clustered in the vicinity of a place where retouch and tool manufacture had taken place were swept aside when the living surface was cleared a few hours later for sleeping. The large angular rock used as a chopper for detaching a wood slab from a mulga tree near camp was soon picked up and used elsewhere as a pounder. Although larger appliances like seed-grinding slabs and features like the elongated hearths character-istic of earth ovens tended to remain intact and in place, smaller or lighter residues became progressively separated from their original

A Western Desert Aborigine task-specific site a few miles from Tikatika. A slab of wood was removed from this mulga tree (*Acacia aneura*), and the impromptu handaxe (or chopper-plane) was abandoned at the base of the tree along with some wooden wedges when the job was finished. In this case, the wooden slab came off short and was rejected. It lies on the ground to the right of the base of the tree. Here the discards' last resting place is also the place where the activities that produced them occurred.

place of production. That is, a process of general homogenization of smaller site residues took place as different activities impinged upon each other in the day-to-day living arrangements of Aboriginal families. This homogenizing tendency was further increased by the fact that Aborigine habitation campsites in the Western Desert tended to be reused, since they were always situated close to the relatively limited water sources there. The mulga boughs from last year's shade shelter would be torn down and used for firewood this year, and the stirring and scuffing actions of people moving about and clearing off places to sit down or sleep would mix the residues from different sequential periods of habitation.

By contrast, task-specific sites – even when used repeatedly as in the case of hunting blinds at choice waterholes and quarries containing desirable lithic materials – were not subject to anything like the degree of interference from other tasks that occur on habitation campsites. Once abandoned as a by-product of the particular task that produced it, an item or group of items tended to remain at or near the place where that task took place. Its place of original production was also its ultimate context of discard. Long after the mulga tree and wood debris decomposed or were eaten by termites, the stone chopper originally used to extract the wood slab remained where it was originally dropped near the base of the tree. Similarly, chipped stone adze slugs tended to accumulate at hunting blinds, since one of the principal activities there was last-minute resharpening of wooden spearpoints (and, consequently, occasional discard of worn out stone adzes used for that operation). Task-specific sites, while dispersed widely over the landscape and numerically not as rich in artifact residues or site features as habitation campsites, proved to be more reliable indicators of the specific loci of particular activities than did the clusterings of by-product residues within habitation campsites. Indeed, what clusterings of these residues did occur in the context of habitation base-camps were more likely to be due to random recombination arising from some other activities like floor clearance than from any lingering association with the original task that produced them. Suffice it to say that the excavated deposits at both the James Range East and Puntutjarpa Rockshelters, as prehistoric habitation base-camps, were subject to the effects of the Principle of Interference as well as to the disturbing effects of wind erosion and the scuffing and stirring of soil by the human inhabitants during repeated occupations. Thus our efforts to observe and explain differences in behavior at these two sites have depended more up to now upon the nature of the material residues than upon their horizontal patterning or spatial distribution in relation to possible activity- or task-specific areas.

At Trench 1, James Range East, the ancient inhabitants left behind 59.6 stone tools, cores, and retouched fragments per cubic meter of excavated fill, as compared with 65.4 stone tools, cores, and retouched fragments per cubic meter of excavated fill at Trench 2, Puntutjarpa. Since all but twenty of the stone tools, cores, and re-touched fragments at James Range East were derived from the James Range II phase, we can see in a gross way that finished stone tools and identifiable artifacts were relatively more abundant in the post-Pleistocene levels of this Central Desert site than they were at Puntutjarpa, where they required over 10,000 years (that is, twice as long) to accumulate. Yet this relationship is reversed when one looks at the relative densities of stone waste flakes per cubic meter at these two sites. It seems clear that more finished tools were brought to James Range East and used there than was the case at Puntutjarpa, where more tools were actually manufactured at the site. The princi-pal exception to this general interpretation arises in the case of sand-stone seed-grinding implements, which, for at least the last 2,000 years, were being manufactured in the North Cave at James Range East. The relatively greater proportion of finished tools at James Range East coincides with the wider variety of tool types seen there as compared with Puntutjarpa. The overall diversity of rock art tech-niques and motifs at James Range East is also greater than was seen at Puntutjarpa, although other techniques and styles are known from nearby Central Desert sites that are not seen there at all.

Perhaps at this preliminary level of analysis, we should consider the possibility that different special tasks, such as the manufacture of stone tools as opposed to their use and discard, were more spread out or separated in time and space than was true at Puntutjarpa in par-ticular or in the Western Desert generally. While comparable to James Range East in the range of general activities represented there, Pun-tutjarpa is more fully representative of the full range of special tasks that comprised these activities as observed in relation to the ethno-graphic behavior of the Western Desert Aborigines than is the case for James Range East when compared with what we know from the literature about the Central Desert Aborigines. In the Western Desert the limited and spotty occurrence of relatively reliable water sources restricted the number of localities where habitation base-camps could be sited. Such sites were revisited often, as, indeed, they had to be, since there were no other places where people could establish their base-camps. Based on the risk-minimizing model proposed earlier, one would predict that all or most of the specific tasks that comprise each general activity would be represented within the confines of each habitation base-camp, since there were not enough water sources over the landscape to permit relatively task-specific sites of long duration.

For example, when considering the general activity of stone tool-making in the Western Desert, we can see why a large part of the manufacture as well as the use of stone tools had to occur in the habitation base-camp. Most natural sources of isotropic stone in the Western Desert are too far from a water source to allow Aborigines to spend more than a short time at them collecting and reducing lithic raw material. In the Central Desert, however, the relative abundance of reliable water sources made it possible for more tasks related to manufacturing stone tools to take place in different localities from those where these stone tools were used. The inverse correlation of stone chipping debris at James Range East in relation to finished tools implies just such a physical separation of tasks within the overall framework of this general activity.

So in the case of lithic technology, it is not hard to see why such locational flexibility in relation to specific tasks might prove advantageous. If one can establish habitation campsites at or near quarries, one can take more time to improve tools by experimenting with materials and by trying out new techniques. The factor of wastage is less critical than it would be under circumstances that require a stay of very limited duration at the quarry. Such a "one night stand" is insufficient to accomplish more than basic selection of material and core reduction, with the major consideration always being to find some way to limit what one has to carry back to camp to a manageable load that will not include too much waste stone. If, instead, one can stay at the quarry site long enough to produce finished or nearly finished tools in a wide variety of forms, then one can develop the skills necessary to produce a wider variety of tools and at the same time can reduce the load for further transport to an efficient minimum. If one accepts this line of reasoning, then it becomes easier to see how the availability of water at or near quarry sites could lead to greater technological efficiency in stone toolmaking and, at the same time, to a wider variety of tool types. I am positing that this latter process was taking place in the Central Desert and that it could account for the relatively high proportion of finished stone artifacts at James Range East in relation to lithic waste material as compared with Puntutjarpa. One way to test this idea would be to survey the region around the James Range East site complex to see to what extent quarry localities occur near water sources and have habitation base-camps nearby. If this hypothesis is correct, the difference between task-specific and habitation base-camps in the Central Desert will prove to be less distinct than it is in the Western Desert, especially in situations where lithic residues are present. The risk-minimizing model for the Western Desert Aborigines leads one to predict a greater combining of tasks included within the general activity of lithic technology at habitation base-camps than would be true for the Central Desert, where water catchments were more widely available.

It is possible, too, that one might see a greater reliance upon lithic materials from quarries as opposed to nonlocalized sources in a place like the Central Desert. As in the Western Desert, gibber plains and creekbeds containing redeposited isotropic stone are common over the landscape. Like the Western Desert "gibbers," these tend to be technically poorer materials than one usually finds in quarries. Given the wider availability of water catchments in the Central Desert, these quarries (like the kangaroos discussed earlier) would be generally more accessible to human exploitation. A simple utilitarian argument would lead us to predict, therefore, that the Aborigines of this region would have exploited these superior materials to a greater degree than their Western desert counterparts. This argument will be examined as analysis of the James Range East lithic inventories continues

The explanation for increased variety in the ground stone tool inventory, especially seed-grinding implements, is more problematical. It is possible that different types of implements in the Central desert were used for processing different plant and seed foods, although a review of this problem (Blake, 1974) based on the existing ethnographic and botanical literature revealed no significant correlations in the Central and Western Deserts between different types of this class of extractive tool and various floristic boundaries and distributions for various species of edible plants that might require such processing. However, this negative result may be as much due to deficiencies in the available literature on this subject as it is to a true lack of correlation. Alternatively, some or all of these plant species may ripen and become available on an essentially random, nonseasonal basis in different parts of the desert according to where rains happen to occur, just as they do in the Western Desert, in which case different seed- and plant-processing implements might be expected to follow a similarly randomized pattern of spatial distribution. Further studies along these lines based on documented museum collections of ethnographic seed- and plant-processing implements and the steadily improving botanical knowledge of arid Australia should be considered. Systematic botanical studies in the vicinity of the James Range East site complex[13] in 1974 showed a sharp difference in the occurrence of edible species of certain kinds on rocky terrain in contrast to the adjacent sandhills and sandplains, although these results must be tempered by recognition of the fact that the flora of the sandhill and sandplains country in this region has been considerably affected by cattle grazing and will require an element of reconstruction before it is well understood.

The increased variety of rock art styles and techniques in the Central Desert and at James Range East is also hard to explain in any convincing way at the present time. The generally increased abundance of rock art in this region probably is related to overall larger human populations as a result of improved availability of water and game. On the basis of historic and ethnographic evidence, Yengoyan (1968: 190) posits an overall average population density for the Central Desert Aborigines of 12.5 people per square mile, which is roughly 2.8 to 3.2 times that for the Western Desert. As a consequence, there may have been relatively more artists at work in the Central Desert. Also, with the increased number of water catchments, we should expect to find more rock art localities there than in the Western Desert. With reliable water sources distributed more widely over various parts of the landscape, there were more potential localities for habitation base-camps where people could reside together long enough to do this more elaborate sort of painting. The increased availability of water sources in the Central Desert increased the opportunities for a more varied rock art, although increased population and geographic distribution of water catchments did not necessitate this increase in the variety of rock art relative to the Western Desert. Perhaps as the symbolic and stylistic grammar of this art is better understood, we shall be able to posit some convincing ideational explanations for these elaborations.

Although we still have not achieved satisfactory explanations for all of the anomalies observed in the material residues at James Range East, we can point to at least two sets of explanations – those relating to faunal and lithic residues – that demonstrate the value of the argument by anomaly. These explanations show that relative stability of residence in a relatively wide variety of locations, thanks to the increased availability of water in surface catchments over the landscape (in contrast to the necessity for greater nomadic movement, shorter-term residence at many localities, and other constraints upon settlement and access to game in the Western Desert that are part of the risk-minimizing model of human adaptation proposed for that region), can make a recognizable difference in the material residues at archaeological sites. These differences are the archaeological signatures of their respective modes of adaptation. But, as the case of faunal and lithic anomalies at James Range East also shows, these signatures do not constitute absolute entities in themselves but are meaningful only in relation to general propositions based upon ecological and geographical relationships that are understood and controlled for. An archaeological signature, once recognized by means of living archaeology, constitutes a relativistic statement of behavioral relationships that can achieve wider utility in archaeology only by continued comparisons with other, similarly controlled evidence from other places and periods. So perhaps at this point it would be advisable to extend the argument by anomaly further by looking at other recent work in Australia in the light of this approach.

9

Antipodean anomalies

The last decade has witnessed an impressive expansion of research in Australian prehistory, and the results so far have been important not just in a quantitative sense but with respect to certain qualities that tend to set these results apart from those of archaeologists working in many other areas. There is an anthropological dimension to Australian archaeology that should be recognized and appreciated in the context of the opportunities for research historically afforded by the antipodes.

There is no necessary reason for archaeologists to seek anthropological explanations for their findings. As I suggested earlier, one could easily limit one's view of archaeology to matters of chronology and typology, with an emphasis on refinements in techniques of excavation and analysis. In some quarters, such an emphasis is archaeology. A quick foray into the nearest academic bookstore or library reveals how many different and special kinds of archaeology there are as one encounters titles like: "Industrial Archaeology," "Rescue Archaeology" (or its American counterpart, "Salvage Archaeology"), "Marine Archaeology," "Romano-British Archaeology," "Classical Archaeology," "Landscape Archaeology," "Experimental Archaeology," and "Public Archaeology," (the last has to do with public policies and programs for site conservation and mangement of cultural resources, and is a term that is starting to see wide use in America). In Britain today, one even finds books on "Aviation Archaeology," which have mainly to do with the recovery of crashed World War II aircraft. This proliferation of specialties reflects the growing "grassroots" interest in archaeology in Britain and elsewhere, but it has relatively little to do with anthropology or with anthropological ideas about human behavior.

In the United States the alliance between archaeology and anthropology, at least in academic contexts, came about largely as a result of a historical coincidence. Stratigraphic archaeology got underway in America at a time when there were still traditionally-oriented American Indian populations present in the vicinity to be interviewed and observed. This happened mainly in the American Southwest, where scholars like Hodge (1897) and Fewkes (1893) sought explicitly to test Indian oral traditions by means of archaeology. The earliest systematic attempt at sequence-dating of pottery in North America was made by A. L. Kroeber (1916) at Zuni, also with the aim of investigating traditional oral histories of Puebloan settlement. The presence of living societies of American Indians in various parts of North America – not to mention the Eskimos, whose ethnographic behavior also came under archaeological scrutiny before long – was a stimulus to archaeologists to look for relationships between the behavior of living and historic groups and their archaeological findings. The denial of such relationships during the previous century in the guise of the "Mound Builder" myth (Silverberg, 1968) and other purported non-Indian origins for the antiquities of the New World was sharply reversed at this time. No longer could homespun antiquarians like Caleb Atwater (1820) declare that the earthworks and artifact remains of the Ohio River Valley, for example, were the products of "Hindoos and Tartars," nor could scholars seriously attribute these remains to a lost Israelite tribe, Norse invaders, or the legendary Welsh Prince Madoc.

Although Australia, too, has its share of proponents for theories that derive the origins for their prehistoric antiquities from such faraway peoples as the Egyptians (Terry, 1968), the situation in the twentieth century has been comparable to what it was in certain parts of North America during the American Indian "Reservation Period" in the late nineteenth and early twentieth centuries. As Jones (1971: 63) has noted, "In the entire Pacific region, the prehistoric record is truncated by historically recorded societies, so that there is a direct link between the most recent archaeology and ethnography," and this observation is especially true in Australia. In America, the awareness of the living indigenes in close proximity to one's archaeological surveys and excavations led to the development of the direct historical approach (Steward, 1942), which was commented upon in Chapter 2 as a kind of continuous analogy. Such continuities exist in Australia and have encouraged archaeologists to consider anthropological explanations for their findings. Australia, in other words, was subject to the same historic coincidence as North America, and the application of scientific archaeology there has become increasingly involved with contemporary ethnography.

But historical coincidences like this do not require us to assume that contemporary ethnography is the best or only way to explain the archaeological evidence. For example, the juxtaposition of living, traditionally-oriented Aborigine societies and the archaeological residues of prehistoric Aborigines was not universally perceived in Australia as an opportunity for an integrative, ethnoarchaeological approach. No less a figure than A. R. Radcliffe-Brown opposed such efforts, stating that:

> It would save a great deal of unnecessary misunderstanding of ethnology on the one hand (related as it is to archaeology and history) and social anthropology and comparative sociology on the other, were they recognised for what they are, two different disciplines having different aims, different methods, and different interests in field investigations. [1935: 535]

There is no question that Radcliffe-Brown's dictum influenced many of his colleagues in Australia, and one can conclude from this that there is no historical necessity for assuming that, even given the opportunity, archaeologists and ethnographers will see any value in integrating their efforts. The burden of this book has been to show how ethnographic observations can enable archaeologists to propose and test valid explanations. But the value of ethnography for archaeology cannot be assumed, even in places like Australia and North America where we are confronted by living societies that are linked directly to our archaeological sequences. The value of living archaeology for the study of human behavior has to be demonstrated anew and on a basis that does not depend upon analogies. The argument by anomaly has been proposed as an alternative basis for establishing convincing explanations of archaeological evidence in relation to contemporary processes of human behavior, and archaeologists today are finding that Australia is full of interesting anomalies.

Access to axes

Even when the weather is clear, a cold, strong wind scours the exposed grassy slopes of the Mt. William Axe Quarry in southern Victoria. This remarkable site is the largest of several axe quarries in southeastern Australia, and it served as a major source of Cambrian greenstone for axes that were traded over wide areas of Victoria and hundreds of miles into South Australia and parts of the Murray-Darling River region. The site was still in use as an Aboriginal axe quarry in the 1830s, and the last Aborigine responsible for controlling access to the quarry and procurement of stone there was a Wurundjeri man named Billibilleri, who died in 1846. A visitor there today can still see many extraction areas, mainly shallow pits where unweathered stone was dug out, and concentrations of smaller debris that indicate work areas where further reduction and shaping of the greenstone axe blanks was done. Not surprisingly, the work areas tend to be located along the slopes of Mt. William that are in the lee of the prevailing winds, although the extraction areas are located wherever suitable stone occurred naturally. Only archaeologists and sheep seem to show much interest in the place today, although there is evidence to show that this was once an important center of aboriginal trade and exchange.

Recent studies by Isabel McBryde and her colleagues (McBryde and Watchman, 1976; McBryde, 1978) point to certain anomalies that can be considered usefully in relation to ethnographic and ethnohistorical evidence. Although the site of Mt. William itself shows internal complexities that suggest a greater degree of separation between tasks than one usually finds at Australian Aborigine stone quarries, McBryde's studies have focused mainly on the geographical spread and distribution of axes made of Mt. William greenstone into different parts of southeastern Australia. Along with this, she has examined axes from other Aboriginal greenstone quarries in Victoria and compared their patterns of geographic occurrence with those from Mt. William. One limitation of McBryde's studies is the relatively small number of well documented ethnographic or archaeological specimens available in museum collections, so she has had to rely heavily upon surface finds of greenstone axes, many of which lack complete documentation or controlled archaeological provenance, in order to boost her sample of specimens to a valid size for statistical comparisons. Altogether, about 1,400 axes were examined from a wide area that includes portions of the states of Victoria, New South Wales, and South Australia. Inevitably one cannot expect to learn much about chronological changes in axe-distribution patterns from such a study, but other kinds of relationships emerge that raise wholly new questions in the prehistory of southeastern Australia.

Techniques used in this study included X-ray diffraction and major trace element analyses, although thin-section analysis proved especially useful. Some ambiguities in identifying greenstone from particular quarries arose, nevertheless, and these are discussed by McBryde and Watchman (1976). One of the first questions to arise was whether the widespread dispersal of greenstone from Mt. William reflected special technical qualities of the material that made it more prized than more locally available greenstone. Samples from the various quarries were subjected to aggregate impact value tests by the Blue Metals Industries' Laboratories, because the mechanical tests applied to stone used in highway surfacing have proved to be applicable to evaluating the hardness and durability of stone used in making axes. All of the greenstone samples from the different quarries received low percentge aggregate impact values, ranging from 8 to 14 (stone from Mt. William had a rating of 10), showing that all of these rocks were hard and possessed high cohesion under stress – ideal qualities for axemaking, but with little variation from one quarry to another. The Mt. William sample also showed a low aggregate abrasion value of 1.4 percent in these tests, which reflects high resistance to abrasion – another desirable quality for axemaking – although there is every reason to expect that the other greenstones and usable basalts from Victoria would score equally low in such tests. From these test results, McBryde (1978:358) concluded that the quality of the material is an important causal factor in the distribution of greenstone for axemaking, but cannot be invoked alone to explain the nature of the dispersal.

One could argue that, given raw material of more or less equally ideal qualities for axemaking, a simple utilitarian model would predict a wide but more or less even pattern of dispersal of axes in all directions from the quarry source. However, such uniformity of dispersal of greenstone from Mt. William is emphatically what one does not find in southeastern Australia. By setting up a series of concentric circles, each 100 kilometers (62 miles) wide, from each quarry site and counting the numbers of axes from that site occurring within each concentric zone, McBryde (1978: 360–1) showed that the relationship between numbers of axes and the distance from the source was not constant for all quarries. Some quarries had wider overall distributions than others. Mt. William material traveled farthest, occurring as much as 600–700 kilometers (370–430 miles) from the quarry. On the other hand, material from the Jallukar quarry site got no farther than 200 kilometers (125 miles) from its source. In at least one case, too, the numbers of specimens actually increased with distance up to 500 kilometers (310 miles) away, then fell off sharply. But even more dramatic anomalies appeared when the occurences of axes from particular quarries were plotted on a map and tabulated on a directional distribution table (constructed on eight segments of a circle centered on the quarry). The principal trends of axe distribution revealed by these maps and tables were to the north and to the southwest. Conversely, axe specimens from these quarries were almost totally absent from eastern Victoria. Other, lesser anomalies in distribution also appeared, especially in the northwestern Wimmera/Mallee district of Victoria, where greenstone axes were also rare or absent altogether.

In fact, as Ian Hodder[14] (pers. comm.) has suggested, it may still be possible to posit a technological explanation for the principal anomalies in this case, namely, the absence of greenstone axes from eastern Victoria and other areas. We need to know more about the kinds of stone the Aborigines of eastern Victoria (i.e., Gippsland) and these other areas were using to make their axes, and we also need to know more about their sources for these materials. Given adequate sources of raw materials for axemaking in Gippsland and such areas as the Wimmera/Mallee district, one might not expect greenstone axes from Mt. William and other quarries to penetrate these regions. There is at least a suggestion that this may have been the case, when we read in Howitt (1904: 312) that:

> Stone tomahawks and axes are made either from water-worn pebbles or pieces split from larger blocks of stone. The former was the practice in Gippsland, where suitable material is very plentiful in the mountain streams ... A Kurnai man having found a waterworn stone suitable for his purpose, first of all chipped or pounded the part intended for the cutting edge with a hard rounded pebble, then having brought it somewhat into shape, he rubbed it down on a suitable rock in the bed of a stream until he had produced a good edge.

On the other hand, Howitt (1904: 312) also reports that the Kulin tribes of central Victoria used both greenstone from Mt. William and stream pebbles in their axemaking. So we must ask: Are there any significant differences in the technological characteristics of quarried greenstone versus stream cobbles for axemaking and axe use? Further work will be needed on this point before the utilitarian explanations for the spatial anomalies in greenstone axe distribution in Victoria can be laid to rest.

A geographic argument fares only slightly better than the technological one, since greenstone axes are well represented in a linear distribution along certain areas where river valleys and other geographic features provided good communications between regions; yet the Wimmera River, which could also have provided such access to the north, was lacking in axes. Another argument that was considered had to do with the distribution of aboriginal human populations in different subregions, but, here, too, the correlation was only partial. Although axes were poorly represented in the Wimmera/Mallee, which is an area of open plains with little reliable surface water lying between better watered districts to the south, in Victoria, and the Murray River to the north, and where human population densities were low and presented relatively little in the way of archaeological remains, the reverse was not true of Gippsland, to the east and southeast, where some of the highest densities of human population in aboriginal Australia probably occurred. Greenstone axes, in other words, were absent or relatively scarce in both the best and the worst areas for aboriginal human settlement in Victoria. So much for the idea of a simple relationship between numbers of greenstone axes and density of human settlement.

At this point in her argument, McBryde turns to ethnohistory for evidence of tribal and/or linguistic boundaries and traditional patterns of alliance or hostility within Victoria that might correlate with the asymmetrical pattern of greenstone axe distribution there. Here a significant correlation does emerge. Nineteenth-century ethnographers described hostile and competitive relations between two major groupings of tribes within Victoria: the Kurnai of Gippsland to the east and southeast and the Kulin of central Victoria. All of the greenstone axe quarries, including Mt. William, lie within the geographic area occupied by the Kulin group, and axes from these quarries are rare or absent in the Kurnai area. Thus McBryde observes:

> This distribution seems to reflect clearly the isolation of the Kurnai from contact or trading relations with the Kulin tribes or access to the greenstone resources of their territory. This aspect is one shared by all quarries investigated ... certain features of the distribution patterns, such as the absence of examples from eastern Victoria, can be explained in terms of interrelationships between tribal groups in the nineteenth century, especially the hostility between the Kulin and Kurnai. It also suggests that material evidence may well reflect certain social relationships. Such social factors may over-ride those of technological convenience ... [1978: 363]

Of course, we do not know the age of many of the axe specimens used in this study, since they lacked archaeological context and were not accurately dated. Moreover, we cannot assume that prehistoric patterns of hostility and alliance were similar to those of the nineteenth century in Victoria. We could even stand this argument on its head and suggest that it was differential access to stone for axemaking that led to this ethnographic pattern of mutual hostility in the first place. As Hodder suggests (pers. comm.), this pattern of exclusivity and boundary behavior could have been the historical product of competition between these groups for a scarce resource – namely, greenstone. Having come this far by examining anomalies in the geographic distribution of material residues, we cannot invoke ethnographic analogy as an explanation without seriously weakening the argument. Are there alternative relationships between human behavior and materials that we should consider in trying to explain this anomaly?

For such a possible alternative we can turn briefly to work done recently by Hodder (1977) in the Baringo District of Western Kenya. Hodder studied the ethnographic distribution of material items such as pots, stools, articles of personal adornment, wooden containers, baskets, shields, spears, and other implements in a border area between three different tribal groups – Tugen, Njemps, and pastoral Pokot. The Njemps are Masai speakers, while the Tugen and Pokot speak related languages belonging to a group called Kalenjin. Masai speakers and Kalenjin speakers have separate oral traditions deriving their origins, although the nature of the social organization of all three tribes is similar. Hodder observed how various material items moved or were restricted in their movement across the borders of these three tribal groups.

Many items, it was found, did not cross the Tugen-Njemps border at all. These included Tugen wooden eating bowls of two types, Tugen drinking cups and honey pots, Njemps stools, and other items such as male and female articles of personal adornment, despite the fact that there was considerable movement by members of both groups and constant interaction across this border almost daily. From this observation, Hodder concludes:

> This freedom of movement across the Njemps-Tugen boundary makes the breaks in the distribution of certain material culture items even more remarkable. The evidence suggests the idea (cf. Barth 1969) that group identities are not necessarily broken down by interaction and contact. Quite the opposite may be the case. [1977: 259–60]

Thus the discontinuities in distribution of certain material items at this tribal boundary do not necessarily signal isolation between these groups, and this cautionary point must also be considered in relation to the explanation for greenstone axe distribution at the Kulin-Kurnai border in Victoria. People from one group can alter their material behavior in order to conform to expectations on the other side of the border, although, as the Tugen-Njemps case also shows, this does not necessarily occur evenly and to the same extent on both sides of the boundary (Hodder, 1977: 261–2). Moreover, these alterations can sometimes take a definite form, as in the Tugen-Njemps case, where some male-associated items (the three-legged stool, ear ornaments, spear types, and cloth of various colors) moved more freely across this border than female-associated traits (Hodder, 1977: 262–3). From this case, it seems clear that, as Hodder (pers. comm.) points out, material items always convey information of a social nature, even when these material items are primarily utilitarian. In the case of the Tugen and Njemps societies in West Kenya, these items served in various ways to identify ethnic groups, and Hodder is presently exploring how stress, in the form of competition for scarce goods (mainly cattle), can lead to such use of materials for ethnic identification.

The main implication of Hodder's studies for aboriginal greenstone axe distribution patterns in Victoria is that it would be premature to treat the absence of axes of this material in the southeast part of Victoria as the signature for an ethnic boundary analagous to that of the nineteenth century Kulin and Kurnai groups. McBryde's studies have posited the existence of an anomalous situation in which the geographic distribution of greenstone axes in Victoria was probably the product of something more than simply utilitarian factors, thereby leading us to a new order of questioning about these material residues. The question now is whether or not we can find ways to specify which of a variety of possible social or ideational factors most effectively account for this anomalous distribution. To do this we shall need to know more about the chronology of prehistoric axes and axe-making in southeastern Australia, and we will need to consider the geographic distribution of other material residues in relation to this presumed Kulin-Kurnai boundary. Were greenstone axes the only items excluded from the Kurnai region? Or were there differential movements of material items across this boundary in one or both directions? McBryde's research in this area is continuing, but it has already progressed far enough to indicate how useful distributional anomalies in material residues can be in ascertaining when nonmaterial factors were at work and in directing further inquiries about those factors.

Tasmania: A land-bridge too far?

Of all the ethnographic Aborigines inhabiting the southeastern part of Australia, none have fascinated Europeans more consistently than the Tasmanians. At first encounter, everything about these geographically isolated people seemed anomalous. The historic Tasmanian Aborigines lacked the dog, the spearthrower, the boomerang, the ground stone axe, and bone implements, although they possessed certain other traits, such as cremation or partial cremation burial, which were not seen among ethnographic Aborigines of the southeast Victorian mainland. Above all, the historic Tasmanians did not fish, despite the fact that the coastal waters around Tasmania abound with scaled fish, expecially parrot fish (*Pseudolabrus sp.*). Anthropologists of the late nineteenth and early twentieth centuries characteristically sought to explain these anomalies as products of arrested cultural–evolutionary development due to geographic isolation – that is, a survival from an earlier stage of cultural evolution.

As Rhys Jones has shown, this widespread and dogmatic view of Tasmanian Aborigines as an unchanging people inhabiting an unchanging environment had a chilling effect on the development of prehistory in Tasmania. For example, A. L. Meston discovered the Mt. Cameron West rock art site in the early 1930s, and Jones (1971: 45) notes that: "This latter find finally clinched an old problem derived from the dialectic of the evolutionists as to whether or not the Tasmanians were advanced enough to have possessed art." Meston also did some excavating at a locality called Rocky Cape, in northwestern Tasmania, where he discovered a parrot fish premaxilla at a depth of twelve to thirteen feet. Bone artifacts were also found in these deposits, and these finds opened up the prospect of discovering changes in the prehistoric cultural sequence of Tasmania.

With this prospect in mind, Jones was led to carry out detailed archaeological excavations in two stratified caves with overlapping sequences at Rocky Cape in 1965, from which he derived an 8,000-year-long cultural sequence culminating in the historic Tasmanian Aborigines. Although his sequence did not extend back into Pleistocene times, its implications were clear: Aboriginal man must have reached Tasmania at some time during the Pleistocene before the submergence of the land-bridge connecting Tasmania to mainland Australia around 11,000 years ago when sea levels rose worldwide as the great continental ice sheets melted. This presumption has since been amply validated by further archaeological discoveries of human habitations in Tasmania and on Hunter Island, a remnant of the ancient land-bridge off the northwest coast of Tasmania, that extend well back into the Pleistocene. At Cave Bay Cave on Hunter Island, radiocarbon dates associated with artifacts of bone and quartz extend back to about 22,800 years ago (Bowdler, 1976: 32), and sites of comparable antiquity have also been found on the main island of Tasmania.

Perhaps the greatest single change, and at the same time the most compelling anomaly, in the Rocky Cape sequence is the disappearance of fishing sometime between around 4,500 and 3,800 years ago. In the basal unit in the South Cave (8,000–6,000 years ago) fish accounted for almost 50 percent of the numbers of bones in the faunal assemblage and about 5 percent by weight. By 5,100–4,500 years ago fish bones had increased to 70 percent of the numbers of bones and 13 percent of the total weight, and this general pattern continued until 3,800 years ago, when we see the "...sudden and total disappearance of scale fish..." in the diet (Jones, 1971: 603). The remaining 3,800 years of human habitation at Rocky Cape produced only a single fish vertebra, although remains of other fauna were abundant.

Regardless of the disappearance of fishing, the subsistence economy at Rocky Cape remained firmly committed to coastal-marine resources, although this pattern declined somewhat during the latter part of the sequence there. At first, seal bones accounted for 85 percent of the dry weight of bones and 37 percent of the numbers of bones in the total faunal assemblage, although with the increase in fish remains around 5,100–4,500 years ago, seal bones declined to 75 percent by weight and 15 percent by numbers. In the next phase, to about 3,800 years ago, seal declined further to 60 percent by weight and 12 percent by numbers of bones. But, following the disappearance of fish at the site shortly after this time, seals regained their former importance. Overall, however, there was an absolute decline in the weight and numbers of seal bones, so that by the last 2,500 years of human habitation at Rocky Cape, seal bones accounted for only about 25 percent of the numbers and 50 percent of the weight of the total fauna recovered. Meanwhile, terrestrial game, represented by marsupial bones, increased in this latter phase to around 20–30 percent of the numbers and weights of bone. Despite the decline in the importance of seal, mainly fur seals (*Arctocephalus doliferus*) and southern elephant seals (*Mirounga leonina*), in the diet of the prehistoric Tasmanians at Rocky Cape,". . .seals provided the decisive element in the non shell-fish meat diet in all units" (Jones, 1971: 550).

As this statement implies, shellfish were also a major component of the Aboriginal diet at Rocky Cape, although it is inherently difficult to compare shells to bones and arrive at a realistic estimate of their relative dietary importance. In terms of numbers of shells, shellfish were the most numerous component of the faunal assemblage throughout the Rocky Cape sequence. The most common species was turbo (*Subninella undulata*), although two species of abalone and other shellfish species like *Dicathais textilosa* and limpets were also well represented.

In one part of the site it was possible to excavate the undisturbed remains of a midden floor and make reasonable estimates of the relative importance of shellfish in the diet at a particular time. The South Cave contained an enclosed chamber that was discovered during the excavations. In the chamber were five small hearths, two pounding stones (one resting on top of the other), as well as human feces, bracken fern, and abalone shells that had been swept into peripheral rubbish piles around the sides of the chamber. Abalone shells were almost completely absent from the ashy midden area in the center of the chamber, yet they accounted for up to 70 percent of the weight of the immediately adjacent shell dumps. The discovery of the enclosed chamber and the exceptional care taken in its mapping and analysis revealed something of the extent of rearrangement of faunal and other debris within a prehistoric habitation campsite and constitutes, among other things, an elegant archaeological example of the operation of the Principle of Interference discussed in Chapter 8. The central area of the chamber, where people presumably sat, slept, prepared and ate some of their meals, and perhaps did some stone toolmaking or at least used tools, was fairly clear of large objects. There were more stones in the dump material around the margins of this cleared area and banked against the cave walls than there were in the center, yet we can be sure that the tasks that gave rise to these residues did not occur next to the cave walls where the residues are now located. Radiocarbon dating indicated that the midden floor was abandoned when the cave was sealed off by rising deposits accumulating at the entrance around 6,700 years ago. Jones estimates that shellfish provided at least half and perhaps slightly more of the meat supply for the people who lived there at this time, and this estimate could be extended – with due caution – to all of the excavated levels at Rocky Cape.

So, while the ancient inhabitants of Rocky Cape stopped eating scale fish around 3,800 years ago, they continued to rely heavily upon a wide variety of coastal marine resources, augmented by terrestrial game and locally available plant foods. Northwest Tasmania was one of the more optimal hunter–gatherer environments in Australia, and Jones (1971: 619) sees no convincing ecological explanation for the disappearance of fishing among the Aborigines there in the prehistoric past or its continued absence from the historic aboriginal diet. Scaled fish of various sorts, especially parrot fish, abound today in Tasmanian coastal waters and are easily caught from or close to shore. On the other hand, the principle of neutral determinism applies in this case, for as Jones (1971: 620) points out, ". . .the prohibition on the eating of fish could be tolerated by the Tasmanians because, although it may have been inconvenient, it did not vitally affect their livelihood." In other words, this change represents a true anomaly, since it cannot be explained on purely utilitarian grounds. Jones goes on to propose that the absence of fish in the last 3,800 years at Rocky Cape (and Tasmania more generally) was the result of some kind of cultural avoidance, like a food taboo of the sort known to have occurred among ethnographic Aborigines in many parts of Australia, including Tasmania.

The anomalous character of this change in the diet of the ancient Tasmanians compels us to consider some kind of social or ideational factors in our explanation. But, as in the case of greenstone axes in Victoria, can we then specify the social or ideational mechanism or combination of factors that best accounts for this anomaly? Jones's argument implies a kind of societywide, blanket prohibition on eating fish, which, although a logical possibility, would have been unusual when considered in relation to the food taboos of other Australian Aborigine societies. In most cases, if not all, such food taboos were specific to particular individuals or subgroups within a tribe, and there were sometimes occasions when even the individuals involved could consume their tabooed species with the approval of the group as a whole. The other ethnographic examples of food taboos in Tasmania cited by Jones sound more like the specific prohibitions already familar to scholars of Australian Aborigines than the sort of blanket dietary restrictions one finds today among several major world religions. So we have not only the burden of accepting Jones's food-taboo hypothesis but the additional requirement of explaining why a blanket taboo of this kind should occur in Tasmania and virtually nowhere else in ethnographic Australia. On this question of geographic isolation, Jones (1978: 47) concludes:

> Perhaps these historical events in Tasmania constitute a specific case within a general proposition that *the number of ideas in a cultural system is a function of the number of minds interacting within it.* To test this we need to look at other islands, at other histories of isolation, at the evolution or breakdown of other human information exchange systems.

Of course, one cannot argue that just because the historic Tasmanians and other Aborigines did not usually prohibit the consumption of entire species in a societywide manner, neither did the prehistoric Tasmanians. But are we entitled then to argue that the avoidance of fish in the Tasmanians' diet was a "maverick element," or the product of "random and sometimes irrational propositions" (Jones, 1971: 620)? Food taboos are, admittedly, a possibility, but are they an explanation?

Perhaps the real value of this discovery lies in the way it challenges a commonplace assumption that hunter–gatherers always exploited the wild resources of their respective habitats as fully as the ecological and technological circumstances of their situations would permit. The Tasmanians clearly could afford to give up this potential food staple, since their habitat was both abundantly supplied with alternative food resources and stable with respect to that abundance. Some nonmaterial factor must have brought about the abandonment of fishing; and it did so under conditions where the abandonment of that primary resource would not be maladaptive to any serious degree. But we may never know what specific stimulus prompted this behavior around 3,800 years ago. Jones's suggestion (1971: 618) that isolation was a factor is also worth considering. Once cut off from the mainland of southeastern Australia, where fishing continued as an important aboriginal economic activity into historic times, the Tasmanians were left alone as an entirely self-sufficient group for the entire post-Pleistocene period. Traditional ties with mainland groups were severed, and any further influences these relationships may have had were over. Fishing might have continued if Tasmania had remained attached to the mainland of Australia simply on the strength of these relationships. Perhaps, as Jones has suggested, this anomaly and some of the other "curious discontinuities" (1971: 618) of Tasmanian prehistory, like abandonment of the use of bone implements, were the products of social and ideational imperatives in a provincial setting. They could happen more easily in a self-sufficient, island setting than as part of a more cosmopolitan network of social relations.

One aspect of Aboriginal Tasmanian behavior that was not anomalous was the choice of lithic raw materials in stone toolmaking. In his analysis of the excavated materials from the North and South Caves at Rocky Cape, Jones identified nine different types of lithic raw material that were used in making stone artifacts. Four of these materials – quartzite, red and yellow quartzite, quartz, and indurated fine sandstone and argillite – were available from local sources at Rocky Cape, although the last occurred there only in small amounts. Silicified chert breccia was derived from localities about 24–32 kilometers (15–20 miles) west and 64 kilometers (40 miles) east of Rocky Cape, as were various cherts. Spongolite was brought in from small outcrops on the west coast of Tasmania at least 80 kilometers from Rocky Cape. The final type, classified as "igneous," is a kind of residual category for single, unique examples. The source for these is uncertain. Thus chert breccia, chert, and spongolite were all materials derived from sources more than a day's walk distant from Rocky Cape (i.e., 24–32 kilometers), and Jones regarded these as "exotic" in contrast to the locally available types of stone. Table 13 (after Table 39 in Jones, 1971) shows the relative percentages of local versus exotic lithic raw materials used at Rocky Cape by cultural units throughout the archaeological sequence there.

From this table, one can see that there was a tendency for the percentage of exotic materials to increase through time, especially in the later part of the sequence. Jones (1971: 290) goes on to note:

> In the formulation of an economic strategy, a balance has to be struck between the increased efficiency of a particular material on the one hand, and the effort which must be invested in its import on the other. The more specialised the industry the more stringent are its requirements . . . the stone technology at Rocky Cape became more refined in the later part of the sequence, with an increased use of specialized, well made tools. The superior performance of these tools made it worthwhile to invest more effort into the exploitation and transport of excellent raw materials.

In particular, Jones shows how the typologically amorphous and varied stone tools at Rocky Cape tended toward more efficient use of raw material, as reflected by the length of retouched edge per unit weight of material. The Rocky Cape stone assemblage in fact consisted mainly of a variety of scrapers – five main types were distinguished by Jones – with variations primarily in the worked edge rather than the implement as a whole.

Jones noted a small but cumulative change in the steep-edge

Table 13. *Relative percentages of local versus exotic lithic raw materials used in stone toolmaking at Rocky Cape sites, Tasmania*[a]

Site	Cultural unit	Age		Total number	Relative percentage of stone	
					Local	Exotic
North cave	1	400	B.P.	207	64	36
	2	2500–400	B.P.	239	96	4
	3	<3800–3500	B.P.	239	90	10
South cave	5	4500(?)–3800	B.P.	1,873	98	2
	6	5100–4500(?)	B.P.	869	100	0
	7	8000–7500 to 6000	B.P. B.P.	816	99	1

[a] After Jones (1971: Table 39).

scrapers (Type 2) toward more restricted and possibly more standardized shape. Among other things, these implements tended to become smaller and showed less step flaking through time. Finely retouched round-edge scrapers (Type 1) increased in numbers to become the dominant tool type in the uppermost levels of the North Cave (Jones, 1971: 447). There was little change in the technical and typological attributes of the other retouched implements in the South Cave sequence, and, in fact, most of the changes in these items occurred within the last 2,500 years in the North Cave sequence as part of what Jones (1971: 312) characterizes as "a slow but steady tendency through the entire sequence towards more efficient use." Unlike the rest of Australia, Tasmanian sites so far excavated contain no signs of a small tool tradition, thus supporting the view that the Tasmanian Aborigines were isolated from the Australian mainland as the sea rose during late Pleistocene times and severed the land-bridge before techniques of small tool manufacture and use had reached Tasmania (Jones, 1973; Mulvaney, 1975: 210–12). So with a fair degree of certainty we may regard all of these changes in the stone toolkit as purely indigenous and independent developments by the Tasmanians, culminating in the stone tools observed by the earliest Europeans to visit Tasmania. These historic assemblages contained no hafted implements of any kind.

There is every reason to accept Jones's argument that tendencies toward increased standardization and improvement in the prehistoric stone assemblages at Rocky Cape led to an increased demand for lithic materials that were better suited for this finer work than was possible with locally available stones. The use-wear and edge-damage studies already carried out by Jones could be combined with an experimental program to observe the mechanical efficiency of each of these lithic raw materials vis-à-vis particular tasks as a final test of this technological hypothesis. But at this stage the hypothesis seems reasonable simply on the basis of inspection of these different types of stone, and we can provisionally accept it as a basis for further conclusions. Increased technical efficiency required raw materials that could be obtained only from distant sources, and it looks as if this explains the correlation at Rocky Cape between increased technical improvement of stone tools and the percentage of exotic stones used to produce those tools, especially in the later units of the North Cave sequence. Thus a strictly utilitarian argument, based on a materialist approach to the lithic residues at Rocky Cape, offers an adequate and satisfying explanation for this correlation.

But the materialist approach works well at another level of explanation, too. As the earlier discussion of dietary remains from the Rocky Cape caves indicated, these ancient hunter–gatherers were living in a fairly optimal habitat in which stress, in the form of direct imposition of a limiting factor like scarcity of water or a key food resource, was less critical than it was in more marginal areas like the Central and Western Deserts. Tasmania, although geographically isolated, was large and varied enough in terrain and resources to provide a base for economic self-sufficiency that sustained the Aborigines there throughout the post-Pleistocene period. It was not until the arrival of Europeans that this stable and successful way of life was abruptly and catastrophically terminated. Given the abundance and reliability of most basic resources there, the ancient Tasmanians probably had little need for widely ramified social networks of the sort we observed in use in the Western Desert to reduce the risks prompted by uncertain resources. The increasingly widened networks for transporting and/or trading exotic raw materials at Rocky Cape still extended no farther than can be efficiently explained by the technological needs posited by Jones. Even within the circumscribed area of the Tasmanian landmass, social networks did not need to extend far, and it is even possible that most of the exotic stones at Rocky Cape were obtained and transported within the ambit of nomadic movement ordinarily followed by the single group or cluster of groups that habitually visited Rocky Cape. Thus the relatively restricted scope of lithic raw material procurement, even when one includes exotic stones, denotes an adaptive condition over at least the last 8,000 years that is a complete opposite to the conditions we observed earlier in the Western Desert.

The final irony of this story appears in the conditions at the time of European settlement in Tasmania during the early nineteenth century. By using fire as a means of clearing areas of scrub and increasing the extent of plains and parkland, the aboriginal Tasmanians had created or enhanced vegetational conditions that were ideal for European use of the land for cultivation and grazing. Commenting on this long-term process of land clearance by the Aborigines, Jones notes:

> Ironically, the landscape had been kept in this condition [i.e., cleared and ideal for European exploitation] and even partially moulded, by the fire sticks of the Aborigines, who had unwittingly eased the task of their invaders. [Jones, 1971: 10]

The very adaptive success of the Tasmanian Aborigines proved in the end to be their downfall, since it fostered conditions that made Tasmania attractive for early European settlement. The conflict between European settlers and the Tasmanian indigenes has been documented in detail (Turnbull, 1948; Howells, 1977), and fighting, together with introduced epidemic diseases and lowered fertility, assured the total extinction of Aboriginal Tasmanian society by the mid-nineteenth century. As Jones concludes, "Within their terrible lifetime, an entire people with a distinctive history going back to the end of the Ice Age, was snuffed out" (1971: 16). The self-sufficient human adaptation that had succeeded in isolation for so long proved exceptionally vulnerable when that isolation was finally overcome. The subsidence of the Pleistocene landbridge that was to preserve Tasmanian society for thousands of years also served, in the end, to seal these people into a geographical trap from which there was no escape after European contact.

Toward a "signature" in shells

In relation to world prehistory, the sites excavated at Rocky Cape were unusual in that they were stratified rockshelters containing shell midden deposits. But the interpretive problems surrounding these shellheaps were similar to those one encounters more commonly in open-air shell midden sites. There were uneven concentrations and zones of various kinds of shell, sometimes packed together in distinct lenses, and sometimes stirred in with soil, shells, and debris. The internal stratification of shell middens has always presented difficult problems for archaeologists, and the Rocky Cape caves were no exception. One cannot safely assume anything like even or regular rates of deposition, nor can one make simple assumptions about the horizontal dispersal of shells over the site surface at any given time. Jones (1971: 128) observes, for example, that:

> Middens . . . owe much of their weight and if well preserved, even more of their volume, to direct human activities . . . A thick lens or even an elongated band of shells could theoretically result from a single visit. As an example, 2,000 *Subninella* shells could easily be consumed at

a base camp by half a band over two days, and it is conceivable that in a periodic domestic sweep-out such as I
have observed in the field in Arnhem Land (1970), that
these could be piled up into a single heap away from the
living area. Thus a single stratigraphic feature, may be the
result of a few days occupation.

Recognition of complexities like this at Rocky Cape led Jones to
work with Betty Meehan among the Anbara Aborigines of Arnhem
Land, in an effort to monitor exploitation of shellfish as a resource
and the discard of shell residues. In Chapter 4 we looked at the
Anbara mode of adaptation, with emphasis on shellfish-gathering
strategies, and now I would like to return to the Anbara case, as
studied by Meehan and Jones, to examine the differential residues
of shell that arise from such strategies.

Shells resulting from Anbara consumption of shellfish occur at
three kinds of sites described by Meehan (1975: 166): (1) "dinnertime" camps; (2) home bases; and (3) processing sites. "Dinnertime"
camps were located on or near beaches close to a river mouth, pref-
erably under a shady tree. Such camps consisted of a cleared central
area with one or two hearths and discrete piles of shells and other
debris such as grass and leaves upon which the shellfish were placed
during and after cooking around the periphery. Sometimes these
localities were revisited, with the result that sitting areas would be
swept off and new hearths and shell heaps would form. Home bases
were a complex expansion of the pattern observed for "dinnertime"
camps, occurring over several months of occupation. Debris continued to be piled around the periphery of each hearth complex,
and at regular intervals, generally once every week or two, the entire
camp area was cleaned up with rakes and sticks or swept by foot. By
this means, rubbish was dumped in areas that were unimportant
with respect to use or access, and quite large banks of debris formed
in these places. The process of scraping and heaping continued intermittently as long as the camp was occupied, and at times the
rubbish from previous occupations was disturbed and became incorporated into contemporary debris piles (Meehan, 1975: 168). Processing sites contained only the shells of *Batissa violaca* and *Crassostrea
amasa,* which were cooked at these localities. The cooked flesh was
carried to the home base and the shells were left behind. These
localities generally resembled "dinnertime" camps except for the fact
that there often was no source of freshwater nearby.

Thus the bulk of shells deposited at home bases represented only
part of the total amount of shellfish eaten during the period of
observation. "Dinnertime" camps and processing sites also accounted
for large amounts of shell discard (Meehan, 1975: 170). This was not

222 *Antipodean anomalies*

the only anomaly noted for base-camps. The main factors that governed the frequency of shellfish gathering from various home bases were the distance of camps from shellfish beds, the seasonal cycle, and ceremonial obligations. Interaction of these variables was complex and did not conform to strictly utilitarian expectations. Meehan (1975: 112) noted, for example, that one home base, the camp of Ngalidjigama:

> ... presented us with a paradox. It was occupied during the dry season and while it was situated only 1 km. from the sea, the main shell beds lay about 3 km. away. Yet there was a higher frequency of shellfish gathering from this camp – 16 days or 81% of the days of observation – than from any of the other sites [i.e., sites that were closer to the shellbeds]. There was a cultural explanation for this high frequency, which overrode spatial and seasonal factors.

The heavy use of Ngalidjigama base-camp at a time when other localities would have been more convenient to the main shell beds was attributed to the requirements of a Kunapipi ceremony that culminated, as these traditionally do, during a night of full moon. There was little time for the men to hunt while these ceremonies were in progress, and it was the women who were called upon to provide the bulk of the food for the assembled group. They did this in two ways: by collecting and preparing *Cycas media* and by collecting shellfish. The use of this particular home base locality was a compromise between the timing of this important ceremony and the locational demands of two basic but quite different food resources. As Meehan concludes, "There is no simple mechanistic explanation for the relationship between the location of camp sites and the frequency of shellfish gathering" (1975: 113).

Another way to look at shellfish residues is to weigh them and see what relation these weights bear to different strategies of shellfish collecting. The Anbara collected at least 6,700 gross kilograms of shellfish on 194 days in 1972–3, of which approximately 1,500 kilograms consisted of edible flesh. The principal shellfish species collected by the Anbara, *Tapes hiantina*, was sampled and weighed by Meehan on five separate occasions, and the flesh weight was found to vary from 26 to 47 percent of the weight of shell. The second most important shellfish species in the Anbara diet, *Batissa violaca*, has a flesh weight of approximately 25 percent that of its weight of shell, although shellfish species of lesser importance in the menu vary in this percentage of flesh/shell weight from as much as 70 percent to as little as 20 percent (Meehan, 1975: Figs. 9:1 and 9:2).

Using these figures and volumetric estimates, Meehan calculated the size of the midden the Anbara would have accumulated during 1972–3. A 9-liter bucket will hold approximately 9–10 kilograms of *T. hiantina* representing about 320 individual animals. Extrapolating from the 6,700 kilograms collected during the 334 observation days, Meehan esitmated that the Anbara collected a total weight of about 7,300 kilograms of shellfish for the whole year, which represents about 234,000 individual animals of a volume of about eight cubic meters. By taking Meehan's figures for *T. hiantina,* we can further calculate that this gross weight and volume would represent a total of between 3,570 and 4,584 kilograms of shell. But is it possible to refine this figure for purposes of a trial archaeological prediction?

Here it may be useful to consider the distinction proposed earlier between habitation base-camps and task-specific sites. Because Meehan's contrast between home base and "dinnertime" camps is drawn mainly with reference to the exploitation, consumption, and discard of shellfish, the differences between these types of sites are probably greater than her descriptions would indicate. It seems likely that a wider range of domestic activities was carried out by a larger segment of Anbara population at home bases than at "dinnertime" camps. Relative to their home bases, Anbara "dinnertime" camps appear to be more task-specific, and this task specificity is as great or greater for processing sites. With this framework in mind, we can explore the degree to which these differences in scope of activity and personnel can be correlated quantitatively with the discard of shell. In essence, we will look at Anbara sites where shell is a significant human residue, without considering other types of task specific sites that do not contain shell. We are assuming, of course, that these three kinds of sites account for all or virtually all of the shellfish residues that flow through the Anbara cultural system.

Tapes hiantina accounted for 61 percent of the total Anbara shellfish intake by weight in 1972–3, with *Batissa violaca* running a poor second at 18 percent. This latter species, however, has a heavy shell, so it was advantageous for the Anbara to cook them and remove the flesh at an intermediate locality near the collecting area (the processing site), thereby reducing the load that had to be carried back to the home base. The other species treated in this way, *Crassostrea amasa,* accounted for less than 15 percent of the total shellfish collected by weight (Meehan, 1975: 121). The other important species collected by the Anbara included *Modiolus micropterus* (5%,) *Anadara granosa* (5%), *Mactra meretriciformis* (5%), and *Melo amphora* (1.2%), with the remaining 25 species of shellfish (including *C. amasa*) contributing less than 5 percent of the total shellfish intake by weight. These shellfish, except for *C. amasa* and *B. violaca,* were cooked and the shells discarded either at "dinnertime" camps or at the home base.

So, using Meehan's 1972–3 figures, we can calculate that the portion of the shellfish intake represented by *T. hiantina* converts into between 2,178 and 2,797 kilograms of shell. For *B. violaca* this would translate into about 608 kilograms of shell. The three remaining major species (*M. micropterus, A. granosa,* and *M. meretriciformis*) resulted in averages of approximately 137, 178, and 290 kilograms of shell each, respectively, for a total of 605 kilograms. No figures are available for shell/gross weights for *M. amphora,* nor do we know the actual percentages by weight represented by each of the remaining 23 species beyond the fact that together they accounted for only 4.8 percent of the total. Perhaps the simplest way to deal with these residual species would be to note that their combined total would have to be less than 438 kilograms or 6 percent of the total gross weight of shellfish collected by the Anbara in 1972–3.

With the 1972–3 season as our case-study, we would expect the home base and "dinnertime" camps to contain between 2,783 and 3,402 kilograms of shells of *T. hiantina* and the other main species plus an undetermined but small amount (less than 438 kilograms) of shells belonging to the remaining 24 species that were a minor component of the shellfish diet at that time. Only two species, *C. amasa* and *B. violaca,* would appear in the context of processing sites, and these would account for only slightly more than 608 kilograms of shell. Aside from evidence for other activities, the presence of 83 percent of the shellfish species accounting for approximately 85 percent of the total weight of shell occurred in the context of home base and "dinnertime" camps. Processing sites, as the most task-specific sites in relation to shellfish procurement, contained 17 percent of the shellfish species representing approximately 15 percent of the total shell weight. While shellfish residues were archaeologically ambiguous with respect to the difference between home bases and "dinnertime" camps, the processing sites were anomalous and stood out both in terms of amounts of shell and types of species represented.

Of course, this case study does not attempt to control for the mixing of shells and other residues reported by Meehan when each of these respective types of sites was reoccupied. But, as in the Western Desert, one would expect that extreme examples of task-specific sites would be less affected by mixing than localities where multiple activities and tasks took place. Processing sites should stand out, both quantitatively and qualitatively, in relation to the shellfish residues present, while other criteria will be needed in order to distinguish home bases from "dinnertime" camps. Nor does this case attempt to compensate for unusual seasons, like the 1973–4 eco-disaster, when the Anbara relied mainly upon *B. violaca* and *C. amasa* as their main wet-season shellfish staples. Stressful seasons like 1973–4 could be expected to produce dramatically different patterns of shellfish refuse, since these two mangrove area species are precisely the ones that require processing camps. While no hard data is yet available for this, one can at least propose that expanded processing camps would represent the "signature" of stressful conditions of the sort experienced by the Anbara in 1973–4, when two relatively minor shellfish species in the usual diet assumed much greater importance as alternate sources of protein.

To my knowledge, the research done by Meehan and Jones has provided the first and, as yet, only empirical model in the world of shellfish collecting, consumption, and discard that allows one to make trial archaeological predictions of the sort attempted here. In this case, shellfish remains provide only a partial "signature" for various types of sites and adaptive relationships, but work on this project is continuing, and much useful data has been gathered on camp structure, technology, and other aspects of the subsistence economy. As this work proceeds, it should be possible to distinguish additional residue patterns that could serve to identify the Anbara mode of hunter–gatherer adaptation.

Burke's Cave and beyond

In his archaeological exploration of the Darling River drainage of interior southeastern Australia, Harry Allen (1972) discovered a stratified Aborigine habitation site in the rocky uplands of the Scrope's Range to the east of the mining town of Broken Hill, New South Wales. This site lies in semiarid country (with an annual average rainfall of less than 10 inches) to the west of the Darling River, but the range in which it lies is visible from the river. The excavations here took place in part of an open-air habitation area, so, despite its name, this site does not represent a rockshelter excavation. Only about 1 percent of the total volume of the site was excavated (i.e., 3 cubic meters or 105 cubic feet), so any conclusions based upon this work must be regarded as tentative. A larger excavated sample will be needed before any firm conclusions can be reached, although the results so far at Burke's Cave are well worth considering.

One is tempted to compare this site directly with those described already from the Western and Central Deserts, since, here, too, we have evidence of aboriginal human habitation under desert or semi-desert conditions. However, the stratigraphic differences between Puntutjarpa and James Range East on the one hand and Burke's Cave on the other are considerable and cannot be ignored. For one thing, Burke's Cave, despite its name, is an open-air site. And the fill at Burke's Cave appears to be largely waterborne, while the other desert sites had histories of aeolian deposition. The deposits at Burke's Cave, in fact, more closely resemble other open-air habitation sites that have been excavated in the Western and Central Deserts, but these lie beyond the scope of the present discussion.

Table 14. *Summary of "industrial units" at Burke's Cave site, New South Wales*[a]

Unit		Number of stone implements	Number of unmodified flakes	Flake implement ratio
1	European and Aboriginal artifacts present	524	5,098	10:1
2	No European artifacts. Aboriginal implements include core tools and scrapers, adzes and slugs, backed blades, and pirri points	449	4,658	11:1
3	No adze slugs or pirri points. Core tools and scrapers present, also greater density of artifacts per unit of volume compared to Unit 4	857	5,160	6:1
4	No backed blades, no adze slugs, no pirri points. Core tools and scrapers only	273	5,675	20:1
	Total	2,103	20,591	(Average for all units) 10:1

[a] After Allen (1972: 148–52, Tables 6:2–7).

Cultural materials were excavated at Burke's Cave to a depth of 66 inches, and Allen (1972: 148) organized these into four sequential "industrial units" that appear in Table 14. With an average density of 200 stone artifacts per cubic foot of excavated fill, Allen (1972: 153) did not exaggerate when he claimed that "Burke's Cave must be one of the largest and richest open sites in Australia." As at James Range East, the low ratio of flakes to implements suggests that many implements were being manufactured elsewhere and brought to the site (Allen, 1972: 158). In general, the core tool and scraper component of the various industrial units did not change during the sequence, but adze slugs, pirri points, and backed blades (in other words, "small tools") were all absent from the lowest levels at Burke's Cave. The association of large core tools (including the so-called "horsehoof" core), adze slugs, pirris, and backed blades with European implements in Unit 1 implies that all of these Aboriginal tools were still being used at the site after European contact in this region

(Allen, 1972: 159). Only a single radiocarbon date of 1850 ± 240 B.P. was obtained at Burke's Cave, from charcoal at a depth of 24 inches below the surface in the upper portion of Unit 4.

What is especially interesting about Burke's Cave are the particular anomalies that parallel those observed in the Western and Central Desert sites and suggest that similar factors of stress were operating in a somewhat comparable manner, especially when we compare some of the finds at Burke's Cave with much earlier materials from the Lake Mungo area nearby. Lake Mungo and the other Willandra Lakes sites present the earliest and longest archaeological sequence so far discovered in Australia. Some of these sites date back to at least 32,000 years ago and have been described elsewhere (Bowler, Jones, Allen, and Thorne, 1970). Allen's unpublished report (1972), however, remains the most comprehensive archaeological account of the prehistory of the Willandra Lakes region, especially in relation to such details as the selection and use of different lithic raw materials for stone toolmaking. A comparison between the Pleistocene-age patterns of stone procurement in the Willandra Lakes-Lake Mungo area sites with those of the post-Pleistocene at Burke's Cave leads one to recognize that exotic stones were used to a considerably greater degree during the post-Pleistocene period in this region than had been true earlier, during the Pleistocene.

At Lake Mungo, 27 stone artifacts were found in situ and 440 more on the surface, of which 295 possessed a thick coating of carbonate, suggesting that they were derived from the Mungo unit close to a carbonate zone in soil associated with a 26,000 B.P. date. A total of 95 percent of these artifacts were made from coarse-grained silcrete of light olive color, and the remainder were made from fine-grained silcrete. Both types of silcrete were available from local exposures near the Mungo homestead, about 13 kilometers (8 miles) from the site (Allen, 1972: 264). At that time there was fresh water in the Willandra Lakes, including Lake Mungo (Bowler, 1971), and air temperatures averaging 5–8 degrees centigrade lower than at present would have reduced evaporation considerably. Thus the virtually total dependence upon local lithic raw materials for stone toolmaking at Lake Mungo by prehistoric Aborigines was correlated with a period of optimal availability of moisture and amelioration of aridity in this region.

By contrast, the post-Pleistocene procurement of lithic raw materials at Burke's Cave was more heavily dependent upon exotic stones. Allen located deposits in the Scrope's Range containing four types of usable stone: (1) fine sandstones (for seed-grinding implements); (2) quartzite pebbles (held in a conglomerate matrix); (3) cobbles of quartz and granite (also contained in a conglomerate); and (4) shales and interbedded limestones containing chert. Many artifacts at

Burke's Cave were made of silcrete, but this raw material does not occur naturally in the Scrope's Range and can be treated as an "exotic." When we turn to Allen's 1972 report (Table 6:5), we find that silcrete was the preferred raw material for stone toolmaking throughout the Burke's Cave site sequence, accounting for from 55 to 77 percent of the tools there, with an overall average of 65.5 percent. Silcrete also dominated the category of unmodified flakes at the site in all industrial units except No. 1, where it accounted for 38 percent of the flakes present. But there were relatively more cores made from quartz than any other raw material, although silcrete came a close second in this category, too. It would be interesting to see how many of the implements classed as adzes and adze slugs were made from local versus exotic stone at Burke's Cave, but this information was not provided in Allen's report. Although we cannot, on the basis of the evidence presented, exclude an explanation for the preference for silcrete on simple technological grounds, we can at least suggest that the increased post-Pleistocene use of exotic stone in the Darling River basin was, alternatively, a product of social networks that expanded with the final onset of more arid and stressful conditions in this region between 15,000 and 10,000 years ago (as determined by Bowler, 1971).

It would be easy to test this proposition by first subjecting the different types of stone occurring at Burke's Cave to various mechanical experiments, especially in relation to working hardwood (vis-à-vis the use of stone adzes, since the ones at Burke's Cave are closely comparable with those found at Puntutjarpa and James Range East). If such experiments demonstrate that silcrete is technically superior for these tasks than the locally available varieties of stone, a technological explanation should be adequate. But if, for some reason, silcrete is less than ideal in relation to the local materials, then we once again have an anomaly that is more economically explained by a social-ideational than a utilitarian argument, namely, the social network hypothesis advanced earlier in relation to the risk-minimizing model of hunter–gatherer adaptation in the Western Desert.

10

Surprise package

As the Australian examples discussed earlier show, anomalies in the patterning of material residues prompt us to ask new kinds of questions about relationships between human behavior and material residues. They do not, however, always present us with obvious answers, and there are still many unanswered questions in these Australian cases. What specific social mechanisms, for example, best account for the anomalous geographic distribution of greenstone axes in aboriginal Victoria? Or explain why the ancient Tasmanians stopped eating fish? It is a truism in science to point out that the more we learn, the more we increase our ignorance. Anomalies discovered by means of ethnographic studies compel archaeologists to expand their explanations in many cases to aspects of the social-ideational realm of human residue behavior that are still incompletely understood even by social–cultural anthropologists. With this increased ignorance comes the possibility of new discoveries in hitherto unforeseen directions, and it is here that the rewards of interaction between archaeology and anthropology become most apparent.

Three personal experiences
Three personal experiences will serve to expound this claim. None of these is final or conclusive, but each one shows how the attitude engendered by living archaeology can give rise to new kinds of anthropological questions about human behavior. On a recent visit to Hong Kong, my wife and I were shown the market at the Chinese town of Sai Kung in the New Territories by a couple of social–cultural anthropologists[15] who have had considerable field experience in this area and speak Cantonese well. Thanks to this guided tour and a detailed briefing before we left Hawaii by another colleague in social–cultural anthropology who has worked extensively in this particular community,[16] we were in a position to appreciate the complexities of social life in Sai Kung, which is a shoreside community that consists of two major ethnic Chinese groups – land people (mainly merchants) and boat people, many of them quite

prosperous. The market in this town is located at the water's edge and serves both ethnic groups. This association is symbolized by the presence of public temples to serve both ethnic groups located side by side close to the market precinct.

As we walked from one row of stalls to another within the market, a pattern began to emerge in relation to the materials occurring together within each stall. As a naive observer, without any ability to discuss or ask questions in the local language, I was forced, as it were, to rely upon physical appearances for my initial understanding of what was happening. One of the most forceful of these impressions had to do with the different groupings of items presented for sale. Each stall contained items of a widely different nature, yet united by some essential similarity of raw material. For example, we encountered a papergoods stall containing everything from temple hangings and lanterns used for ceremonial occasions to toilet paper. To use a Durkheimian distinction widely applied to Australian Aborigines, here were objects of a sacred and profane nature – and what could be more mundane than toilet paper? – resting together in direct association in the same stall and, in some cases, on the same shelf. Similarly, another stall contained a wide variety of dried and processed roots, some of which were materia medica while others were for everyday cooking. These juxtaposed extremes (in one sense) were visibly united from the point of view of living archaeology by the nature of the materials involved. We did not pursue the matter then, but it looks as if one could ask, as we have done in this book, about the grammatical structure of material relations implied by this behavior. Perhaps these material relations could be the starting point for making discoveries about the social and ideational relations that produced them. Material relations of this kind have not been the usual starting point for social anthropological studies of Chinese culture.

Another example of the new perspective afforded by living archaeology can be seen in the material residues studied by "aviation archaeologists" – those enthusiasts mentioned in the last chapter who dig up the wreckage of crashed World War I and II aircraft (Robertson, 1977). At first glance, there does not seem to be very much that is anthropological about this activity, which in many cases is more a kind of historical treasure hunt than an active part of social science. Yet this apparently arcane activity could acquire an anthropological dimension when looked at from the point of view of living archaeology, as is true in fact whenever we look at human residues in their final context of discard. Recently I paid a visit to the Essex Aviation Group, a volunteer organization whose principal workshop is located at the Duxford Airfield, Cambridgeshire. Essex contains many wrecked World War II aircraft, and this group concentrates on excavating these wrecks and documenting them as fully as possible. Their efforts are matched by those of similar organizations in other parts of England and in Scandinavia.

I made this visit with the aim of pursuing a question: To what extent can wrecked aircraft be regarded as unwritten statements of national policy? Certainly we can see how today, in areas like the Middle East, sales or aid in military aircraft are a material expression of foreign policy by countries like the United States and U.S.S.R., with direct consequences upon the balance of power (Sampson, 1977). This has been true ever since air power became a decisive element in warfare. In places like southeast England, where aerial combat was intense during World War II, aviation archaeologists can expect to find the remains of airplanes made in England, Germany, the United States, and, to a lesser extent, Italy. One even finds the wreckage of airplanes that were manufactured in the United States for sale to England, and of components like aircraft engines of identical design that were manufactured both in England and in the United States during the war. At their Duxford facility, the Essex Aviation Group has a display area containing bits and pieces of different combat aircraft representing these different categories.

At Duxford I was shown identical parts of the same type of engine from two different airplanes that had crashed in Essex during the war. This was the famous Merlin engine designed by Rolls Royce and used during the Battle of Britain by the Royal Air Force in fighters like the Spitfire and Hurricane. Later in the war, this same engine was fitted to an American-designed fighter, the P-51 Mustang, with such success that the Merlin became the standard engine for the Mustang. To meet this demand, the Merlin engine was mass-produced by the Packard Motor Company in the United States. One of the engines I was shown was a Rolls Royce-produced Merlin from a Spitfire that crashed at Great Leighs, Essex, sometime after 1943, while the other was a Packard-built Merlin from an American P-51B that crashed in Lawling Hall, Essex, in August 1944. Both airplanes were badly smashed, and both came to rest in wet, heavy clay soils. Yet the components of the Rolls Royce engine were in dramatically better condition, especially in relation to rust and corrosion, after resting in the ground for over 30 years, than those of its Packard-built counterpart. The American-built engine parts were heavily pitted and darkened from corrosion, and no amount of work could restore their original finish, while the Rolls Royce engine parts that survived the crash were almost as good as new and required minimal restoration work.

Many factors could account for this difference. The conditions under which the airplanes crashed could vary, especially if one airplane burned while the other did not. And differences in the chemistry and moisture content of the soils in which the airplanes came to rest might provide an explanation. Then, too, these are just two cases, and a larger sample of similar wrecks would be needed to see if any kind of pattern exists in such differences. So far, aviation archaeology has made only halting steps toward controlling these kinds of variables, although diligent archival work (something that has already begun in most amateur groups of this kind), detailed recording of the soil conditions in which the wreck occurred, and excavation of similar wrecks to establish an adequate sample for comparison, respectively, are all feasible steps that could be taken to control for such differences.

Having controlled for such physical factors, however, one may find that they still do not fully account for differences in preservation like those observed in the Merlin engines at Duxford. Many of the enthusiasts who have excavated and restored such wrecks insist – admittedly on subjective grounds – that consistent differences in preservation exist (*Quest*, 1977: 8), and there is speculation at Duxford and elsewhere that these differences reflect different manufacturing standards arising from conscious or unconscious policies by the manufacturers of these aircraft and engines. Were German airplanes better built than British ones? Were American airplanes produced under contract to their allies better or worse built than those of the same type constructed for American use? Could the requirements of rapid mass production have overridden the need for quality control or durability in the finished product? If approached in the same controlled and systematic manner as archaeology more generally, aviation archaeology could explain such differences and provide a circumstantial basis for drawing inferences about nonmaterial aspects of national behavior that may have influenced these material outcomes. But aviation archaeologists will be encouraged to apply such controls in their recovery of data only if questions of this kind are asked.

A final personal experience that shows the value of observing behavior from the point of view of living archaeology concerns Mr. Fred Avery, a resident of the town of Brandon, Suffolk. This town is well known to archaeologists as the principal center in England for the manufacture of gun-flints, and Mr. Avery is the only person left in Brandon who still practices this craft. The methods he uses are identical to those reported in the literature (Skertchly, 1879; Clarke, 1935; Knowles and Barnes, 1937), which is not surprising since he was taught the craft by his father-in-law, who was one of the professional gun-flint knappers when this activity still went on in a big way in Brandon.

If one gets off the train at Brandon and walks through the town, the first impression one has is that this is an ordinary, medium-sized

East Anglian town, with the usual small shops and big trucks crowded in the center. But there are signs that this town is different. A closer look reveals that an unusually large number of houses and garden walls contain blocks of dressed flint instead of bricks or other kinds of building stone. Indeed, many of the better walls in Brandon are made of polyhedral flint cores with the striking platforms lined up to form the smooth outer facing (something which is unusual in East Anglia, where flint is a common building material). By the time one reaches the Flint Knappers Hotel, a pub near the town center, the material residues of this town's former flint-knapping industry are all around. A further walk toward the outskirts brings one to Mr. Avery's home, complete with workshed in the back yard and a large cement crock filled with pieces of dark gray and black East Anglia flint.

People have been chipping East Anglia flint since at least Middle Paleolithic times, although of course Mr. Avery's methods differ from those of the Paleolithic in some important ways. He uses a blunt-tipped metal hammer instead of a hammerstone for his core-reduction, and he uses a sharp-tipped metal hammer for flake removal and a small metal anvil on a table for the final shaping of his gun-flints from the elongated flakes obtained during the core-reduction process. He works rapidly, with the sureness of someone whose motor patterns reflect long practice, accurately producing gun-flints of different sizes, which he places in different canisters according to size. Mr. Avery is a professional bricklayer and sometime stonemason (he dresses flint blocks for wall construction), but he devotes about 1½ hours each day to making gun-flints and says he produces approximately 150,000 – 200,000 gun-flints each year. Most of these are sold in the United States, and it appears that Mr. Avery is the principal and possibly the only regular supplier of gun-flints to American gun clubs, who, among other things, restore and fire antique flintlock muskets, rifles, and pistols.

Mr. Avery obtains his supply of flint from chalk quarries located in Thetford, a few miles from Brandon. The quarrymen there put aside any nodules of flint they encounter, and Mr. Avery periodically collects this material in his station wagon and takes it to his regular workshop, about three-quarters of a mile from his home. He says that he used to be able to get better quality flint. But good-quality, dark-colored raw material can only be mined from depths that are greater than the quarrymen usually go. When there were large numbers of flint-knappers in Brandon such mining was commonplace, but today Mr. Avery has to settle for slightly inferior material.

Mr. Avery's work presents us with an interesting anomaly. His flint-knapping, while exacting, is not especially laborious. Unlike his predecessors in Brandon, he does not work all day, nor does he have to excavate deep shafts in the ground to obtain raw material. He is able to carry on the craft as a sideline to his principal occupation, and he does not require equipment beyond a few basic hand tools. Yet his products are marketed at distances ranging from 4,000 to 8,800 kilometers (2,500 to 5,500 miles) away. Predictions based on a general law of supply and demand would argue that the distance a given product travels from its point of production should increase in direct relation to the energy or labor expended in producing it. Scarcity is no answer either, since usable flint is found in many parts of North America. Seen in relation to such predictions, Mr. Avery's gun-flints travel much farther than one would expect, given the rather modest amount of labor and capital investment required to produce them. What arguments might best explain this anomaly?

For one thing, there is the factor of skill. Perhaps a machine could be designed to produce gun-flints, but the expense of building such a machine would be prohibitive, and it would probably require a long period of development and testing before it produced reliable results. Mr. Avery's special skills, which are in turn a product of a long tradition of flint-knapping in Brandon, are the key factor that makes it possible to produce usable gun-flints in Brandon today without recourse to extravagant capital expense. Another important factor is the specialized and "curational" nature of the demand-structure of this industry. Guns like Kentucky long rifles and other firearms that in some cases are over 200 years old are, in Binford's (1973) terminology, curated items that have been retained far beyond their normal use-life. In more orthodox archaeological parlance, these flintlock firearms represent a contemporary example of an archaism in material culture. Mr. Avery's skills and those of his predecessors have had the related effect of freezing a specialized technology in order to maintain such archaisms. That is, the technology of gun-flint production at Brandon has changed very little, if at all, during the last 100+ years, and this conservatism is linked to the peculiarly archaic demands of a "curational" market. From this case one could even propose that prolonged curation implies increased conservatism in those technologies needed to maintain the class of item being curated. Another argument, albeit one based on subjective impressions rather than hard evidence, is that the demand for gun-flints in North America is strong enough, as it were, to "pull" these gun-flints thousands of miles from their place of production. Here the key factor seems to be the specialized nature of the demand. Mr. Avery produces flints in Brandon that will fit within a fairly narrow range of tolerance into the fixtures on the flintlock mechanisms of the guns in North America, and there do not seem to be many other people who are able or willing to do this. So it is not just skill but the specialized nature of the skill that explains the anomalous distances that these gun-flints travel before being used. Mr. Avery's relations with his customers are essentially anonymous and are carried out in a manner quite different from the personalized social networks that we observed in operation in the Western Desert, but in each case we can note the presence of exotic lithic materials in use and as eventual residues. The specialized demands of curation in a complex, modern society act to produce material residue patterns that are comparable to those occurring as a response to ecological stress in a relatively less complex, nonindustrial society in the Australian desert. As emphasized earlier, archaeological "signatures" like the presence of exotic lithic raw materials are not absolute but are relative to the ecological and social context in which they occur. As such, they must be discovered and explained as anomalies in relation to the regularities in material behavior that exist in those respective contexts.

The final anomaly connected with this case is that Mr. Avery is indeed the last Brandon flint-knapper, despite the continued and possibly even growing demand for gun-flints in America. I asked him why no younger people are learning the craft from him now. He said that there had been several who were interested and wanted to learn but that they had been discouraged by their parents because they all knew that many of the old flint-knappers died at a relatively early age of lung damage due to silicosis contracted from breathing flint dust while they worked. Mr Avery is aware of this danger. He tries to work in a well ventilated room and only for relatively short periods, unlike the old-timers at Brandon who often worked together all day in large groups inside a closed and stuffy shed. But apparently no one else is willing to take this risk. If the Brandon gun-flint industry should cease, it will probably be for this reason rather than any based on a decline in the demand-structure, scarcity of raw material, or any other utilitarian explanation based on the material and economic relations of this industry. This particular material anomaly compels us to ask questions and recognize factors of a wholly different order from those of a simple materialist nature.

In an effort to encourage students to explore this way of looking at human behavior through the study of material relations and residues, a graduate seminar in ethnoarchaeology was organized six years ago at the University of Hawaii. Students enrolled in this seminar carried out limited living archaeology field projects in settings that ranged from public campgrounds to home kitchens. A brief description of a few of these projects gives some idea of the scope and imagination shown by these students in trying out this approach.

> —A study of the contents of a Chinese herbalist's shop in Honolulu.[17] The argument by anomaly worked especially

well here, where it was found that various traditional material medica, mainly from plants that could be (and
sometimes were) grown locally, were being obtained
from Taiwan and mainland China. The extra effort and
expense to procure these materials from China was a
good measure of the extent to which traditional values
relating to curing remained important in a Chinese-
American community of long standing.
— A field study of fences and other boundary and spacing
mechanisms in a close-knit Church of the Latter Day Saints
community in Laie, on the north shore of Oahu.[18] This
project is intended to test hypotheses about spatial relations and boundary behavior in Mormon communities proposed by Leone (1973), and the work is continuing.
— An examination of kitchen equipment and contents in
middle-class Honolulu homes.[19] One of the more interesting anomalies to arise in this study was the extent to
which equipment and materials not specifically related to
kitchen use were regularly stored within the physical
confines of this rather specialized part of the house.
Another was the frequent use of kitchen activity-oriented
implements for nonkitchen-related tasks (such as the
chopsticks that were used more often for stirring paint
than for eating).
— Inventory and analysis of the contents of a rural store in
a small pineapple growing community on West Molo-
kai.[20] In this study, interesting anomalies emerged in the
relationship between the distance various goods traveled
from their point of manufacture and the time and effort
expended in their production. Not all goods in the store
conformed to simple expectations of greater distance for
items representing larger energy investments, and these
deviations provided a ready entrée into the social imperatives of the demand structure of this community.

These studies, like the personal experiences described earlier, provide an indication of how living archaeology can ask new questions
about human behavior through the study of material residues and
associations. They parallel such major research projects as "Le Projèt
du Garbage" (Rathje, 1978) and various student-run studies carried
out at the University of Arizona (Schiffer, 1976: 187–90). The ethnographic study of human residue formation provides a point of
departure for discovering how social as well as economic imperatives
operate, both in particular societies and in the human species more
generally, that has until now been little used by anthropologists.

In adopting this approach, however, we must be careful not to fall into the classic and much-discussed trap of the "functionalist fallacy." That is, we cannot assume a priori that any human society necessarily presents a totally harmonious integration of its components in a manner that is adaptive to its surroundings. Cautionary tales of a social–anthropological nature have appeared in the literature, ever since Malinowski's pioneering studies in functionalism among the Trobriand Islanders, that show how human societies often operate in inconsistent and dysfunctional ways that even go beyond the limits of the principle of neutral determinism. In response to these critiques, living archaeology needs to examine relationships within the society being studied for possible adaptive and materialist explanations to the utmost on the one hand while, on the other hand, accepting the possibility that some kinds of behavior may in fact prove to be maladaptive, even when referred to a higher level of explanation. As archaeologists we have to appreciate the likelihood that there were societies in the past that, for reasons we have yet to discover in most cases, were unable to adapt in the face of changing circumstances and persisted in maladaptive behavior until they became extinct. As anthropologists we need to be able to recognize and examine processes in present-day societies that account for such behavior. For example, the "overkill hypothesis" presented by Paul S. Martin (1967; Martin and Wright, 1967) to explain the extinction of Pleistocene megafauna in different parts of the world as the result of man's activities as a superpredator can be looked at not only in terms of archaeological, faunal, and paleoclimatic studies but also in relation to processes of overkill that occurred in the historic past and ethnographic present. Can recent and present-day occurrences of overkill and overexploitation of resources generally provide us with predictions about the material residues arising from such behavior that can be tested against the prehistoric evidence? Certainly we cannot expect to deal effectively with questions like this if we assume beforehand that all contemporary societies operate in an adaptive manner the way we think they should, instead of finding out how they really do behave.

In describing the Western Desert Aborigine mode of adaptation, I have emphasized those relationships that can reasonably be explained most economically as adaptive in one way or another. The picture presented so far has been one of a highly integrated society in which virtually all aspects of behavior bear a consistent relationship to the requirements imposed by ecological constraints. Ironically, however, as we have successfully explained more and more Aboriginal behavior in adaptive terms, we have also been forced to recognize aspects of behavior that continue to defy such explanations. The choice in such instances is usually between a convoluted and unconvincing ecological argument or the admission that, given our present state of knowledge, ecological explanations do not always suffice. These are the ultimate anomalies, and the Western Desert Aborigines present us with at least two examples. Each cries out for some kind of explanation that will effectively resolve the potentially maladaptive nature of the behavior involved, but it would be presumptuous of me to propose final explanations. At this stage all I can say is that the argument by anomaly should lead us to recognize that these are new kinds of questions that could lead to important discoveries as Australian Aboriginal studies continue.

The question of canine commensalism
Utilitarian or economic-rationality explanations for the association of dingoes with Desert Aborigines have not been a howling success. Among many present-day hunter–gatherers dogs are an important hunting aid, but as Meggitt (1965: 24) has noted:

> The available evidence, limited and uneven as it is, suggests that over wide areas of Australia the tame dingo was by no means an effective hunting dog and that it contributed relatively little to the Aborigines' larder. It seems that only in ecologically specialized regions where particular kinds of game were abundant (as in the tropical rain forests) was the tame dingo a significant economic adjunct to the family hunting unit.

This rather cautious statement does not contradict the eyewitness accounts by individuals like Finlayson (1935: 67) and Hackett (1934; 1937: 288) that dingoes were used for hunting by Western Desert Aborigines, but it raises questions as to the economic importance of tame dingoes as economic providers. Later assertions by Hayden (1975) notwithstanding, it is surprising how few firsthand accounts there are for the use of dingoes in hunting in this region when one reads the large number of early accounts by explorers, travelers, and ethnologists who visited the desert while traditional Aborigines were still living off the land. Also, these accounts sometimes show how incidental the dingo was in relation to overall hunting strategies. On at least three occasions reported by Hackett (1934: 25, 32, 39), camp dingoes captured small animals on their own that were quite literally snatched from their jaws at the last moment by an Aborigine who caught up with them.

At Warburton, the Aborigines denied ever having used dingoes in hunting, especially when pursuing large animals, and this view was echoed by Jankuntjara informants (another Pitjantjatjara-speaking group in the Everard Range, South Australia, at the southeastern end of the Western Desert) interviewed by Hamilton (1972: 290).

Nor were dingoes ever used for hunting by the desert-dwelling Aborigines we observed in the Clutterbuck Hills-Tikatika region in 1966–7 or at Pulykara, near Mt. Madley, in 1970. Camp dingoes did, as Hayden (1975: 14) correctly notes, hunt on their own for small game, and sometimes people would take these small animals from them to eat for themselves, but should this be regarded as purposeful use of dogs in hunting?

The question of dingoes for hunting in the Western Desert is like the case of the proverbial elephant being examined by several blind men, each of whom perceived a different aspect of its total character. We have anecdotal accounts from the earliest period of European contact and further, more systematic accounts from ethnographers who studied the Western Desert people at a time when European contact was considerably more advanced. Descriptions from different times and places vary, and one can claim, as does Hayden (1975: 14), that the dingo was important to the economic life of pre-contact Aborigines in the Australian desert. But this claim lacks consistent support, either from the early accounts of such use of dogs, which are rare and ambiguous as to the true role of the dog in hunting, or from later evidence that denies the importance of dingoes in hunting in most parts of the desert. Moreover, the early accounts give us no clear quantitative picture of the importance of dingoes in the total hunting aspect of the economy. At present, it seems easier to argue that the relative rarity, ambiguity, and apparently minor importance of dogs in hunting by Western Desert Aborigines noted by both early and late observers is, in fact, a true reflection of their insignificance as providers of meat.

As indicated in Chapter 3, most hunting of large animals that we observed in the Western Desert was done by stealth, either by concealment behind a blind or, less commonly, by stalking. The Aborigines possessed impressive skills in stalking, although their rate of success at this was poorer than from blinds – this in spite of the fact that many men increasingly used shotguns and .22 caliber rifles instead of spears and spearthrowers. At no time did we see any attempt at hunting by pursuit across open or rocky ground. The moment a kangaroo or emu that was being stalked or watched during its approach toward a blind bolted and began to run away, the hunters would emerge or stand up and begin conversing, as often as not joking about "the one that got away." They did not even consider pursuit, with or without dogs. Nor were dogs used in tracking game. This was done entirely by means of observing tracks in the sand and soft soil, and the dog's sense of smell was not exploited as a potential asset in hunting. As Hayden (1976: 12) states, "if one decides to hunt with a dog the strategy adopted will be suited to hunting with the dog," whereas among the people studied in the Western

Desert the converse was equally true, namely, that the Aborigines had adopted strategies that did not make use of the dog. This was understandable, since the presence of dingoes in or around a hunting blind or during a stalking episode would frighten away the game. Contrary to Hayden's assertions that dingoes do not bark (1975: 13), the dingoes we encountered among desert-dwelling Aborigines at Pulykara, which at least to all appearances were true dingoes unaffected by interbreeding with European dogs, barked, howled, and whined often and with little provocation. So did the dingoes we encountered at the Aboriginal reserves at Wiluna, Laverton, Warburton, Leonora, Papunya, and Docker River. This is true also for wild dingoes, as anyone who has camped in the Western Desert will have occasion to know. Among the desert-dwelling people we observed, dingoes did not accompany the hunters but were sent with the women instead.

There were exceptions to this general rule. One was a young man living at Pulykara in 1970 who liked to take his favorite dog, named Pitjipitji, with him on hunts. But he trained the dog not to follow the hunters too closely, and Pitjipitji would skulk along a quarter of a mile behind the hunters while they were on the move. If he came too close, the hunters would throw sticks at him, shouting "Payi!" until he retreated. I was told that Pitjipitji was not allowed to come along on hunts that were planned from blinds, but I never had the opportunity to test this statement by observing a hunt of this kind when this man was present.

The other exception was the increasing use of large hunting dogs by Aboriginal women on desert reserves during the 1960s. The dogs in this case were big and powerful mongrels derived from mating between dingoes and station dogs (probably greyhounds or other similar breeds), and, unlike the usual Aboriginal behavior toward dingoes, these dogs were fed regularly and provided with kennels fashioned of brush or a section cut from a 44-gallon metal drum. These hunting dogs were clearly a post-European contact phenomenon and occurred typically within the context of the reserve settlement in close proximity to Europeans. For this reason these dogs were often kept licensed and leashed to a chain – something never done for ordinary dingoes – and they were trained by their women owners not to chase sheep. This was done by attaching a joint of mutton to a collar tied around the puppy's neck and allowing the puppy to wear the piece of rotting meat until the odor became so strong that, we were told, the dog would never again go near a sheep. Such measures were essential in order to minimize potential conflict with European station owners, who often accused the Aborigines of allowing their dogs to ravage their herds. I first encountered hunting dogs being kept by women at the Wiluna Aboriginal Reserve, on the western fringe of the Western Desert, in 1966, and later my wife and I observed the use of such dogs by women at the Laverton Reserve in 1966–7. These dogs would accompany the women on foot or be carried in a vehicle until a kangaroo was seen. Even if the kangaroo started to hop away, the dogs were loosed and they caught and killed it with such inevitability that one of the women would start gathering wood for the roasting fire before the animal had even been caught. The first pair of hunting dogs reached Warburton from Laverton in 1970, and we were present to observe the event, which aroused considerable excitement among the Aboriginal women living at Warburton. The use of hunting dogs was more efficient than traditional hunting methods, at least in relation to labor and time expended and in the certainty of a kill. But, as of 1970, Aborigine men at these localities steadfastly refused to adopt this new method (although they were happy enough to share in meat from kills made by these dogs) and preferred to hunt in a traditional manner, modified by the increased use of guns and vehicles. European-bred dogs were also used for hunting by Western Desert Aborigines at Yalata Reserve (White, 1972: 201) and in the Everard Range, South Australia (Hamilton, 1972: 290). Hayden (1975) reports the use of a dog for hunting by a Western Desert Aborigine man at Cundeelee Mission, Western Australia. But he does not specify whether this was a dingo or a European-bred dog, and this pattern of behavior sounds suspiciously like another case of post-European change in the use of hunting dogs. Men also used dogs as hunting aids at Ooldea, South Australia (Berndt, 1942: 162).

Dogs served other purposes among the desert Aborigines besides their dubious function as hunters' helpers, although these do not help us much when it comes to explaining the persistent association of man and dog in this part of Australia. Wild dingoes were sometimes hunted and eaten, and tame dingoes were eaten, too, although people stated that they did this only with extreme reluctance during serious emergencies. On cold nights, dogs were used to drape around one's body to keep warm. They gave warning by barking and howling whenever strangers approached the camp. Dogs were said to be capable of seeing ghosts (*mamu*) at night, and their tendency to bark in the night for no apparent reason was usually attributed to this cause. But, as with the hunting explanation, we would be reaching if we were to attempt to rationalize the persistence of dogs in desert Aborigine communities on such a flimsy basis. The warning role of dogs, for example, should not be overstressed, since there are no dangerous predators in the Australian bush. So unless one accepts the sort of extreme eco-utilitarian arguments proposed by Hayden, it would be better to try to understand the more realistic appraisals by Meggitt and Kolig, who noted recently, mainly with reference to the presence of dingoes among Aborigines of the Kimberley District:

> The apocryphal utility of dogs can hardly account for the scores of dogs that can be found in every camp. If only one or perhaps two dogs out of a dozen have any, if only the faintest, value as hunters, why are Aborigines prepared to maintain this lopsided ratio? [Kolig, 1978: 92]

Although dogged attempts to provide utilitarian explanations have met with little success, we can at least show that dogs were not grossly maladaptive in relation to Aboriginal ecology. As long as people were careful to keep food out of reach, dingoes did not make significant inroads into the Aboriginal diet or otherwise interfere with food-getting. Unlike European dogs, dingoes, as noted by Hackett (1934) and Hayden (1975), can forage for their own food and hunt small game by themselves even when living in association with man, so:

> Under pre-contact conditions, it seems that the maintenance of dingoes in Aboriginal camps would have been considerably less of a drain on human resources and energy than the corresponding maintenance of European dogs among contemporary groups. [Hayden, 1975: 14]

By this argument, the use of European-bred dogs for hunting by contemporary Aborigines living on reserves and other settlements in close proximity to Europeans is understandable, since these dogs must, as it were, pay their own way by making some sort of positive contribution to the Aborigine diet. If dingoes were such great hunters in pre-contact times, as Hayden claims, why would Aborigines wish to acquire European-bred dogs for hunting nowadays? European-bred dogs have not acquired greater importance in the overall food procurement by some desert Aborigines so far because there are so few of them. The process of introduction and acceptance was just under way in the mid-1960s at Wiluna, where there were only 5 hunting dogs for a resident population of slightly over 200 people, and at Laverton, where there were 2 hunting dogs for a population of about 300 people. Hunting dogs did not even reach Warburton until 1970. The problem is not to explain the present acceptance of European-bred dogs, which appear to be gaining a position of importance in hunting, but the pre-contact presence and persistent association between man and dingoes in the Australian desert.

Having concluded that dingoes were important neither as providers nor consumers in relation to the Aborigine diet, we should also note that desert dingoes are chronic cringers and skulkers. At no time did I ever see or hear of a person being bitten by one. Evidence from Papunya, Northern Territory, suggests, too, that dingoes and other dogs in contemporary Aborigine settlements are not vectors for disease in humans (Hamilton, 1972: 293). Perhaps, then, we are faced with a case of what evolutionary biologists refer to as commensalism, in which two organisms "eat from the same plate" without affecting each other's well-being, either for good or ill. Like the sea anemone attached to the shell in which a hermit crab lives, the two species *Homo sapiens* and *Canis familiaris* lived in an association that was neither parasitic nor symbiotic but neutral in its mutual effects.

Commensalism, however, is more a label than an explanation. If, for the sake of argument, we agreed to regard the association of aboriginal man and dingoes in the Australian desert as a case of commensalism, then we are still faced with explaining the association. Unlike the hermit crab, who has nothing to say about the sea anemones that reside on the shell be occupies, the Aborigines play an active role in maintaining their association with dogs. The real question is, to what extent do the Aborigines control that association? Could they get rid of their dogs if they wanted to? In theory perhaps they could, but in fact they cannot. Let us consider the alternatives.

Hamilton (1972) has offered an affective theory for the association of aboriginal man and dog that may seem far-fetched to some. She stresses the idea that puppies are regarded as surrogate infants and are "mothered" in a manner similar to human babies. Puppies are fondled and carried in a manner identical to infants (i.e., draped over the small of the woman's back) and are even suckled. Aboriginal women are more involved in affective behavior than men, but both men and women readily declare their fondness for puppies. This theory is attractive in the way it accounts for such behavior and attitudes; and earlier, in Chapter 3, I suggested that such affection toward puppies could easily lead to imprinting that would encourage dogs to remain close to the Aborigines even after this "mothering" has ceased. In our own work, my wife and I have encountered extreme cases of such "mothering" behavior, the most notable one being a woman we christened the "Dog Lady" at Pulykara (Gould, 1970). This elderly woman looked after a pack of some dozen dingoes, most of them full grown, with extraordinary solicitude. She rearranged boughs to provide each dog with shade during the heat of the day and covered its eyes whenever she ate something and did not want the dog to see the food (although she did not go so far as to feed the dog). This behavior fits well with Hamilton's affective theory, but we must keep in mind the danger of ethnocentrism that lurks in such a viewpoint. It is all too easy to equate this "mothering"

Love and hate. The ambivalence of Western Desert Aborigines toward their dogs is reflected in this scene near Mt. Madley, where the woman covers her dog's eyes so it will not see the piece of candy (which I gave her after this picture was taken) that she is about to eat. She likes her dog well enough not to want to hurt its feelings but not well enough to feed it.

behavior with the kind of extreme attention we sometimes see being paid to pets in our own society by lonely women or sentimental men. Hamilton's picture, while accurate as far as it goes, is not the whole story.

As Kolig (1978) shows, Aborigines in fact have a strong love–hate relationship toward their dogs. The affective theory here is expanded to include all behavior toward dogs, including periodic episodes of extreme hostility. Dogs hover and skulk about the Aboriginal camp constantly awaiting the chance to dart in and seize a morsel of unattended food – food in this case meaning practically anything (i.e., soap, boots, clothing, etc., as well as more conventional edibles) – and are constantly being driven away by shouts of "payi" and thrown objects. On one occasion in 1967 at Warburton I saw a Ngatatjara woman go berserk after being hounded, quite literally, by a pack of camp dogs who were trying to get at a bundle of food she was attempting to unwrap. It was a hot summer day, the flies were bad, and tempers were short. As she drove one dog away from her bag, another darted in and snatched a piece of damper, and then another would make its move. As more and more dogs were attracted to the scene, the woman suddenly picked up a metal rod she used as her digging-stick and, with a piercing scream, proceeded to smash it down on every dog she could reach. The uproar of her screams and howls of dying and maimed dogs was terrific, and instantly the whole camp was aroused. Some people cheered her on while others shouted to her to desist, and in the end she had killed three dogs outright and maimed at least five more (they probably died, too, for their backs were broken). The particular irony of this episode was that only a few minutes before this happened I had used the last piece of film I had with me to photograph this same woman's tolerant petting and nuzzling of some of these very dogs before she started to open her bundle!

Of course, as Kolig (1978: 97) and R. and C. H. Berndt (1964: 288) correctly note, killing someone else's dog is an offense that demands reparation. But the fact that such reparations, with their implicit notions of private ownership, are institutionalized among Aborigines is some indication of how frequently such hostility toward dogs occurs. No other aspect of private property is treated with such seriousness by Aborigines. Kolig (1978: 98) describes episodes of this kind from his field area in the Kimberleys and goes on to note the character of dogs as represented in Aborigine myths, which he views as a kind of social statement about the ambivalent attitudes Aborigines have toward them. While dogs were accorded privileged treatment by being allowed to roam freely through the precincts of a sacred ceremony (though other animals were chased away), they were consistently represented in myths as figures of social disorder

(Kolig, 1978: 101–3), and Aborigines who ignore marriage rules – a serious offense – are often said to act like dogs (Maddock, 1972: 97). As Kolig demonstrates, "the dog's myth image shows it to be loaded with detrimental, uncanny attributes. The dog appears as a vicious, murderous creature, a destroyer par excellence" (1978: 101). Such strong love – hate emotions toward dogs were manifested by the Western Desert people at least as strongly as they were in the Kimberley District.

So the commensalism of man and dog in arid Australia is not an emotionally neutral relationship. The "ties that bind" are strong, but these emotions by themselves cannot explain the persistence of the bond. The strength of this bond is evident in observations like the following one from the Everard Range:

> When one man complained bitterly of the depradations of his nine dogs I suggested he might shoot some of them. He turned in horror. "Kill the dogs?" he exclaimed. "Do men kill their children when their own hands brought them up?" [Hamilton, 1972: 294]

In this statement one can also perceive something of the structural factors that govern this persistent man – dog association. Presumably the Western Desert man interviewed by Hamilton would not only refrain from killing his own dogs in any effort to reduce the general canine population, but he would also resist attempts by other Aborigines to kill his dogs. At Laverton in 1966, my wife and I arrived shortly after a "cleanup" campaign had just been carried out on camp dogs at the Reserve by officers of the Department of Native Welfare. Unlicensed dogs were shot on sight, although many dogs escaped and the canine population there quickly regained its former size. The Aborigines we spoke with then were ambivalent about these efforts to reduce the doggie population. They unanimously agreed that the dog population was excessively large and had become troublesome, and they felt that something should be done to reduce the number of dogs. But no one wanted his own dogs to be killed, nor was anyone willing to kill someone else's dogs for fear of offending the owner and having to pay reparations of some kind.

In short, it would have been impossible for these Aborigines to do anything effective themselves to reduce the number of dogs in their camps, and there is every reason to think that this was true for dingoes in pre-contact times as well. Even under ecological conditions that favored hunting strategies that minimized the role of the dingo as a hunting aid, such as we find in large areas of the Western Desert, we can posit compelling reasons of a nonutilitarian nature for the continued association of man and dog from the ethnographic observations that are available to us. The case of canine commensalism in the Australian desert is complex and anomalous in many respects, but it is not inexplicable. Given certain ecological conditions and an acephalous society in which no effective restraint on the canine population is possible (other than the occasional tendency of dingoes to become feral, which is problematic as far as real numbers are concerned), we can at least begin to consider what the prehistoric role of dingoes might have been in arid Australia without being dogmatic about it.

Without waterbags

While the presence of dingoes does no more than suggest the possibility of behavioral anomalies among the desert Aborigines that might be maladaptive, the absence of waterbags as a function of roasting all large animals in their skins is decisive. Here is a truly dysfunctional aspect of behavior that, according to the arguments developed in this book, should not occur. Skin waterbags with capacities of as much as 19 liters (5 gallons), usually made from the skins of kangaroos, euros, or wallabies, have been reported sporadically from early studies of Central Desert Aborigines like the Aranda (Gillen, 1896: 186), Wongkonguru (Horne and Aiston, 1924: 50–1), and an unspecified group in the vicinity of Tennant Creek, Northern Territory (Spencer, 1922: 49). More recently, O'Connell (pers. comm.) was told by his Alyawara informants that kangaroo-skin waterbags were used by them as well, and he was able to arrange to have one made for him by Alyawara Aborigines living at Macdonald Downs Station, Northern Territory. In July 1974, O'Connell brought this waterbag to our archaeological field camp in the James Range and demonstrated its ability to hold water and be carried effectively. What is surprising is that an artifact of this kind, which offered undeniable advantages to nomadic desert hunter–gatherers, should be produced in the Central Desert of Australia and not in the Western Desert, where stresses imposed by scarcity and unreliability of water resources were greater.

In the Western Desert all large game is roasted in its skin in earth-ovens. The fur is singed first and then the carcass is laid in the coals of the earth-oven for however long it takes the coals to cool – usually about 40–45 minutes. This pattern of roasting game, described elsewhere in greater detail (Gould, 1967), is rigidly adhered to in those areas of the Western Desert we visited in 1966–7 and 1969–70 and is reported in the literature as the sole method for roasting large game in this region. The Aborigines I observed considered it unthinkable to prepare large game in any other way, although they did not cite any ritual sanctions or mythological precedents for their behavior. This method of roasting has some possible advantages. For one thing, it helps retain moisture in the meat (which, as the reader may have already inferred, is greatly under-

Singeing the fur of a red kangaroo. This is invariably done by
Western Desert Aborigines prior to roasting the animal, and it
effectively eliminates any possibility of using kangaroo skins for
waterbags, cloaks, or footwear.

cooked by European standards). Juiciness in the meat is certainly
desirable in an arid environment. Butchering is also made easier by
the way the skin is stiffened together with the carcass as a whole
after roasting. Roasting in this way, however, does not keep grit out
of the meat, since the meat is not actually consumed until after the
butchering has been accomplished and the meat transported to the
habitation base camp. By then it has acquired its characteristic
"crunchy goodness" that most Europeans would find hard to take.
But, set against the possible advantages is the overwhelming disad-
vantage this method has in destroying the skin of the animal.

Kangaroo skins constitute a class of material with many potentially
adaptive uses in the Western Desert. Skin footwear, cloaks, and
baby-carriers would be useful, but skin waterbags could have made a
real difference in overcoming or minimizing risks inherent in obtaining water in the Western Desert. Waterbags could have provided
the extra margin of safety for people traveling along chains of
ephemeral waterholes, and they would have enabled a greater degree of penetration of high-risk areas where water sources are unreliable than was possible with the traditional technology. They would

have extended the effective range of hunting. Wooden bowls used for carrying water in the Western Desert had very limited capacity (rarely more than one or two gallons) and were subject to sloshing and spilling. Their usefulness in transporting water did not rival that of skin waterbags.

In the Central Desert, roasting methods included techniques that allowed people to skin the animal first and make use of the skin as well as the meat. Moreover, information about alternative roasting methods and skin waterbags was available to the Western Desert people, since we have numerous instances of contact and interaction between these regions. It is safe to assume that the exchange of incised sacred boards and stones *(churinga)* from the Central Desert from one patrilineage to another into the Western Desert in historic times, for example, provided opportunities for the exchange of information of all kinds, including the use of skin waterbags. The existence of a model, in the form of Central Desert waterbags made of skin, plus the presence of social networks necessary to communicate this model, makes it likely that this particular technological innovation was known to the Western Desert people but was rejected by them, either consciously or unconsciously. So this particular anomaly of material behavior cannot be due to ignorance. It appears, instead, that Aboriginal conservatism connected with roasting large game in the Western Desert was genuinely maladaptive in obstructing the adoption of skin waterbags, not to mention other useful articles made of skins. Perhaps people do not have to live on islands or otherwise be as isolated as the ancient Tasmanians to present us with examples of gross anomalies in material behavior.

Instead of trying to explain away this anomaly, we might do better to ask how much tolerance an adaptive system like that of the Western Desert Aborigines has for maladaptive behavior. The Western Desert people were obviously surviving without the aid of skin waterbags throughout the post-European contact period, so the absence of this item of technology was not fatal to the society as a whole. Nevertheless, this particular absence constitutes a profound anomaly in relation to our expectations based on the ecological requirements for living in this region and the risk-minimizing model of human adaptation described there. At the very least, this case should caution us from assuming that all aspects of an adaptive system – even one as highly integrated as that of the Western Desert people – are optimally or even minimally consistent with the ecological constraints imposed upon that system. No answer to this problem can be found until we first recognize anomalies like this and start to ask questions based upon them. While we may not be able to resolve this anomaly yet, we are compelled by it to ask a new order of question that has not, to my knowledge, been asked before about the Aborigines of this region.

What now?

Twenty years ago I could agree with the now-famous and often quoted statement by Willey and Phillips (1958: 2) that, "archaeology is anthropology or it is nothing," without really understanding what it meant. Like quotations from the Bible or the sayings of Chairman Mao, this statement is subject to interpretation. Today, however, we cannot accept such a statement unless we can specify what kind of anthropology we are talking about. Not all anthropology is appropriate to the aims of archaeology, and, what is perhaps even more important, we cannot allow archaeology to be presented as a kind of imperfect anthropology of the past.

Archaeology sailed perilously close to this particular intellectual iceberg during the 1960s when it set out to discover matrilineal pottery and other "signatures" of prehistoric social organization. I concur with Roland Fletcher's[21] recent arguments (pers. comm.) that such efforts created false expectations for archaeologists while at the same time demeaned the discipline of archaeology. It is unrealistic for us to expect to discover the remains of prehistoric bands, tribes, systems of cross-cousin marriage, or other abstractions described and analyzed by social and cultural anthropologists. Partly, this is due to the basic limitations of archaeology referred to in the Introduction, but it is also because these abstractions are the constructs of social anthropology and, as such, are subject to varying degrees of inexactitude in relation to the realities of behavior in contemporary, ethnographic societies. Like the problem of "culture with a capital K," these abstractions are not always the kinds of approximations of reality in human behavior that can be usefully studied by archaeology. For example, I would not wish to argue that bands exist among the Western Desert Aborigines, any more than Lee (1976) would claim they exist among the !Kung Bushmen of the Kalahari, and there are serious doubts in some quarters about the validity or usefulness of the concept of the tribe (Fried, 1975). Even such concepts as cross- and parallel-cousin marriages are rarely absolute in any given society but usually exist as statistical preferences and are highly manipulable in different social situations. If archaeologists are not careful, they will fall into a subtle kind of ethnocentrism by basing their hypotheses upon these kinds of anthropological abstractions. If archaeologists are going to make effective use of ethnographic evidence, they must apply the same critical standard of judgment to the ethnographies they use as they do already toward archaeological reports and interpretation.

So we must consider just what sort of anthropology is most appropriate to the aims of archaeology. As a first step toward a unified theory of ethnoarchaeology, I have argued that archaeology is concerned primarily with the anthropology of human residues in relation to behavior. The "signatures" of such residues in contemporary societies must be approached at the level of first principles if they are not to be treated as analogues. Having demonstrated the inadequacies of the argument by analogy, I offered the argument by anomaly as a more satisfying alternative approach. The operations needed to carry out the data collecting and reasoning for discovering and explaining anomalies in human material and residue behavior are what I have termed living archaeology.

These operations are best carried out in two steps: (1) observation and modeling of adaptive behavior in contemporary societies, both with respect to short-term strategies and long-term changes in the total system, with the aim of recognizing and attempting to explain anomalies as well as consistencies in the total adaptive system; and (2) establishment of convincing linkages between particular kinds of adaptive behavior and unambiguous "archaeological signatures" in human residues that identify these kinds of behavior. In a preliminary way, my aim has been to demonstrate the explanatory power of this approach in relation to data gathered mainly in Australia, and I have emphasized the more obvious or gross patterns that can serve as archaeological signatures in particular cases. This does not contradict the efforts by other ethnoarchaeologists like Yellen (1977) and O'Connell (1977) to discern such signatures of behavior in data that are more subtle or statistically opaque. But, in a field like ethnoarchaeology, which is just beginning to develop into a self-conscious subdiscipline, it may not always be necessary to go to the extremes of applying high-level statistical manipulations to basic data in order to perceive such signatures. In many cases, as my review of recent Australian evidence shows, these signatures may be fairly unsubtle and can stand out clearly in relation to the behavior that produced them once the logical and empirical links between them have been established. Of course, there is always a basic requirement for careful measurement of primary data, and scholars like Yellen and O'Connell are to be commended for carrying out such measurements as part of their research programs. Careful measurements of critical evidence lies at the heart of even the most obvious archaeological signatures before they can be regarded as convincing.

The first person to call himself an "ethnoarchaeologist" was Jesse Fewkes (1900), an archaeologist who worked extensively in the American Southwest attempting, among other things, to test contemporary Indian oral traditions by means of archaeology. While interest by archaeologists in ethnology is thus of long standing, living archaeology, as described in the preceding chapters, is a relatively new approach that can lead to a new order of questioning in archaeology. The results of this approach so far in Australia are promising, and living archaeology now is clearly applicable to the study of general principles that determine material relations in any human society. It even offers the opportunity of making reliable discoveries in the realm of ideational behavior. As long as living archaeology addresses problems related to general principles in human residue behavior, it will serve as the baseline for archaeology as a social science.

However controversial my arguments may be to some, they should open doors for archaeologists who are genuinely interested in understanding and explaining human behavior. If my efforts here are successful, I would expect to see and perhaps be involved in debates on these and related issues in the years to come. When I was in the Army some years ago, I was told by various NCOs that there was something wrong with my "attitude". Somehow, being told this didn't bother me too much. However my colleagues may regard the attitudes expressed in this book, I shall be pleased if there is debate and disappointed if there is none. At the risk of appearing to be a renegade archaeologist, I have tried to present an individualized but coherent point of view that should serve to enliven our discipline.

Notes

Introduction

1 Stile's (1977: 97) distinction between *doing* and *using* ethnoarchaeology is relevant here.

Chapter 3

1 It can be argued that *M. titan* is not extinct but only reduced in size as *M. giganteus* (O'Connell, pers. comm.).

2 These observations are reported on more fully in Gould (1967) and were made among groups of Aborigines found within 97 kilometers (60 miles) of either the Warburton Ranges Mission or Laverton, Western Australia. These people had the use of guns and, in some cases, vehicles. So it is arguable whether these observations apply strictly to desert-dwelling Aborigines.

3 I am grateful to Mrs. Phyllis Nicholson for suggesting that I examine this idea in relation to my ethnographic field data from the Western Desert.

Chapter 4

4 I am indebted to Rhys Jones of ANU for this suggestion.

Chapter 5

5 Although this term is widely used by ethnoarchaeologists now, I first heard it voiced by J. O'Connell in discussions at the Australian National University, Canberra.

6 Dr. Barbara Luedtke, Department of Anthropology, University of Massachusetts, Boston.

7 I am grateful to Michael Schiffer, Department of Anthropology, University of Arizona, for proposing what became the prototype for this rule (or, in his terms, "law").

Chapter 7

8 It would be a fair criticism to argue that I am talking about simple differences here rather than anomalies. The problem lies with the preliminary nature of the research results being described. The differences we are presently observing between archaeological assemblages in the

Western Desert and the Central Desert may, in fact, prove to be entirely consistent and expectable in relation to basic variations in ecology – thus qualifying as extensions of regularities observed earlier. But there may also be true anomalies, as, for example, in the case of kangaroo-skin water bags discussed in Chapter 10. Our analysis of the Central Desert archaeological material has not progressed far enough for us always to be able to tell the difference between variability and anomaly, and I urge the reader at this point to take a provisional view of my use of the word, anomaly. At this stage in the research, I think the important thing is to be prepared to recognize an anomaly when one appears.

9 Curator of Archaeology, The Australian Museum, Sydney.

Chapter 8

10 By Dr. Helene A. Martin, School of Botany, University of New South Wales, Sydney.

11 By Dr. Patrick C. McCoy, Department of Anthropology, Bernice P. Bishop Museum, Honolulu.

12 By Dr. Michael Archer, School of Zoology, University of New South Wales, Kensington.

13 By Ms. Nancy Bronstein, Exhibits Department, California Academy of Sciences, San Francisco.

Chapter 9

14 Department of Archaeology, Cambridge University.

Chapter 10

15 Dr. James Watson, School of Oriental and African Studies, University of London, and Mrs. Rubie Watson, Graduate Student in Anthropology, London School of Economics.

16 Dr. C. F. Blake, Department of Anthropology, University of Hawaii, Honolulu.

17 Mrs. Susan Jane Wheeler.

18 Mrs. Patricia Beggerly.

19 Ms. Barbara Moir.

20 Mr. Paul Cleghorn.

21 Department of Anthropology, University of Sydney, N. S. W.

Bibliography

Alkire, William H. (1972). An introduction to the peoples and cultures of Micronesia. *Addison Wesley module in anthropology*, no. 18, 56 pp.

Allen, Harry (1972). *Where the crow flies backwards: Man and land in the Darling Basin*. Ph.D. dissertation, Department of Prehistory, Australian National University, Canberra.

 (1974). The Bagundji of the Darling Basin: Cereal gatherers in an uncertain environment. *World Archaeology*, 5, 309–22.

Anonymous (1977). Enemy within. *Quest*, 48, 8–9.

Archer, Michael (1977). Faunal remains from the excavation at Puntutjarpa Rockshelter, in Puntutjarpa Rockshelter and the Australian desert culture, R. A. Gould, *Anthropological Papers of the American Museum of Natural History*, 54, 158–65.

Ardrey, Robert (1975). *The hunting hypothesis*. Atheneum, New York.

Ascher, R. (1959). A prehistoric population estimate using midden analysis and two population models. *Southwestern Journal of Anthropology*, 15, 168–78.

Atwater, C. (1820). Description of the antiquities discovered in the state of Ohio and other western states. *American Antiquarian Society, Transactions and Collections*, 1.

Bailey, Geoffrey N. (1975). *The role of shell middens in prehistoric economies*. Ph.D. dissertation, Department of Archaeology, Cambridge University.

Barth, F. (1969). *Ethnic groups and boundaries*. Little, Brown, Boston.

Basedow, Herbert (1925). *The Australian Aboriginal*. F. W. Preece, Adelaide.

Beaton, John M. (1977). *Dangerous harvest: Investigations in the late prehistoric occupation of upland south-east central Queensland*. Ph.D. dissertation, Department of Prehistory, Australian National University, Canberra.

Bennett, John W. (1969). *Northern plainsmen*. Aldine, Chicago.

Berndt, Ronald M. (1959). The concept of "the tribe" in the Western Desert of Australia. *Oceania*, 30, 81–107.

Berndt, R. M., and Berndt, C. H. (1964). *The world of the first Australians*. Ure Smith, Sydney.

Bigalke, E. H. (1973). The exploitation of shellfish by coastal tribesmen of the Transkei. *Annals of the Cape Provincial Museum (Natural History)*, 9, 159–75.

Binford, Lewis R. (1962). Archaeology as anthropology. *American Antiquity*, 28, 217–25.

 (1964). A consideration of archaeological research design. *American Antiquity*, 29, 425–41.

 (1967). Smudge pits and hide smoking: The use of analogy in archaeological reasoning. *American Antiquity*, 32, 1–12.

(1968). Methodological considerations of the archaeological use of ethnographic data. In Lee, R. B., and DeVore, I. (eds.), *Man the hunter*. Aldine, Chicago, pp. 268–73.

(1973). Interassemblage variability – the Mousterian and the "functional" argument. In Renfrew, C. (ed.), *The explanation of culture change: Models in prehistory*. Duckworth, London, pp. 227–54.

Binford, Sally R., and Binford, Lewis R. (1969). Stone tools and human behavior. *Scientific American*, **220**, 70–82.

Birdsell, Joseph B. (1975). A preliminary report on new research on man-land relationships in Aboriginal Australia. *American Antiquity*, **40**, 34–7.

Blake, Christine M. (1974). *An analysis of the seed-grinders of the desert regions of Central and Western Australia*. B.A. Honors thesis, Department of Anthropology, University of Hawaii, Honolulu.

Bonnichsen, Robson (1973). Millie's Camp: An experiment in archaeology. *World Archaeology*, **4**, 277–91.

Bordes, François (1972). *A tale of two caves*. Harper & Row, New York.

Bowdler, Sandra (1976). Left high and dry. *Hemisphere*, **20**, 29–33.

Bowler, J. M.; Jones, R.; Allen, H. R.; and Thorne, A. G. (1970). Pleistocene human remains from Australia: A living site and human cremation from Lake Mungo. *World Archaeology*, **2**, 39–60.

Bowler, J. M. (1971). Pleistocene salinities and climatic change: Evidence from lakes and lunettes in Southeastern Australia. In Mulvaney, D. J., and Golson, J. (eds.), *Aboriginal man and environment in Australia*. Australian National University Press, Canberra, pp. 47–65.

Carnegie, David W. (1898). *Spinifex and sand*. Mansfield & Co., New York.

Carneiro, Robert L. (1970). A quantitative law in anthropology. *American Antiquity*, **35**, 492–4.

Carson, Rachel (1962). *Silent Spring*. Houghton Mifflin, New York.

Chapman, Valerie C. (1977). *The Jindabyne Valley in southern uplands prehistory: An archaeological investigation*. M.A. dissertation, Department of Prehistory, Australian National University, Canberra.

Cipriani, Lidio (1966). *The Andaman Islanders*. Praeger, New York.

Clarke, D. L. (1968). *Analytical archaeology*. Methuen, London.

Clarke, Rainbird (1935). The flint knapping industry at Brandon. *Antiquity*, **9**, 38–56.

Collingwood, R. G. (1946). *The idea of history*. Oxford University Press.

Coombs, H. C. (1977). The Pitjantjatjara Aborigines: A strategy for survival. *Centre for Resource and Environmental Studies Working Paper*, Australian National University, Canberra, **1**, 56 pp.

Crabtree, Don E. (1970). Flaking stone with wooden implements. *Science*, **169**, 146–53.

Crawford, I. M., and Tonkinson, R. (1969). Report on sites lying within the area leased by International Nickel in the vicinity of Wingellina, which are thought to be sacred to Aborigines. To the Advisory Panel to the Minister for Native Welfare, Perth, Western Australia, 15 pp.

Darlington, Philip J., Jr. (1965). *Biogeography of the southern end of the world*. McGraw-Hill, New York.

Dawson, T. J. (1977). Kangaroos. *Scientific American*, **237**, 78–89.

Deetz, James (1967). *Invitation to archaeology*. Doubleday, New York.

(1968). Hunters in archaeological perspective. Discussion in Lee, R. B., and DeVore, I. (eds.), *Man the hunter*. Aldine, Chicago, pp. 281–5.

Dortch, C. E. (1973). Human occupation of Devil's Lair, W.A. during the Pleistocene. *Archaeology and Physical Anthropology in Oceania*, **8**, 89–115.

Edwards, Robert (1968). Prehistoric rock engravings at Thomas Reservoir, Cleland Hills, western South Australia. *Records of the South Australian Museum,* **15,** 647–70.

Elkin, A. P. (1949). Pressure flaking in the Northern Kimberley, Australia. *Man,* **130,** 110–13.

(1964). *The Australian Aborigines.* Doubleday, New York.

Eyre, E. J. (1845). *Journal of expedition of discovery into Central Australia.* Boone, London, 2 vol.

Fewkes, J. W. (1893). A-wa'-to-bi: An archaeological verification of a Tusayan legend. *American Anthropologist,* **6,** 363–75.

(1900). Tusayan migration traditions. *Bureau of American Ethnology Report for 1897–98,* **19,** 577–633.

Finlayson, H. H. (1935). *The red centre.* Angus and Robertson, Sydney.

Fitzpatrick, E. A., and Nix, H. A. (1973). The climatic factor in Australian grassland ecology. In Moore, R. M. (ed.), *Australian grasslands.* Australian National University Press, Canberra, pp. 3–26.

Flannery, Kent V. (1968). Archaeological systems theory and early Mesoamerica. In Meggers, B. J. (ed.), *Anthropological Archaeology in the Americas.* Anthropological Society of Washington, Washington, D.C., pp. 67–87.

Flood, Josephine M. (1973). *The moth-hunters.* Ph.D. dissertation, Department of Prehistory, Australian National University.

(1976). Man and ecology in the highlands of southeastern Australia. In Peterson, N. (ed.), *Tribes and boundaries in Australia.* Australian Institute of Aboriginal Studies, Canberra, pp. 30–49.

Frazer, J. G. (1898). *The golden bough.* Macmillan, London, 2nd ed. (abridged ed. 1923).

(1913). *The belief in immortality.* Macmillan, London.

Freeman, L. G. (1968). A theoretical framework for interpreting archaeological materials. In Lee, R. B., and DeVore, I. (eds.), *Man the hunter.* Aldine, Chicago, pp. 262–67.

Fried, Morton H. (1975). The myth of tribe. *Natural History,* **84,** 12–20.

Frith, H. J., and Calaby, J. H. (1969). *Kangaroos.* F. W. Cheshire, Melbourne.

Fysh, Catherine F.; Hodges, K. J.; and Siggins, Lorraine Y. (1960). Analysis of naturally occurring foodstuffs of Arnhem Land. In Mountford, C. P. (ed.), *Records of the American-Australian scientific expedition to Arnhem Land.* Melbourne University Press, **2,** 136–43.

Gardner, C. A. (1944). The vegetation of Western Australia. *Journal of the Royal Society of Western Australia,* **28.**

Gentilli, J. (1972). *Australian climate patterns.* Thomas Nelson, Melbourne.

Gibbs, W. J. (1969). Meteorology and climatology. In Slayter, R. O., and Perry, R. A. (eds.), *Arid lands of Australia.* Australian National University Press, Canberra, pp. 33–52.

Gillen, F. J. (1896). Notes on some manners and customs of the Aborigines of the McDonnell Ranges belonging to the Arunta tribe. In Stirling, E. C. (ed.), *Report on the work of the Horn Scientific Expedition to Central Australia, Part IV: Anthropology.* Dulan, London, pp. 161–86.

Glacken, Clarence J. (1956). Changing ideas of the habitable world. In Thomas, W. L., Jr. (ed.), *Man's role in changing the face of the earth.* University of Chicago Press, pp. 70–92.

Gladwin, Thomas (1970). *East is a big bird: Navigation and logic on Puluwat Atoll.* Harvard University Press, Cambridge.

Goodale, Jane C. (1970). An example of ritual change among the Tiwi of Melville Island. In Pilling, A. R., and Waterman, R. A. (eds.), *Diproto-*

don to detribalization: Studies of change among Australian Aborigines. Michigan State University Press, East Lansing, pp. 350–66.

(1971). *Tiwi wives: A study of the women of Melville Island, North Australia.* University of Washington Press, Seattle.

Gould, Richard A. (1967). Notes on hunting, butchering, and sharing of game among the Ngatatjara and their neighbors in the West Australian Desert. *Kroeber Anthropological Society Papers,* **36**, 41–66.

(1968). Living archaeology: The Ngatatjara of Western Australia. *Southwestern Journal of Anthropology,* **24**, 101–22.

(1969). *Yiwara: Foragers of the Australian Desert.* Scribners, New York.

(1970). Journey to Pulykara. *Natural History,* **79**, 56–66.

(1974). Some current problems in ethnoarchaeology. In Donnan, C. B., and Clewlow, C. W., Jr., *Ethnoarchaeology.* Institute of Archaeology, University of California, Los Angeles, Monograph 4, 29–48.

(1977). Puntutjarpa Rockshelter and the Australian desert culture. *Anthropological Papers of the American Museum of Natural History,* **54**, 187 pp.

Gould, Richard A.; Koster, Dorothy A.; and Sontz, Ann H. L. (1971). The lithic assemblage of the Western Desert Aborigines of Australia. *American Antiquity,* **36**, 149–69.

Grey, George (1841). *Journals of two expeditions of discovery in North-west and Western Australia.* Boone, London, 2 vols.

Hackett, C. J. (1934). A letter about an unknown world. Unpublished notes on a field trip to northwestern South Australia. 68 pp.

(1937). Man and nature in Central Australia. *Geographical Magazine,* **4**, 287–304.

Hamilton, Annette (1972). Aboriginal man's best friend? *Mankind,* **8**, 287–95.

Harris, David R. (1977). Subsistence strategies across Torres Strait. In Allen, J.; Golson, J.; and Jones, R. (eds.), *Sunda and Sahul: Prehistoric studies in Southeast Asia, Melanesia and Australia.* Academic Press, London, pp. 421–63.

Hayden, Brian (1975). Dingoes: Pets or producers? *Mankind,* **10**, 11–15.

(1976). *Australian Western Desert lithic technology: An ethnoarchaeological study of variability in material culture.* Ph.D. dissertation, Department of Anthropology, University of Toronto.

(1977). Stone tool functions in the Western Desert. In Wright, R. V. S. (ed.), *Stone tools as cultural markers.* Australian Institute of Aboriginal Studies, Canberra, 178–88.

Heider, Karl G. (1967). Archaeological assumptions and ethnographical facts: A cautionary tale from New Guinea. *Southwestern Journal of Anthropology,* **23**, 52–64.

Helms, Richard (1895). Anthropological notes. *Proceedings of the Linnean Society of New South Wales,* **2**, 387–407.

(1896). Anthropology of the Elder Exploring Expedition. *Transactions of the Royal Society of South Australia.* **16**, 237–332.

Hiatt, L. R. (1965). *Kinship and conflict: A study of an Aboriginal community in Northern Arnhem Land.* Australian National University Press, Canberra.

Hodder, Ian (1977). The distribution of material culture items in the Baringo District, West Kenya. *Man,* **12**, 239–69.

Hodge, F. W. (1897). The verification of a tradition. *American Anthropologist,* **19**, 299–302.

Horne, G, and Aiston, G. (1924). *Savage life in Central Australia.* Macmillan, London.

Howells, William W. (1977). Requiem for a lost people. *Harvard Magazine,* **79,** 48–55.

Howitt, A. W. (1904). *The native tribes of south-east Australia.* Macmillan, London.

Hunten, Donald M. (1975). The outer planets. *Scientific American,* **233,** 130–40.

Isaac, Glynn (1978). The food-sharing behavior of protohuman hominids. *Scientific American,* **238,** 90–108.

Jelinek, Arthur J. (1971). A consideration of the evidence for seasonal patterns in the Paleolithic cultures of the Near East. Paper presented at School of American Research Advanced Seminar on Seasonality in Prehistory, Santa Fe, 32 pp.

(1976). Form, function, and style in lithic analysis. In Cleland, C. E. (ed.), *Cultural change and continuity: Essays in honor of James Bennett Griffin.* Academic Press, New York, pp. 19–33.

Jones, Rhys (1971). *Rocky Cape and the problem of the Tasmanians.* Ph.D. dissertation, Department of Prehistory, Australian National University, Canberra.

(1973). The geographical background to the arrival of man in Australia and Tasmania. *Archaeology and Physical Anthropology in Oceania,* **3,** 186–215.

(1978). Why did the Tasmanians stop eating fish?. In Gould, R. A. (ed.), *Explorations in ethnoarchaeology.* University of New Mexico Press, Albuquerque, pp. 11–47.

Knowles, Francis H. S., and Barnes (1937). Manufacture of gunflints. *Antiquity,* **11,** 201–7.

Kolig, Erich (1978). Aboriginal dogmatics: Canines in theory, myth and dogma. *Bijdragen tot de Taal-, Land- en Volkenkunde,* **134,** 84–115.

Kroeber, A. L. (1916). Zuni potsherds. *Anthropological Papers of the American Museum of Natural History,* **18,** 7–21.

(1952). The superorganic. In Kroeber, A. L. (ed.), *The nature of culture.* University of Chicago Press, pp. 22–51.

Kroeber, A. L., and Kluckhohn, Clyde (1963). *Culture: A critical review of concepts and definitions.* Random House, New York.

Lawrence, Roger (1968). Aboriginal habitat and economy. *Occasional Papers of the Department of Geography, Australian National University,* **6,** 289 pp.

Leakey, M. D. (1971). *Olduvai Gorge: Excavations in Beds I & II, 1960–1963.* Cambridge University Press.

Lee, Richard B. (1966). Kalahari-1: A site report. In *The Study of Man.* Anthropology Curriculum Study Project, New York, 13 pp.

(1969). !Kung Bushman subsistence: An input–output analysis. In Damas, D. (ed.), *Contributions to anthropology: Ecological essays.* National Museums of Canada Bulletin 230, Ottawa, 73–94.

(1976). !Kung spatial organization: An ecological and historical perspective. In Lee, R. B., and DeVore, I. (eds.), *Kalahari hunter–gatherers: Studies of the !Kung San and their neighbors.* Harvard University Press, Cambridge, 73–97.

Leone, Mark P. (1972). Issues in anthropological archaeology. In Leone, M. P., *Contemporary archaeology.* Southern Illinois University Press, Carbondale, pp. 14–27.

(1973). Archaeology as the science of technology: Mormon town plans and fences. In Redman, C. L. (ed.), *Research and theory in current archaeology.* Wiley, New York, pp. 125–50.

Lévi-Strauss, C. (1966). *The savage mind*. Weidenfield and Nicolson, London.
Longacre, William A. (1974). Kalinga pottery-making: The evolution of a research design. In Leaf, M. J. (ed.), *Frontiers of anthropology*. Van Nostrand, New York, pp. 51–67.
Love, J. R. B. (1936). *Stone-Age Bushmen of to-day*. Blackie, London.
Luedtke, Barbara Ellen (1976). *Lithic material distributions and interaction patterns during the Late Woodland Period in Michigan*. Ph.D. dissertation, Department of Anthropology, University of Michigan.
McBryde, I. (1978). Wil-im-ee Moor-ing: Or, Where do axes come from? In Specht, J., and White, J. Peter (eds.), *Trade and exchange in Oceania and Australia*. Australian Museum and Anthropological Society, Sydney, pp. 354–82.
McBryde, I., and Watchman, A. (1976). The distribution of greenstone axes in southeastern Australia: A preliminary report. *Mankind*, **10**, 163–74.
McCarthy, F. D. (1939). "Trade" in Aboriginal Australia, and "trade" relationships with Torres Strait, New Guinea and Malaya. *Oceania*, **9**, 405–38.
Macintosh, N. W. G. (1974). Early man and the dog in Australia. In Elkin, A. P., and Macintosh, N. W. G. (eds.), *Grafton Elliot Smith: The man and his work*. Sydney University Press, pp. 83–94.
Maddock, Kenneth (1972). *The Australian Aborigines: A portrait of their society*. Penguin, London.
Maiden, J. H. (1889). *The useful native plants of Australia*. Turner and Henderson, Sydney.
Martin, Paul S. (1967). Pleistocene overkill. *Natural History*, **76**, 32–8.
Martin, P. S., and Wright, H. E., Jr. (eds.) (1967). *Pleistocene extinctions: The search for a cause*. Yale University Press, New Haven.
Mathews, R. H. (1903). The Aboriginal fisheries at Brewarrina. *Journal of the Royal Society of New South Wales*, **37**, 150–3.
Meehan, Betty (1975). *Shell bed to shell midden*. Ph.D. dissertation, Department of Prehistory, Australian National University, Canberra.
   (1977a). The role of seafood in the economy of a contemporary Aboriginal society in coastal Arnhem Land. Report to the Joint Select Committee on Aboriginal Land Rights in the Northern Territory, Canberra, 12 pp.
   (1977b). Man does not live by calories alone: The role of shellfish in a coastal cuisine. In Allen J., Golson, J., and Jones, R. (eds.), *Sunda and Sahul: Prehistoric studies in Southeast Asia, Melanesia and Australia*. Academic Press, London, pp. 493–531.
Meggitt, M. J. (1957). Notes on the vegetable foods of the Walbiri of Central Australia. *Oceania*, **28**, 143–5.
   (1962). *Desert people*. Angus and Robertson, Sydney.
Menzel, Dorothy (1956). Archaism and revival on the south coast of Peru. In Wallace, Anthony F. C. (ed.), *Selected papers of the Fifth International Congress of Anthropological and Ethnological Sciences*. University of Pennsylvania Press, Philadelphia, pp. 596–600.
Micha, Franz Josef (1970). Trade and change in Aboriginal Australian cultures: Australian Aboriginal trade as an expression of close culture contact and as a mediator of culture change. In Pilling, A. R., and Waterman, R. A. (eds.), *Diprotodon to detribalization: Studies of change among Australian Aborigines*. Michigan State University Press, East Lansing, pp. 285–313.

Mitchell, T. L. (1838). *Three expeditions into the interior of eastern Australia.* Boone, London, 2 vol.

Mountford, Charles P. (1941). An unrecorded method of manufacturing wooden implements by simple stone tools. *Transactions of the Royal Society of South Australia,* **65,** 312–16.

(1976). *Nomads of the Australian Desert.* Rigby, Adelaide.

Mulvaney, D. J. (1966). The prehistory of the Australian Aborigine. *Scientific American,* **214,** 84–93.

(1975). *The prehistory of Australia,* Penguin Books Australia, Melbourne.

Nagel, E. (1961). *The structure of science: Problems in the logic of scientific explanation.* Harcourt Brace Jovanovich, New York.

Naroll, Raoul (1962). Floor area and settlement population. *American Antiquity,* **27,** 587–9.

Nelson, N. C. (1909). Shellmounds of the San Francisco Bay region. *University of California Publications in American Archaeology and Ethnology,* **7,** 309–56.

Newsome, A. E. (1965a). The abundance of red kangaroos, *Megaleia rufa* (Demarest), in Central Australia. *Australian Journal of Zoology,* **13,** 269–87.

(1965b). The distribution of red kangaroos, *Megaleia rufa* (Demarest), about sources of persistent food and water in Central Australia. *Australian Journal of Zoology,* **13,** 289–99.

(1965c). Reproduction in natural populations of the red kangaroo, *Megaleia rufa* (Demarest), in Central Australia. *Australian Journal of Zoology,* **13,** 735–59.

(1971). The ecology of red kangaroos. *Australian Zoologist,* **16,** 32–50.

O'Connell, James F. (1974). Spoons, knives and scrapers: The function of yilugwa in Central Australia. *Mankind,* **9,** 189–94.

(1977). Working in mysteries without any clues: Thoughts on the role of ethnographic analogy in Australian archaeology. Prehistory Seminar, Australian National University, August 12.

Odum, Eugene P. (1975). *Ecology.* Holt, Rinehart and Winston, New York.

Peterson, Nicolas (1976). The natural and cultural areas of Aboriginal Australia: A preliminary analysis of population groupings with adaptive significance. In Peterson, N. (ed.), *Tribes and boundaries in Australia.* Australian Institute of Aboriginal Studies, Canberra, pp. 50–71.

Petri, Helmut (1954). 'Sterbende Welt in Nordwest-Australien,' *Kulturgeschichtliche Forschungen,* vol. 5, A. Limbach, Braunschweig, West Germany.

Pfeiffer, John E. (1972). *The emergence of man.* Harper & Row, New York.

Plog, Fred (1973). Laws, systems of law, and the explanation of observed variation. In Renfrew, C. (ed.), *The explanation of culture change: Models in prehistory.* Duckworth, London, pp. 649–61.

Pryor, L. D. (1976). *The biology of eucalypts.* Edward Arnold, London.

Radcliffe-Brown, A. R. (1935). Kinship terminologies in California. *American Anthropologist,* **37,** 530–5.

Rathje, William L. (1978). Archaeological ethnography . . . Because sometimes it is better to give than to receive. In Gould, R. A. (ed.), *Explorations in ethnoarchaeology.* University of New Mexico Press, Albuquerque, pp. 49–75.

Riley, Denis, and Young, Anthony (1966). *World Vegetation,* Cambridge University Press.

Robertson, Bruce (1977). *Aviation archaeology.* Patrick Stephens, Cambridge.

Rowe, J. H. (1959). Archaeological dating and cultural process. *Southwestern Journal of Anthropology,* **15,** 317–24.

(1962). Chavin art: An inquiry into its form and meaning. Museum of Primitive Art, New York.

Sampson, Anthony (1977). *The arms bazaar.* Hodder & Stoughton, London.

Sandall, Roger (1967). Walbiri ritual at Ngama (film, 23½ min., color and sound). Australian Institute of Aboriginal Studies, Canberra.

Schaller, George B. (1973). *Golden shadows, flying hooves.* Knopf, New York.

Schenck, W. Egbert (1926). The Emeryville Shellmound: final report. *University of California Publications in American Archaeology and Ethnology,* **23,** 147–282.

Schiffer, Michael B. (1972). Archaeological context and systemic context. *American Antiquity,* **37,** 156–65.

  (1975). Archaeology as behavioral science. *American Anthropologist,* **77,** 836–48.

  (1976). *Behavioral archaeology.* Academic Press, New York.

  (1978). Methodological issues in ethnoarchaeology. In Gould, R. A. (ed.), *Explorations in ethnoarchaeology.* University of New Mexico Press, Albuquerque, pp. 229–47.

Shawcross, Wilfred (1967). An investigation of prehistoric diet and economy on a coastal site at Galatea Bay, New Zealand. *Proceedings of the Prehistoric Society,* n.s., **33,** 107–31.

Silverberg, Robert (1968). *Mound builders of ancient America: The archaeology of a myth.* New York Graphic Society, Greenwich, Connecticut.

Skertchly, Sydney B. J. (1879) 'On the manufacture of gunflints; the methods of excavating for flint; the connection between Neolithic art and the gunflint trade.' *District Memoir of the Geological Survey of Great Britain and Ireland,* London.

Skolnik, Merrill I. (1962). *Introduction to radar systems,* McGraw-Hill, New York.

Smith, Bruce D. (1976). "Twitching": A minor ailment affecting human paleoecological research. In Cleland, C. E. (ed.), *Cultural change and continuity: Essays in honor of James Bennett Griffin.* Academic Press, New York, pp. 275–92.

Smyth, R. Brough (1878). *The Aborigines of Victoria.* Government Printer, Melbourne, 2 vols.

Sollas, W. J. (1915). *Ancient Hunters.* Macmillan, London, 2nd ed.

Spaulding, Albert C. (1953). Statistical techniques for the discovery of artifact types. *American Antiquity,* **18,** 305–13.

Spencer, Baldwin (1914). *Native tribes of the Northern Territory of Australia.* Macmillan, London.

  (1922). *Guide to the Australian ethnological collection exhibited in the National Museum of Victoria.* Government Printer, Melbourne.

Spencer, Baldwin, and Gillen, F. J. (1899). *The native tribes of Central Australia.* Macmillan, London.

  (1904). *The northern tribes of Central Australia.* Macmillan, London.

  (1927). *The Arunta.* Macmillan, London.

Stanislawski, Michael B. (1969). What good is a broken pot? An experiment in Hopi-Tewa ethnoarchaeology. *Southwestern Lore,* **35,** 11–18.

  (1973). The relationship of ethno-archaeology, traditional, and systems archaeology. Paper read at 72nd annual meeting of the American Anthropological Association, New Orleans (revised, 1973), 11 pp.

  (1975). What you see is what you get: Ethnoarchaeology and scientific model building. Paper presented at the annual meeting of the Society for American Archaeology, Dallas, 22 pp.

Steward, Julian H. (1942). The direct historical approach to archaeology. *American Antiquity,* **7,** 337–43.

Stickel, E. Gary, and Chartkoff, Joseph L. (1973). The nature of scientific laws and their relation to law-building in archaeology. In Renfrew, C. (ed.), *The explanation of culture change: Models in prehistory.* Duckworth, London, pp. 663–71.

Stiles, Daniel (1977). Ethnoarchaeology: A discussion of methods and applications. *Man,* **12,** 87–103.

Strehlow, C. (1920). Die Aranda-und Loritja-Stämme in Zentral Australien, Part V (material culture). Stadtisches Völker-Museum, Frankfurt am Main.

Strehlow, T. G. H. (1965). Culture, social structure, and environment in Aboriginal Central Australia. In Berndt, R. M., and Berndt, C. H. (eds.), *Aboriginal man in Australia.* Angus and Robertson, Sydney, pp. 121–45.

Sturt, C. (1833). *Two expeditions into the interior of southern Australia.* Smith, Elder & Co., London, 2 vols.

Terry, Michael (1968). Were these the first Australians? *Today's People,* **19,** 2–8.

Thomas, David Hurst (1974). *Predicting the past: An introduction to anthropological archaeology.* Holt, Rinehart and Winston, New York.

Thomson, Donald F. (1939a). The seasonal factor in human culture, illustrated from the life of a contemporary nomadic group. *Proceedings of the Prehistoric Society,* n.s., **5,** 209–21.

(1939b). Remarkable fishing methods used by the Aborigines of Arnhem Land. *The Illustrated London News,* July 15 & August 19, pp. 101–4, 302–3.

(1949). *Economic structure and the ceremonial exchange cycle in Arnhem Land.* Macmillan, Melbourne.

(1964). Some wood and stone implements of the Bindibu tribe of central Western Australia. *Proceedings of the Prehistoric Society,* n.s., **30,** 400–22.

Tindale, Norman B. (1925). Natives of Groote Eylandt and of the west coast of the Gulf of Carpentaria, parts 1 and 2. *Records of the South Australian Museum,* **2–3,** 61–102, 103–34.

(1965). Stone implement making among the Nakako, Ngadadjara, and Pitjandjara of the Great Western Desert. *Records of the South Australian Museum,* **15,** 131–64.

(1974). *Aboriginal tribes of Australia.* University of California Press, Berkeley.

Tuggle, H. David, Townshend, Alex H., and Riley, Thomas J. (1972). Laws, systems, and research designs: A discussion of explanation in archaeology. *American Antiquity,* **37,** 3–12.

Turnbull, Clive (1948). *Black war: The extermination of the Tasmanian Aborigines,* Cheshire, Melbourne.

Tylor, E. B. (1899). *Anthropology: An introduction to the study of man and civilization.* Appleton, New York, (orig. 1881).

Vavilov, N. I. (1926). *Studies on the origin of cultivated plants.* Institute of Applied Botany and Plant Breeding, Leningrad.

Washburn, Sherwood L. (1976). Foreword to *Kalahari hunter–gatherers: Studies of the !Kung San and their neighbors,* ed. Lee, R. B., and DeVore, I., Harvard University Press, Cambridge, xv–xvii.

Watson, Richard A., and Watson, Patty Jo (1969). *Man and nature: An anthropological essay in human ecology.* Harcourt Brace, Jovanovich, New York.

White, Carmel, and Peterson, Nicolas (1969). Ethnographic interpretations of the prehistory of Western Arnhem Land. *Southwestern Journal of Anthropology*, **25,** 45–67.

White, Isobel M. (1972). Hunting dogs at Yalata. *Mankind*, **8,** 201–5.

White, J. Peter (1967). Ethno-archaeology in New Guinea: Two examples. *Mankind*, **6,** 409–14.

(1971). New Guinea and Australian prehistory: The "Neolithic problem." In Mulvaney, D. J., and Golson, J. (eds.), *Aboriginal man and environment in Australia*. Australian National University Press, Canberra, pp. 182–95.

White, J. Peter, Modjeska, Nicholas, and Hipuya, Irari (1977). Group definitions and mental templates: An ethnographic experiment. In Wright, R. V. S. (ed.), *Stone tools as cultural markers*. Australian Institute of Aboriginal Studies, Canberra, pp. 380–90.

White, J. Peter, and Thomas, David Hurst (1972). What mean these stones? Ethnotaxonomic models and archaeological interpretations in the New Guinea Highlands. In Clarke, D. L. (ed.), *Models in Archaeology*. Methuen, London, pp. 275–308.

White, Leslie A. (1959). *The evolution of culture*. McGraw-Hill, New York.

Willey, Gordon R., and Phillips, Philip (1958). *Method and Theory in American Archaeology*, University of Chicago Press.

Wilmsen, Edwin N. (1970). Lithic analysis and cultural inference: a Paleo-Indian case. *Anthropological Papers of the University of Arizona*, **16,** 87 pp.

Winship, George P. (1896). The Coronado expedition, 1540–1542. *14th Annual Report of the Bureau of Ethnology*, Smithsonian Institution, Washingston, D. C., pp. 329–613.

Wittfogel, Karl A. (1960). Developmental aspects of hydraulic societies. In Adams, R. M., Collier, D., et al. (eds.), *Irrigation civilizations: A comparative study*. Pan American Union, Washington, D.C., 43–52.

Wobst, H. Martin (1978). The archaeo-ethnology of hunter–gatherers, or the tyranny of the ethnographic record in archaeology. *American Antiquity*, **43,** 303–9.

Yellen, John E. (1977). *Archaeological approaches to the present: Models for reconstructing the past*. Academic Press, New York.

Yengoyan, Aram A. (1968). Demographic and ecological influences on Aboriginal Australian marriage sections. In Lee, R. B., and DeVore, I. (eds.), *Man the hunter*. Aldine, Chicago, pp. 185–99.

Index

Halls Creek, Western Australia, 141
Harts Range, Northern Territory, 180
Helms, Richard, 77, 98–9
Hermannsburg Mission, Northern Territory, 165
Hocking Range, Western Australia, 182
"home base" hypothesis, 31–2
Hopi Indians, 5, 114
Hughes Creek, Western Australia, 144–5
Hunter Island, Tasmania, 213
"hydraulic hypothesis," 140

Ica Valley, Peru, 116
Ikulpa site, Northern Territory, 184
Ilpirra Aborigines, 141–2
Inca Empire, 116
increase rituals (among Aborigines), 106–7
index of subsistence effort, 77, 78–9
infanticide, 39
initiation ordeals (among Aborigines), 84, 106–7
in-law avoidance behavior (among Aborigines), 15
"instant tools", 72, 131
interference, principle of, 196–7, 214

Jallukar Axe Quarry, Victoria, 208
James Range, Northern Territory, 164–5; 167–8, 184
Jessie Gap, Northern Territory, 183
joking relationships (among Aborigines), 15

Kaitish Aborigines, 141
Kalahari Desert, 61, 250
Kalahari-1 site, 27
Kalinga (of Luzon), 5, 115
kalpaṛi *(Chenopodium rhadinostachym)*, 63
Kampuṛarpa *(Solanum centrale)*, 8, 17–18, 20, 22, 63–4
Kangaroo Island, South Australia, 177
Kimberley District, Western Australia, 53, 141–3, 242, 246

Kimberley points, 141–3, 177, 179
kulama yam ceremony, 107
Kulin tribes (of Australia), 210–12
Kunapipi ceremony, 222
!Kung Bushmen, 5, 28, 76, 250
Kurnai Aborigines, 88, 209–12

Lake Macdonald, Northern Territory & Western Australia, 130
Lake Menindee, New South Wales (fossil site), 94
Lake Mungo site, New South Wales, 227
Lake Throssel, Western Australia, 148
Late Woodland Period (of Michigan), 135–6
Laverton, Western Australia, 19, 68, 153–4, 240–1, 246
Leonora, Western Australia, 240
Leverrier, Urbain, 139
Leibig's Law of the Minimum, 52, 140
Loritja Aborigines, 165, 185
Lowell, Percival, 139

Macdonald Downs Station, Northern Territory, 247
Macdonnell Range, Northern Territory, 163
Macropus titan, 59
Macumba River, South Australia, 163
Madoc (legendary Welsh prince), 205
maintenance tools, 121, 127, 137
mallee (vegetation), 53, 94
MAM (carcinogenic compound), 103
mamu (ghosts), 23, 241
Marree, South Australia, 163
mental templates, 118, 120
Micronesia, 158–9
Mitchell, Thomas Livingstone, 95
Monaro Tableland, New South Wales & Australian Capital Territory, 57, 97–8
Mound Builder myth, 205
"mountain devil" lizard *(Moloch horridus),* 14
mouse hunting (by Aborigines), 65–6